TECHNOLOGY ENTREPRENEURSHIP AND BUSINESS INCUBATION
Theory • Practice • Lessons Learned

TECHNOLOGY ENTREPRENEURSHIP AND BUSINESS INCUBATION

Theory • Practice • Lessons Learned

Editors

Phillip H Phan
Johns Hopkins University, USA

Sarfraz A Mian
State University of New York at Oswego, USA

Wadid Lamine
Toulouse Business School, France

Imperial College Press

ICP

Published by

Imperial College Press
57 Shelton Street
Covent Garden
London WC2H 9HE

Distributed by

World Scientific Publishing Co. Pte. Ltd.

5 Toh Tuck Link, Singapore 596224

USA office: 27 Warren Street, Suite 401-402, Hackensack, NJ 07601

UK office: 57 Shelton Street, Covent Garden, London WC2H 9HE

Library of Congress Cataloging-in-Publication Data
Names: Phan, Phillip Hin Choi, 1963–   author. | Mian, Sarfraz A., 1952–   author. |
    Lamine, Wadid, author.
Title: Technology entrepreneurship and business incubation : theory, practice, lessons learned /
    Phillip H. Phan (Johns Hopkins University, USA), Sarfraz A. Mian (State University of
    New York at Oswego, USA) & Wadid Lamine (Toulouse Business School, France).
Description: New Jersey : Imperial College Press, [2016]
Identifiers: LCCN 2016013817 | ISBN 9781783269761 (hc : alk. paper)
Subjects: LCSH: Business incubators. | Technological innovations--Economic aspects. |
    New business enterprises. | High technology industries. | Entrepreneurship.
Classification: LCC HD62.5 .P5225 2016 | DDC 338/.04--dc23
LC record available at https://lccn.loc.gov/2016013817

British Library Cataloguing-in-Publication Data
A catalogue record for this book is available from the British Library.

Desk Editors: Dr. Sree Meenakshi Sajani/Mary Simpson

Typeset by Stallion Press
Email: enquiries@stallionpress.com

Printed in Singapore

Contents

Redux: What do We Know about Business Incubation Today?

Phillip Phan, Sarfraz Mian and Wadid Lamine

Introduction

According to Google Trends, interest in business incubators[1] peaked in the mid-2000s in North America.[2] Today, more scholarly and policy interest in business incubators tend to be found in emerging economies such as China, India and Russia or small countries with an interest in technology-based economic development such as Singapore, Israel, Scandinavia, Kenya and South Africa. This is partly due to the accumulation of evidence on their generally positive effects of promoting technology entrepreneurship and economic development (c.f., Audretsch *et al.*, 2015).

While there has been a marked increase in the number of scholarly papers on business incubators in general, there has yet to be an organized volume narrowly focused on their impact on technology entrepreneurship.

---

[1] Although the scholarly literature makes a distinction between various types of incubators, Chapter 1 indeed goes through a long list of forms and definitions, because their purpose is similar, we use the term 'incubator' to refer to all property-based startup sponsoring organizations.

[2] https://www.google.com.sg/trends/explore#q=%2Fm%2F0581_y [Accessed January 16, 2016].

This book represents a first attempt. It reports on selected research from around the world, each focusing on an aspect of business incubation most salient to that part of the world. There are already a number of competent reviews of the scholarly research on incubators from North America and Continental Europe (see, for example, Hackett and Dilts, 2004). Less prominent is the research on incubators from emerging economics such as China, Russia and Brazil or developing economies such as Tunisia and South Africa. Most chapters begin with a definition of the incubators they investigate and take the reader through a short history of their development within the geographic region of interest. Another reason we present business incubation research in this way is to provide the reader a geographically broad view of the field. We note that while incubation is a universal concept, the way it has expressed itself, as these chapters illustrate, differs around the world. We hope that the reader would consider the theoretical and empirical opportunities for advancing this research by seeking out collaborations from these and other scholars around the world.

Research on business incubation has covered topics such as descriptions of different types of business incubators, discussions of the various service models and their implications for value creation, the impact of business incubation on business survival, regional economic development and employment and the policy determinants and implication for the growth of incubators. One of the earliest attempts at articulating the incubator concept is by Smilor and Gill (1986) in which they argued business incubators provided the type of support that startups are not able to obtain on their own from the marketplace, either because they are resource poor, conceptually vague or bereft of the right connections to needed resource pools. The implication of their book is that business incubation is a policy response to market failure and the 'linking' function is the result of policy interventions by governments, corporations, universities, non-governmental organizations or research institutes. Indeed, much of the research following Smilor and Gill (1986) have focused on describing the attempts by various actors to foster entrepreneurial activity using property-based organizations (incubators, science parks, accelerators, and so on). In this research, scholars have focus on the policy rationale for intervention (e.g. La Rovere *et al.*, 2015) or characterize incubators as outcomes of institutional (such as universities and corporations) strategies to create economic wealth (Mian, 1996; Foss and Gibson, 2015).

Other collections of the research have characterized incubators as mechanisms to foster inter-firm collaboration and the exchange of ideas and technology (Mitra and Edmondson, 2015). Yet, others have looked at the connection between regional development and the development of human capital, with incubators as the enabling organizational entity, among others (Baptista and Leitão, 2015).

The above being said, because various business incubation models have rapidly evolved in form over the past more than 30 years, it has been challenging to study the phenomenon from a theoretical and empirical perspective. For example, the early business incubators were conceived as sponsoring organizations that provided low cost space to newly formed technology businesses. The later provision of discounted business services such as accounting, legal advice and business incorporation and business planning was added to render this combination of space and services the basis of the classic incubator model. As the pace of new business creation accelerated with the advent of the *connected era,* incubators that proved they could shorten the time between discoveries and commercialization became more attractive to funders and entrepreneurs.

Hence, a generation of incubators in the biomedical sciences emerged that combined wet laboratory facilities, the most costly type of space and typical incubator services. Wet lab incubators brought the concept of 'cheap rent', which had fallen off as the reason for incubation success, back a full circle because scientist-entrepreneurs could not conduct the needed translational research in university-based labs, usually due to conflict-of-interest, and did not have the financial means to set up private ones. Incubators became magnets for angel investors and venture capitalists looking for 'ground floor' opportunities in such technology domains as biotechnology, materials and information/communications. Today, the original incubator model exists within a constellation of other property-based sponsorship organizations such as science parks, accelerators and 'maker spaces'. Indeed, Google Trends reports that while interest in incubators has abated in Internet searches, interest in Y-Combinator, the prototypical accelerator and its analogs has exploded around the world.[3]

---

[3] https://www.google.com.sg/trends/explore#q=Y%20Combinator [Accessed January 16, 2016].

Overview of the contributions

To begin, Chapter 1 provides definitions, a brief history and a review of the research in business incubation. It describes the typical incubation process, with a focus on the interventions typically encountered in such organizations. The point being made is that incubation in its evolved form is a deliberate, non-market based activity designed to move a nascent enterprise through its natural stages of growth at an accelerated rate, and to protect it from market forces that threaten early survival. To do so requires planning and resources, since growth is naturally constrained by the available resources. Because of being cloistered, startups are also protected from the competitive forces that can prematurely kill them. Whether such protection is efficient in the end or leads to 'zombie' startups has been a matter of debate since the concept was introduced to the literature. That debate continues today, even though in practice incubators have implemented various mechanisms such as term limits, performance targets and stage-gates to mitigate the risks of over-investment in poor ideas.

Chapter 2 turns its attention to business accelerators, a more recent form of incubator. Specifically, they examine the empirical evidence from 13 business accelerators based in London, Berlin and Paris. Accelerators have taken on an importance, in part fueled by the Internet, not seen in earlier discussions of incubators. While accelerators are still an emerging organizational form, and therefore too young to study for their long-term performance, through a comparative case analysis, the authors were able to suggest a number of factors that could improve the odds of success. These are the selection process and criteria for inclusion, comprehensiveness of business support services and presence of networking opportunities for the startup firms. The chapter employs institutional theory to view the data, representing a minority of studies to use theory and worthy of emulation. They suggest that accelerators are more likely to survive if they can legitimate themselves in the eyes of stakeholders. This is because accelerators are an unfamiliar organizational form and hence not accorded the institutional support that familiar forms can take for granted.

Chapter 3 continues the theme with an inductive study of accelerators based in the United Kingdom. They define accelerators as an umbrella term for any program providing structured mentoring, networking opportunities and access to funding. The chapter addresses two related questions, which are how accelerators make a difference in the performance of their tenant firms, and whether they act strategically to position themselves in the marketplace for incubation. Similar to the approach taken by other chapters, the authors begin with a typology of accelerator archetypes, in their case, ecosystem builders, investors and matchmakers. Ecosystem builders are public entities focused on creating business ecosystems that are friendly to startups to attenuate early-stage failures. Matchmakers, on the other hand, are accelerators that help tenant firms find their first customers and are focused on the activities and support structures devote to that aim. The different accelerator models address a wide range of startup types and provide useful indications on how and where to position themselves in the ecosystem.

Chapter 4 employs an ecological perspective to investigate the survival odds of incubator tenant firms in China. They take as given that incubators operate in a market for tenant firms and are therefore connected by resource networks. As a result, they simultaneously collaborate and compete with each other. This mutualism–competition dynamic directly affects tenant firms' performance, so that the task of the incubator manager is to manage this dynamic rather than ignore or suppress it. They look at how this is done in terms of two contextual constraints: government ownership and portfolio specialization. They find that these constraints attenuate the effects of mutualism and competition on tenant firm performance.

Chapter 5 offers a historical view of incubation (or innovation habitats) in Brazil, beginning with early government initiatives to instigate knowledge transfer and exploitation as the means of economic and social development to the present day. The author highlights the importance of academic institutions, a theme that is played out in similar attempts around the world, as creators of knowledge, and sources of energy, imagination and risk taking among young people. The chapter reports on the material and intangible results and discusses the challenges and future prospects.

Chapter 6 reports on the effectiveness of technology incubation mechanisms in Russia. Similar to Chapter 5, it provides an overview of incubator development over two decades. This period coincides with the post-Soviet development of Russia into a market-driven economy. The social changes brought on by the economic shift created the need to unleash entrepreneurial activity as a means to mitigate the job losses brought on by transformations in State-owned enterprises, especially in the oil and gas sector. Their study takes a value-added approach (Mian, 1996) to assess incubator services to the 83 companies they studied in the Nizhniy Novgorod region of Russia. As expected, in regions fostering incubation capabilities in developing environments, the results suggest that main attraction for startups when choosing incubators is the latter's ability to facilitate access to governmental funding.

Chapter 7 reports on a sample of tenant firms from various incubators in Tunisia, and shows that successful startups are associated with entrepreneurs with the educational background and experience in starting companies. As such, those incubators that can extend this learning process for the entrepreneur, by hosting serial startups, are more likely to be associated with successful tenant firms. This chapter represents an interesting take on the role of the incubator, which is that by keeping startups alive longer, they also extend the learning cycle of the founding entrepreneurs, which improves the chances of future successful starts.

Chapter 8 reports on the selection processes used by 24 publicly funded business incubators from South Africa, where incubation is a relatively new phenomenon. Hence, the authors' investigative approach is exploratory and utilizes semi-structured interviews to capture the ongoing dialog between incubator managers and their tenant firms. They find that, beyond standard demographic factors, incubators selected their tenant firms in an interactive, yet, relatively structured manner. This is consonant with a portfolio view of incubation, in which the composition of the tenants firms is as important as the individual competencies or assessment of the probability of success of individual tenants. Composition matters because tenant firms learn from each other and the mature incubator is adept at exploiting this mechanism to accelerate knowledge transfer.

Chapter 9, which is an updated reprint from an earlier paper published in the *Journal of Business Venturing*, looks at the problems with the extant literature on science parks and incubators in terms of three levels of analysis: the science parks and incubators themselves, the tenant firms and tenant entrepreneurs and their teams. It concludes, after reviewing the key literature, that there is no systematic framework to understand these organizations. While there has been a few attempts at such frameworks in the decade since the publication of the paper, the authors' general conclusion remains true today. They argue that the lack of clarity regarding the performance of incubators is associated with problems in defining performance, and by implication, has led to the lack of theoretical rigor in much of the research till and since then.

Conclusion

In summary, the chapters in this volume offer the scholar a retrospective of incubators and the related research, the latest research from regions that are new to the study of this phenomenon and prospective views of the theories and frameworks applicable to future research. Research has also shown that incubation and related forms of sponsoring property-based organizations *can* work to lower the odds of failure among technology startups (Hackett and Dilts, 2004). For example, based on a survey of 19,000 incubated businesses in the US, Amezcua *et al.* (2013) found that successful incubated businesses were those whose resource gaps matched the competencies provided by the sponsoring organization. Hence, from the entrepreneurs' standpoint, incubators offer an opportunity to mitigate the risks of failure through learning-by-doing and vicarious transfer of knowledge from experienced mentors and resource providers.

As the reader will discover, the public policy discussion emerges repeatedly throughout this book, suggesting that incubation has become a popular method to support economic development. From this standpoint, the general evidence suggests reasons for optimism. This is because incubation represents a relatively low cost tool (compared to 1950s-style industrial policy or the five-year plans of centrally planned economies) to experiment with economic development initiatives that do not require long time horizons to realize.

References

Amezcua, A. S., Grimes, M. G., Bradley, S. W., and Wiklund, J. (2013). Organizational sponsorship and founding environments: A contingency view on the survival of business-incubated firms, 1994–2007. *Academy of Management Journal*, 56(6): 1628–1654.

Audretsch, D. B., Belitski, M., and Desai, S. (2015). Entrepreneurship and economic development in cities. *The Annals of Regional Science*, 55(1): 33–60.

Baptista, R. and Leitão, J. (Eds.). (2015). *Entrepreneurship, Human Capital, and Regional Development: Labor Networks, Knowledge Flows, and Industry Growth*, International Studies in Entrepreneurship. Springer Cham Heidelberg, New York, NY.

Foss, L. and Gibson, D. V. (Eds.). (2015). *The Entrepreneurial University: Context and Institutional Change*, Riot! Routledge Studies in Innovation, Organization and Technology. Routledge, New York, NY.

Hackett, S. M. and Dilts, D. M. (2004). A systematic review of business incubation research. *Journal of Technology Transfer*, 29(1): 55–82.

La Rovere, R., Ozório, L., and Melo, L. J. (Eds.). (2015). *Entrepreneurship in BRICS: Policy and Research to Support Entrepreneurs*. Springer Cham Heidelberg, New York, NY.

Mian, S. (1996). Assessing the value-added contributions of university technology business incubators to tenant firms. *Research Policy*, 25: 325–335.

Mitra, J. and Edmondson, J. (Eds.). (2015). *Entrepreneurship and Knowledge Exchange*. Routledge Studies in Entrepreneurship. Routledge, New York, NY.

Smilor, R. and Gill, M. (1986). *The New Business Incubator: Linking Talent, Technology and Know-How*. Lexington Books, Lexington, MA.

Chapter 1

Business Incubation and Incubator Mechanisms[1]

Sarfraz Mian

Introduction

The Oxford dictionary defines incubation as 'the process or an instance of incubating something in a controlled environment' (OED, 1993). The embryonic developments of an animal within an egg, and exposure to an infection or disease with the appearance of the first symptoms are often quoted as examples of the incubation phenomenon. In its business use, incubation is considered as a unique and flexible mix of organized enterprise development processes that enable fledgling new and small businesses by providing critical support to survive and grow in their early stages of development. Therefore, incubation mechanisms also known as incubators are designed to serve as launching pads for young and small business startups, which need access to support services; they serve as business development tools for providing a nurturing milieu. The National Business Incubation Association, the world's largest professional association representing the field in the US provides the following definition: "Business incubation is a business support process that accelerates the successful development of startup and fledgling companies by providing entrepreneurs with an array

---

[1] Updated reprint from the *Handbook of Research on Entrepreneurship*, Alain, F. (Ed.), (2014), pp. 335–366, with permission from Edward Elgar Publishing, Cheltenham, UK.

of targeted resources and services. These services are usually developed or orchestrated by incubator management and offered both in the business incubator and through its network of contacts. A business incubator's main goal is to produce successful firms that will leave the program financially viable and freestanding. These incubator graduates have the potential to create jobs, revitalize neighborhoods, commercialize new technologies and strengthen local and national economies" (NBIA, 2012).

According to the UK Business Incubation association, "Business Incubation provides SMEs and startups with the nurturing environment needed to develop and grow their businesses, offering everything from virtual support, rent-a-desk through to state of the art laboratories and everything in between. They provide direct access to hands on intensive business support, access to finance and experts and to other entrepreneurs and suppliers to really make businesses and entrepreneurs to grow. Business incubation provides a nurturing, instructive and supportive environment for entrepreneurs during the critical stages of starting up a new business. The goal of incubators is to increase the chance that a startup will succeed, and shorten the time and reduce the cost of establishing and growing its business. If successful, business incubators can help to nurture the companies that will form the true creators of a region's or a nation's future wealth and employment" (UKBI, 2012).

Other major business incubation-related professional associations such as the European Business and Innovation Centre Network (EBN), International Association of Science Parks (IASP), German Association of Innovation, Technology and Business Incubation (ATD) and France Technopolis Enterprises Innovation (RETIS), each define the incubation function with slight variation and even use different terminologies for some of the mechanisms employed. For example, in Germany, the innovation center mechanism is more prevalent; this in terms of functionality is equivalent to a technology incubator in the US/UK terminology. In France, the incubator support is generally limited to the business idea development, testing and resources planning stages and ceases prior to the legal set up of the business that is generally carried out in a pépinières or hatchery.

To understand the relationship of each of these mechanisms to the business incubation support process, it is important to envision the steps involved in the startup cycle of a business, which can be directly related to the types of interventions that incubator mechanisms provide (Table 1).

Table 1.   Phases of the Incubation Process and Incubator Mechanisms

PHASE 1: Pre-incubation/Idea development	PHASE 2: Incubation and acceleration	PHASE 3: Post-incubation consolidation and growth
This earlier stage of intervention is intended to help aspiring/potential entrepreneurs in germinating/refining their business ideas. Recommended for risky S&T based startups, it is often provided by university incubators/ innovation centers. The overriding objective is technology commercialization, rather than market opportunity and seeks public funds.	This support stage kicks in when the business plan is being implemented, with a team, and operations have begun. Incubators can help refine the plan, build the team, provide resources and even invest in the company. The company is yet to become profitable and pays for assistance/services. Also known as 'acceleration' in which cases targeted assistance is provided. They often require subsidizing.	This stage provides incubator graduates and R&D units of larger firms to interact and help new technology-based firms consolidate and grow in a customized and often knowledge laden host environment. Science parks and some larger incubators also act as hosts to mature anchor tenants which can be a crucial strategy to help provide know-how as well as financial sustainability by assisting with and subsidizing their other programs.
	Development/Mixed use incubator	
Innovation center/Technology incubator		*Science park/Research park*
	Pépinières and hatcheries	*Technopolis*
	Virtual incubator/Accelerator	
French research/Academic incubator		

Source: Adapted from EU (2002).

Although a comprehensive science park facility equipped with an innovation center/technology incubator may be involved in supporting across the whole incubation continuum covering all three stages, as a germinator/incubator/consolidator, most facilities focus on one or two phases, which allows flexibility and keeps the focus. This leads us to the next section.

A typology of incubator mechanisms

There are different ways to categorize business incubator mechanisms/models. The prominent approaches are (a) based on incubator clients' sectoral/industry focus, (b) based on incubator facility's organizational structure — with wall or brick-and-mortar, without wall or virtual. Incubators are also categorized based on their sponsorship type — privately run for-profit or government supported non-profit incubators. Despite their diverse goals, there are several programmatic overlaps among these types. We define here the following popular incubator models:

Development Incubators: These incubators are aimed at addressing specific economic and/or social development objectives such as industrial restructuring, job creation and empowering women–youth–minority populations. Such initiatives are often funded and/or subsidized by state and/or local governments. Their main goal is to help create and grow new firms by providing nurturing environments.

Mixed-Use Incubators: The main goal of the mixed-use general purpose incubators is to promote continuous regional industrial and economic growth through general business development. While these incubators include knowledge-intensive firms, they also include low technology firms in services and light manufacturing. A main focus of support is access to local/regional sources of technical, managerial, marketing and financial resources.

Technology Incubators: The primary goal of technology incubators is to support the development of technology-oriented firms. They are mainly located at or near universities, large industrial laboratories, innovation centers and science and technology parks with which they have formal links to draw resources. Some specialized incubators also target specific technologies such as biotechnology, agriculture, ICT or software. Technology incubators promote transfer and diffusion of new technology to the marketplace at the same time encouraging academic entrepreneurship. At some places, they serve as mechanisms for corporate entrepreneurship where the focus is on technology-based spin-outs and subsidiaries of established firms.

Accelerators: According to NBIA, people sometimes use the term business accelerator as another term for business incubator in an attempt to differentiate themselves in the market. During the dot-com boom that occurred around 2000, numerous terms like "accelerator" emerged to describe business incubation programs. In the current market, many of these terms have fallen away, but accelerator remains a relatively popular term to describe business incubation programs.

Science Parks/Research Parks: A science or research park can be characterized as a complex set of activities within a limited geographic area around a university campus where high value-added research, industry and capital are combined by entrepreneurs, including academic and research personnel. The IASP further defines science parks as being managed under a formal co-operative agreement with university research centers for the purpose of promoting the establishment and growth of knowledge-based enterprises. A main mechanism is the transfer of technical and managerial expertize to tenant firms. In some countries, the parks aim to attract existing firms as well.

Technology Parks/Technopolis: Often, larger than science parks, a technology park or *technopolis* is a zone of economic activity composed of the universities, research centers, industrial and tertiary units, which realize their activities based on research and technological development. Technology parks are limited in geographic area but maintain network links to large firms and the public research infrastructure at both national and international levels. In Japan and France, the technopolis model extends over the entire surrounding urban area. In the United States, technology parks differ in so far as their main goal is to promote synergy between the surrounding research and industrial sectors and create specific "*centres of competence*".

Pépinières and Hatcheries: In France, generally incubators associated with research and academic institutions provide support services from the idea stage to the legal establishment of a business entity without providing any physical space. Typically, new firms locate at *pépinières d'entreprises* or hatcheries which provide temporary accommodation for individual entrepreneurs and small businesses. These facilities are mainly sponsored by local government and community actors with the goal of stimulating local job creation. A main factor behind this has been the role of regional and local governments in developing incubation mechanisms adapted to their specific economic and territorial needs.

Virtual Incubators: Virtual incubators or incubators without walls are a phenomenon of the late 1990s/early 2000s dot.com bubble. They generally have a central office and do not offer any on-site space to locate client firms. Most of the networking and client support is carried out through the internet. NBIA traditionally has defined virtual incubation as the delivery of incubation services solely through electronic means. However, the term may be used interchangeably with "affiliate program" for services delivered to clients that are not in residence in an incubator. "Virtual incubation" also may be used to denote a program that offers services to clients who are located far away from an incubator, when the program does not offer any multi-tenant space.

Table 2 provides a comparative overview of the types of programmatic activities or key services generally made available in the aforementioned incubator types.

A brief history on the growth of incubators

Historically, the first known business incubator was opened in 1959 in the US, called the Industrial Center of Batavia, New York. It was a privately owned multi-tenant facility established in an abandoned manufacturing building. The Center was hosting a chicken company, whose presence helped coin the name 'incubator' for the facility, according to the founder (NBIA, 1990). Shortly thereafter, in 1964, another US facility, the University City Science Center began operations in Philadelphia. The UCSC facility was the nation's first urban research park and was sponsored by 28 colleges/universities and health centers (*ibid*). These two pioneering

Table 2.   Incubator Mechanisms and Scope of Services/Programmatic Activities

Mechanism type	Physical space	Shared services	Business services	R&D, tech facilities	University connection	Venture funds
Development incubator	Yes	Yes	Limited	No	No	Limited
Mixed-use incubator	Yes	Yes	Yes	Limited	Possible	Limited
Technology incubator/ Innovation center	Yes	Yes	Yes	Yes	Yes	Yes
Science/Research park/Technopolis	Yes	Possible via incubators	Yes	Yes	Yes	Yes
Pépinières and hachries	Yes	Yes	Limited	No	Possible	Possible
Virtual incubator	No	No	Limited	No	No	Possible

facilities which laid the foundation of incubator mechanisms in North America initially started experimenting with limited shared tenant services including rental space.

By 1980, there were 12–15 such facilities in the US, and this 'first wave' of incubator programs that started out in the 1970s primarily aimed at addressing the economic restructuring and job creation needs, essentially provided affordable space and shared services often in abandoned industrial facilities. The apparent failure of the 'smokestack chasing' policies of the US states, and the work of researchers such as Birch (1979) at MIT, which highlighted the importance of new startups and entrepreneurial small firms in job growth and vibrancy of the national economy, helped catalyze the incubation movement (Mian, 2011). In the 'second wave' that prevailed during much of 1980s and 1990s, several new incubation facilities were developed in the US and Europe that offered a richer menu of services including counseling, skills enhancement and networking facilities. According to NBIA (2012), the following public–private sector activities drove incubation industry growth during this period:

- In the mid-1980s, the U.S. Small Business Administration (SBA) encouraged incubator development by holding a series of regional conferences and several publications to disseminate information about incubation.

- In 1982, the state of Pennsylvania established the Ben Franklin Technology Development Program, which included incubators as a key component, and became a pioneer in states' support of business incubation.
- A major private technology firm, Control Data Corporation formed City Venture Corporation (CVC) that developed business incubators in several US cities.

Following this lead, several states and communities in the US and Canada, Europe, Asia and South America embraced the business incubation concept. And during the 'second wave', extensive worldwide activity in establishing business incubation programs was witnessed.

Starting in late 1990s, a new incubation model emerged in parallel. This 'third wave' introduced the internet-based virtual incubation model which helped to provide a convergence of support towards creating growths potential, specialized ventures such as ICT startups. A case in point is the establishment of incubators like Idealab in 1996. This for-profit internet incubator model which mushroomed in a couple of years fell back within few months after the April 2000 Nasdak technology stock failure (NBIA, 2001). However, the wave of specialized incubators such as in biotech and incubators as part of science parks continued to grow. Figure 1 provides an overview of the various incubation models that have been developed over these years.

It may be noted here that during the last quarter century, notable international incubator programs (other than the US) were launched in China, France, Brazil, Korea, Israel, Taiwan, Malaysia and Turkey. Therefore, today, various types of business incubator mechanisms have emerged as successful economic development tools through basic innovative enterprise development in many North American, European and emerging economy Asian and South American nations. Because of the vast variations in the incubator definitions across nations, it is difficult to estimate the total number of incubators in the world. However, a broad search of the webpages of several incubator-related national professional associations show that they are popular in several developed and emerging nations. Table 3 provides a list of the number of facilities operating in various parts of the world. Figure 2 shows the growth of incubators in North America.

Over the past half century during which the business incubation concept has been taking roots, first in the US and then in Europe and elsewhere, the use of various incubator mechanisms has grown rapidly and matured

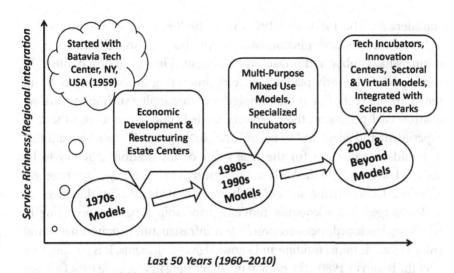

Figure 1. Historic Evolution of the Incubation Mechanism Models
Source: Mian 2012

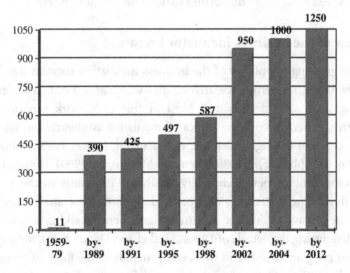

Figure 2. Growth of Incubator Programs in the US
Source: iNBIA

considerably. The 1980s and 1990s were the 'hey days' of the incubation industry experiencing phenomenal growth both in the US and Europe during which public and private entities engaged in a great deal of often ill-considered and poorly planned projects prompting industry's shake-up in the following years. Given the complexity of developing such innovative yet controversial programs, these projects needed time — the time to test, to experiment and adapt and to fail or succeed. Years ago, it was often said that it would take decades for the true value of incubation industry to be known. Fortunately, in the USA, and to a great extent in Europe, that time was afforded.[2] Generally, the 'success' has been attributed to the fact that these are well managed and adequately funded partnership programs operating in relatively developed socio-economic and infrastructural environments and enjoy favorable initial funding and knowledge endowments. It is obvious that after the boom of 1980s, the growth in establishing new science park facilities has plateaued in the USA starting the second half of 1990s (Mian, 2011), which is a sign of relative maturity. However, there are strong indications that the university-related incubation model continues to be a favored policy instrument for technology-driven regional economic development both in the US as well as Europe and beyond (Mian and Hulsink, 2009).

A review of the business incubator literature

With the growing popularity of the business incubation concept starting in the early 1980s, numerous research studies were carried out to review the emerging incubator mechanisms. Most of this early work was primarily descriptive, generally covering topics of incubator configuration, typology and job creation through economic restructuring (Allen, 1985; Smilor and Gill, 1986; Campbell *et al.*, 1988; Allen and McCluskey, 1990). However, with the development of new technology incubator programs in the US and Europe during the 1980s and 1990s, particularly those associated with univer-sities, a new wave of impact assessment and benchmarking studies were conducted during the decade of 1990s (Hacket and Dilts, 2004a). Most of this incubator program assessment work was generally in the form of qualitative case studies, where units of analysis varied from incubators, their tenant firms, sponsoring universities and the surrounding region (Mian, 1991, 1997;

---

[2] Inferred from interviews with NBIA officials and other incubation experts.

Tornatzky *et al.*, 1996; Autio and Klofsten, 1998; Sherman and Chappell, 1998; Thierstein and Wilhelm, 2001). Some of the characteristics studied include key components of an assessment framework for technology business incubators (particularly university related) including goals, partnerships, operational policies and portfolio of value-added services including mentoring and coaching, networking and ease of knowledge flows within and across incubator boundaries, benchmarking measures, regional embeddedness, comparisons of on- and off-incubator firm performance, agglomeration effects, firm credibility and marketing reference, government subsidized versus privately owned facilities and specialized versus general purpose facilities.

Table 4 provides a chorological list of major studies covering the last more than three decades of work in understanding the business incu-

Table 3. Business Incubators Operating in Various Countries

Country/region	Number of facilities	Information source, year[3]	Incubator model types included
USA	1250	iNBIA, 2012	Business incubators, technology incubators, accelerators
Germany	300	ADT, 2012	Innovation centers, technology incubators
UK	300	UKBI, 2012	Business incubators, technology incubators, accelerators
France	113	RETIS, 2010	Public incubators, parks, center of enterprise and innovation
Canada	120	NBIA, 2006	Business incubators, technology incubators, accelerators
China	548	MOST, 2006	High-tech incubators, science and technology parks
Brazil	400	APROTEC, 2008	Technology incubators, innovation centers
Mexico	191	NBIA, 2006	Business incubators, technology incubators, accelerators
World	7000 (estimates)	iNBIA, 2012	All types of incubation programs

[3] The various country professional associations which are the sources of information are NBIA — National Business Incubation Association, USA; ADT ; UKBI — United Kingdom Business Incubation; RETIS; MOST — Ministry of Science and Technology, China; APROTEC.

Table 4.   Business Incubator Perspective and Assessment: Major Studies

Author(s), year, country	Methodology and data	Key findings
Allen (1985), USA	70 incubators and 910 firms (response 56%).	This study pointed out the potential of incubators for regional development. It helped to *define incubator organization types* based on sponsorship, and service categories provided to the tenants. The concept of incubator was described as a network of organizations providing skills, knowledge and motivation, real estate experience, provision of business and shared services.
Smilor and Gill (1986), USA	117 incubators and 211 firms (response NA).	The findings of this research supported much of what was already known and provided new data about the age, education and salary of incubator managers. Using the four *incubator organization types identified* earlier, the study further identified their measures of success.
Campbell *et al.* (1988), USA	13 incubators and 294 firms (response 55%).	In this case study, the *features identified contributing to the incubator effectiveness* were low cost developing and operating; and quality management of facilities.
Allen and McCluskey (1990), USA	127 incubators, response 70%. Regression analysis (dependent variables: log of jobs created and firms graduated).	Occupancy rates around 50% show that incubators are not strong real estate ventures. *Old incubators with accumulated expertize are more successful* than new ones. Incubators that admit light manufacturing firms are more successful in job creation. None of the business support services have significant impact on jobs created and firms graduated.
Mian, (1991, 1996a, 1997), USA	Six established university technology business incubators (UTBIs), 150 tenant firms (response 32%).	As the first university incubator focused work, the study supported the assertion that the *university relationship provides the resource base and environment conducive to the development of NTBFs*. In a series of papers, the work provided a *checklist for successful facilities*, and developed an *assessment framework for managing UTBIs*.

Rice (1993), USA	Nine incubators 36 firms (selected).	The study contended that *managerial intervention is the key* in incubation support, and success is measured by proactive direct intervention. Factors limiting the effectiveness of direct intervention were identified as the availability of time and lack of responsiveness of the firms.
Tornatzky *et al.* (1996), USA	54 incubators (TIs mostly) out of 84 identified through reputational snowballing. Mail questionnaire followed by phone interviews.	The findings of this study describe the best practices for each of the following *technology incubator* domains: management, business planning, finance and capitalization, research and technology, legal and regulatory, physical infrastructure, markets and products and structure/operations. Descriptions supported with data provide *benchmarking measures* in each of the above domains.
Autio and Klofsten (1998), Finland	Case study of two incubators to assess their management policies.	Incubators are *embedded in local context and their success could only be analyzed in the local settings*. 'Success stories' cannot be generalized. Practitioners should be careful in adopting policies that are found to be important in other incubators.
Thierstein and Wilhelm (2001), Switzerland	Case study for nine incubators in Switzerland. Short surveys in 40 incubators. Response 63%.	The *regional economic development aim is missing*. This can be partially explained by the fact that contrary to most countries incubators in Switzerland are *privately owned* in most cases.
Colombo and Delmastro (2002), Italy	45 incubator firms (Response 20%) are matched with 45 similar firms that are outside the incubators. Quantitative analysis on matched sample.	Italian incubators are successful in attracting high skilled entrepreneurs. However, there are *no significant differences between on- and off-incubator firms regarding their innovative output. The on-incubator firms outperformed off-incubator firms in employment growth, education of the workforce, participation in EU-sponsored projects and establishing formal cooperative relations.*

(Continued)

Table 4. (*Continued*)

Author(s), year, country	Methodology and data	Key findings
Hsu *et al.* (2003), Taiwan	Comparison between firms in ITRI incubator (16 firms, response 50%) and firms in other incubators (34 firms 16% RR).	ITRI incubator tenants are more satisfied with incubator services when compared to firms in other incubators. It was found that *agglomeration is important for the development of the incubator firms' success* which implies that complementarities are important in local economic development.
Lee and Osteryoung (2004), Korea	39 Korean university incubators and 20 U.S. university incubators.	14 factors for the effectiveness of incubator systems, among them, goal/operations strategy, physical/human resources, incubator services, and networked program. There are no significant differences between U.S. and Korean incubators, except for goal/operation strategy which were *perceived to be more important to UBIs in the US than in Korea.*
Peters *et al.* (2004), USA	48 incubators: 19 non-profit, 14 universities-based, and 15 for-profits incubators.	There is a significant difference in the number of companies graduating among the three types of incubators (non-profit, for-profit and university-based). *The success of incubators relates mostly to the presence of coaching and access to networks.* Characteristics and quality of networking also varied by incubator types.
Abetti (2004), Finland	Case study of 5 incubators among 16 incubators in Finland. A general assessment for the Helsinki region.	The *survival rates reach to 95%.* The incubators receive little funding from the government but are able to create high skilled cost-effective jobs (government subsidy per created job is €6450 which is much less than the welfare costs per person in Finland). *Average sales growth rose by 160% per year during and after incubation.*
Rothaermel *et al.* (2007), USA	79 tech ventures incubated at Georgia Tech's ATDC.	Knowledge flows from university to incubator firms through contractual and non-contractual ways. The *knowledge flows increased firms' absorptive capacity which positively related to firm performance.*

Etzkowitz *et al.* (2005), Brazil	Case study based on detailed interviews. Qualitative research.	The most important finding is that *university connection allowed Brazilian incubators to create a less costly development strategy that took advantage* of resources, such as academic, available elsewhere.
Wynarczyk and Raine (2005), UK	Surveys in 17 incubators. Quantitative and qualitative evaluation.	Incubators do play an important role in nurturing business and creating jobs. The hands on support provided by the incubator and advisors are found to be vital for firm survival especially in the early stages of the business.
Chan and Lau (2005), Hong Kong	Case study of six incubator firms. Qualitative assessment.	*Rental subsidies and office spaces are found to be critically important for* entrepreneurs. The training programs are also found to be useful for incubator tenants. On the contrary, firms indicate that they do not gain benefits from clustering.
von Zedtwitz and Grimaldi (2006), Italy	Case study of 15 incubators. Qualitative assessment.	Incubator services should be type-specific and the *portfolio of the services provided should match with the objectives of the incubator*. The incubator management should be sufficiently experienced to match service needs to incubator purpose.
Kim and Armes (2006), Korea	Information on 150 incubator managers (response 40%). Qualitative assessment of incubators and managers.	*Qualified incubator managers tend to provide better and specialized services;* use wider range of support services and establish wider support networks. The rapid growth in the incubation business created a shortage of managers and hence had a negative impact on the success of incubators.
Studdard (2006), US and Finland	Survey of 52 firms. Response 18%. Quantitative analysis.	Knowledge acquired by interacting with the incubator manager has no effect on new product development, technological competence and sales cost but it enhances the reputation (defined as *increased credibility and marketing reference*) of the firm.

(Continued)

Table 4. (*Continued*)

Author(s), year, country	Methodology and data	Key findings
Gassmann and Becker (2006), US and Europe	47 interviews. In addition 77 firms from the EC benchmarking survey.	Both the incubator and the *ventures benefit from resource and information flows at the initial phase.* The main corporation benefits at the second phase from intangible and tacit knowledge coming from the for-profit incubators and the firms.
Chandra (2007), China	Case study of 12 incubators. Interviews with managers.	The fact that most incubators in *China* are large in size, high-tech-oriented and rely on state funding made *incubators dependent on government and weakened their capability toward market-oriented incubation.*
Aerts *et al.* (2007), Europe	Data from European Commission Benchmarking study. 107 incubators. Response 18%.	*Tenants' survival rate is positively correlated with the availability of a more balanced screening process.* Reliance on one screening process (market, financial, management screening) is positively related to high failure rate. Incubators role in supporting entrepreneurial spirit by any means is critical for firm survival.
Hytti and Maki (2007), Finland	131 high-tech firms. Response 83%.	Firms that are young and have growth potential benefit more from the incubator services. Older firms tend to be less satisfied with services. *Incubation period should be optimal and flexible according to firm needs.*
Akçomak and Taymaz (2007), Turkey	Matched sample assessment of 48 incubator firms (response 60%).	There are *differences between on- and off-incubator firms in terms of sales and employment but not in innovativeness.* Tangible incubator services and seed funding explain this differential.
McAdam and McAdam (2008), Ireland	18 university incubator firms over 36 months incubation period.	*Tangible incubator resources are important for the development of the firm in the early stages.* Among a set of factors, networking and clustering are rated to be the most important factors behind the firm's success.

Frenkel *et al.* (2008), Israel	12 incubators (6 private and 6 public). Surveys with incubator managers, 60 firms.	Both private and public technology incubators promoted technological entrepreneurship among the immigrants from US and former USSR. *Firms in private incubators seem to benefit from networking with (international) strategic partners and academia.* But private incubators cannot fully substitute public incubators.
M'Chirgui *et al.* (2011), France	A data set of 29 technology incubators, 1200 firms incubatee projects were surveyed.	The resource combinations (tangible and intangible are a relevant factor in explaining inter-incubator variation in their NTBF development performance: *The key incubator resources identified are advisors, financial resources, patents, co-location with university research and science park.*
Said *et al.* (2012), Malaysia	10 year longitudinal study of three incubators in Malaysia's MSC program for IT businesses.	*Partnerships between the state, local and private sectors and among the incubator tenants remain underdeveloped. For more robust results, the incubator management needs improvements and professionalization.*
Schwartz and Hornych (2008), Germany	151 firm incubated in diversified and specialized incubators. Response n.a.	The investigation of the value-added contributions of *specialized incubators*, particularly regarding hardware (premises, equipment) components, business assistance, networking and reputation gains *reveals considerable differences compared to the more diversified incubation models.*

Sources: Mian (1996a), Hacket and Dilts (2004b), Rothaermel and Thursby (2005), Akçomak (2009) and others.

bation concept, facility design, articulating the typology of incubator mechanisms and incubator performance assessment and benchmarking. As shown, only a handful of the studies were comprehensive enough to assess the performance of such mechanism in providing business incubation support. Some of these studies specifically focused on the university technology incubator generally understood to provide a resource base necessary for the development of new technology based firms (Allen and Levine, 1986; Mian, 1991, 1994a).

According to Hackett and Dilts (2004b) during all these years, only a handful of studies use theories developed in various social science disciplines, but they fell short of any serious attempt to develop a theory that may have enhanced our understanding of the business incubation process. These diverse efforts include the market failure argument (Plosila and Allen, 1985), structural contingency theory (Ketchen *et al.*, 1993), network theory (Hansen *et al.*, 2000), social capital theory (Bollingtoft and Ulhoi, 2005), the real-options view (Hackett and Dilts, 2004a), and the resource-based theory perspective (M'Chirgui *et al.*, 2011).

Benchmarking the incubation mechanism: learning from best practices

As stated earlier, business incubators are employed as incubation mechanisms for basic innovative enterprise development in many US, European and other regions of the world. It is therefore important to evaluate the performance of these mechanisms as part of any regional innovation strategy. Despite the steady increase in the number of these mechanisms since the 1980s, first in the US and then Europe, there has been no single framework available to assess how they are working and thereby improve their effectiveness. As noted by Autio and Klofsten (1998, p. 30), "in spite of the rapid increase in the number of evaluations, the available material on the successful management of incubators is largely dominated by documents of the so called 'success story' type". This has placed economic development leaders in a difficult position. On the one hand, the regions that see a wave of activity sweeping the world feel some pressure to follow suit. On the other hand, experts caution that the jury is still out on the effectiveness of incubation mechanisms due to the lack of pertinent experience and hence evidence about their usefulness (Mian, 1997). This is particularly true in light of the numerous questions regarding their impact and organizational self-sustainability. The challenges confronting incubation researchers developing such a framework are summarized by Doutriaux (2001):

- Lack of understanding of the technology business incubation process;
- Lack of consensus on the type of evaluation criteria to be used (OECD, 1997);
- High heterogeneity of the population of science parks and technology incubators with a high variety of sponsors, objectives, science orientation and business models (Bearse, 1998);
- Lack of proper experimental design with an appropriate control group to correct for pre-incubation firm characteristics and external effects (Sherman and Chappel, 1998) and
- Short times series of data for analysis because of the emerging nature and relatively short history of these mechanisms (Zhang, 2004).

Success is relative and depends on expected outcomes. As noted by Bearse (1998), "The definition of a business incubator in terms of its goals and objectives provides the essential starting point for an evaluation". However, not all incubation programs have the same goals and objectives. Whereas an economic development agency may be interested mainly in job creation, a university may look for dynamic research linkages and research funding, whereas a for-profit incubator may insist on profitability and return on investment. Success criteria will therefore generally differ from case to case, making for difficult comparisons and generalizations.

Sherman and Chappell (1998) have proposed four domains of potential incubator impact, each needing its own sets of measurements: "incubator-level impacts, firm-level impacts, community-level impacts, and ancillary community impacts". Studies on "best practices" often use the following criteria: number of jobs created (by tenants and by graduates, locally and globally), number of graduates and survival rate, sales of tenant firms and of graduates (locally and globally), growth in sales and profitability of tenant firms, number of clients served and their geographic distribution, incubator revenue (profitability, sustainability), new technologies brought to market, taxes paid by the incubator and its tenants, local economic impact (direct and indirect impact, in terms of business activity, jobs, regional exports and imports, property values).[4]

The most important weakness of most assessment schemes is the difficulty to find an acceptable control group of outside firms to evaluate the relative impact of the incubation program (incubator, science park) on incubatee firm itself and also control for the new firm's individual dynamics (startup characteristics, management team, business proposition), technology life cycle, sector of activity, external economic and technological factors — that is, how different would have those firms' development be if they had not joined the incubation program?[5]

Typical key success factors reported in the literature and by practitioners include the following:

- A well-researched business plan/feasibility analysis with focus on financial feasibility, sustainability.
- A business management approach with enough financial resources to hire an experienced incubation program manager and to offer competitive staff salaries.
- Local business community support, local businesses having recognized the need to broaden/diversify the local economy.
- Local government ready to champion the concept and acting as stimulator, strategic partner.
- Partnerships with local universities or colleges.
- Strategic partnership between all levels of governments.
- Proactive board of directors with vision and good business/social networks.

To benchmark the performance of a technology business incubation mechanism, a comprehensive assessment framework was proposed by Mian (1997, 1996b), which is based on an in-depth study of multiple US

---

[4] Inferred from presentations made at the 2001 National Business Incubation Association conference, San Jose, CA, May 2001, and also from OECD (1999).

[5] One exception is series of studies conducted in UK where matched-pair samples of on-and-off-park firms were used, for details, see Westhead (1997).

university incubator cases. Given the dynamic and environmentally integrative approach adopted in this framework, it is considered appropriate to use it to assess the effectiveness of incubators in their pursuits of developing regional innovation ecosystems. The following three key sets of variables are employed:

(1) *Performance Outcomes* — the incubation system's performance outcomes are assessed using four elements: (a) program sustainability and growth; (b) tenant firms' survival and growth; (c) contribution to the sponsors' mission; (d) community-related impacts.

(2) *Management Policies and Their Effectiveness* — an assessment of the incubators and science parks' management practices and operational policies in light of the program objectives provides a review of the effective utilization of resources resulting in the success of the program. The key elements assessed include: (a) goals, organizational structure and governance; (b) financing and capitalization; (c) operational policies; (d) target markets.

(3) *Services and Their Value Added* — a review of the actual provision and their perceived value added to the client firms in the form of: (a) the typical shared office services including rental space and other business assistance services; (b) the sponsor institution-related inputs, such as, in the case of a university, student employees, faculty consultants and other institutional support and provision of networking for the TBF.

The framework has earlier been employed to benchmark the performance of the incubation mechanisms assessed in several case studies in North America and Europe (Mian, 1997; Mian and Hulsink, 2009). This framework has been adapted for use by Lofsten and Lindelof (2002, pp. 862–863) for science parks in Sweden. It is comprehensive enough to cover the key variable involved and can easily be adapted for use in accessing most of the incubation mechanism types described earlier in this chapter. To illustrate through actual case study examples, this framework is employed to assess and benchmark the performance of two prominent US incubation programs in the following case studies.

Incubator case studies

The Virginia Tech Corporate Research Center (VT-CRC) is a state university-led science park and incubator situated in Virginia's rural New River Valley Region. Established by the Virginia Technological Institute and State University (Virginia Tech), this rapidly developing modern facility offers multitude of highly developed infrastructure located next to the University campus and offers trained manpower and university R&D results. Not only new firms based on university technology are being nurtured, but outside firms are also being solicited through generous relocation packages. The Park has experienced steady growth in physical facilities and number of tenants since inception providing technology transfer and entrepreneurial training generating substantial innovations.

The Park is a not-for-profit subsidiary of the Virginia Tech Foundation, which is governed by a board with broad regional representation and serves as a focal point in economic development by incubating and capturing technology-oriented firms in this rural region of the state. In the last three years, the Park has grown to accommodate 140 leading-edge high-tech companies engaged in diverse areas of research and technology.

Due to its technology emphasis, the entry policy is restricted toward those firms that can benefit from regional technology resources and the exit policy is kept flexible. With its numerous value-added services, the facility is making sustained efforts to tap university technology by modernizing the area's technology infrastructure though broadband connectivity and leveraging university resources. The VC and seed capital availability is limited and there are conscious efforts to improve this service by co-locating financial institutions on the park facility. The park provides a virtual incubation support through its Business and Technology Center to new and fledgling firms from throughout the state.

A new brick and mortar technology incubator facility VT Knowledge Works was established in 2005 to overcome the need for formal incubation support, however, the original program has continued to operate throughout the region in a virtual incubation fashion. Both of these programs are located in the CRC. In this two-pronged approach, the first pre-launch components are constructed to help market-worthy ventures organize, formulate strategy, obtain outside investment and launch in an efficient manner. In the second enterprise class, members benefit from emphasis on strategic support for ongoing growth, continuing intra-preneurship and professional development for the corporate leader.

The University Research Park in Wisconsin-Madison (URP) is a suburban science park equipped with a maturing incubator facility. The focus is on university-developed technologies managed by its Wisconsin Alumni Research Foundation (WARF), specifically in the biotechnology area. The Park is another state university-led initiative that has been successful in incubating several new firms in partnership with the local private sector that is also funding the incubator operation.

The facility is organized as two not-for-profit corporations, one for real estate operation and the other to run its Science Center. It provides shared space and office services to its client firms. Most business development services including VC and financial referrals and technology support services from university resources are available to the clients. A survey of the client firms showed that they were generally satisfied with the provision of these services. URP is a state-of-the-art award winning park with a relatively new incubator — the Madison Gas and Electric (MGE) Innovation Center.

As a unique public–private partnership for technology development, the MGE Innovation Center houses a number of new startup firms, some of which are experiencing growth and have moved to the Science Center building of the Park which provides a flexible space for expansion. The UW-Madison itself has benefited in multiple ways. Its students and faculty have enjoyed collaborations with the Park companies through student internship programs and part-time jobs, faculty company creation and research partnerships.

The University's drive in technology commercialization and the promotion of its image as a partner in regional economic development has been well served. After three decades of growth on Madison's near west side, in 2009 University Research Park established its presence in downtown Madison with a new Metro Innovation Center targeting nearby UW-Madison talent of university-related entrepreneurs focused on IT and medical devices technologies. In 2010, an ambitious Phase II of the Park project was started that will add 54 building sites on additional 270 acres. The Park Phase 2 is planned to include some mixed use development including residential housing, which will allow enhanced student/faculty entrepreneur-related activities.[6]

Table 5 provides a comparative overview of the benchmarking characteristics of these two US cases described as follows.

In terms of sponsorship, both facilities have partnership arrangements involving university, government and private sectors — they both have

Table 5. Overview of Benchmarking Characteristics of Two Incubator Mechanisms

Surrounding region	Small size city rural area (Blacksburg, VA)	Medium size city semi-urban area (Madison, WI)
Incubator/ Science park	VT-CRC	MGE innovation center/URP, Wisconsin
Facility background	A rural park with a virtual but developing incubator facility. Established in 1985 by VT. About 104 firms and 1800 employees. Broad range of university technology.	A suburban park with maturing incubator. Established in 1984 by UW. About 110 firms and 2300 employees. Focus on biotech and other areas of university technology.
Performance outcome	Experienced fast growth in facilities and tenants since inception. Salient efforts in university tech tr. and enterer. training. Steady tenants generating substantial innovations.	Sustained growth in park over the past two decades. Significant efforts in university tech. tr. though WARF. Created successful firms and partnered with private sector to help incubate new firms.
Management policies and their effectiveness	Park is not-for-profit subs. of VT foundation. Governed by board with regional reps. Strict entry and flexible exit criteria. Serves as a focal point in econ. dev. of the region.	Park is organized as two not-for-profit corps. under university trustees. Strict entry and flexible exit criteria. Serves as a focal point in mobilizing university developed technology for regional development.

(*Continued*)

[6] See http://universityresearchpark.org/Category/URP-news/ [Accessed February 18, 2011].

Table 5.   (*Continued*)

Surrounding region	Small size city rural area (Blacksburg, VA)	Medium size city semi-urban area (Madison, WI)
Services and their value added	Limited shared park services, including tech dev. services, efforts to provide seed cap and VC access, info databases, tech trans., access to university resources. Formal incubator facility is being developed.	Increasingly developed park and incubator shared services, bus and tech dev. services, easy seed cap and VC access, info databases, tech tran., access to university resources. Tenant satisfied with support and avail of resources.
Overall assessment:	A modern and growing park facility with virtual incubation component. Sustained efforts to capitalize on university tech and developing area innovation infrastructure.	A state of the art park with a private sector supported incubation operation. Developing a model tech entrepreneurship infrastructure based on university's R&D strengths.

research universities in leadership positions, which are also producing new knowledge through their R&D centers.

URP has a formal incubator program MGE Innovation Center, while VT-CRC continues to operate its virtual regional incubation ecosystems that provide startup and firm acceleration help and act as tenant capturing tools for their parks. Both facilities are surrounded by several other affiliate organizations providing technical and business advice, laboratories and workshops, seed and venture capital connections, databases and internet sources and entrepreneurial education and training programs.

The Management policies and practices are covered under goals, organizational structure and governance. In terms of goals, they both seek participation in the regional economic development activities by supporting the development of technology-based firms, providing a laboratory for learning entrepreneurial skills, and promoting commercialization of university technology. The study findings of these parks with respect to their past accomplishments show that both have made considerable progress in meeting these goals. In terms of governance, they have boards with representations from the key stakeholders, which provide policy guidance. These are generally run as not-for-profit organizations and typically a director (manager) heads the park management team and the incubator manager reports to the park director.

Marketing practices of targeted technologies and the type and characteristics of entrepreneurs admitted were the key factors reviewed. In terms of targeted technologies, the new and emerging fields, including software, informatics, electronics and biotechnology firms, represented the largest number of tenants; however, the relative marketing emphasis varied according to university strengths and/or regional developmental policies. The participation of university faculty and students as entrepreneurs has been on the rise — university-related entrepreneurs are encouraged to participate in both facilities.

Financing practices have been studied both from the park as well as their client firm perspectives. Whether public or private, most parks and their associated incubator programs have benefited in one form or another from state grants. However, most of the US incubators (including large number of those established in early 1980s) have yet to attain financial self-reliance — a goal espoused by both facilities studied here. The support for the provision of easily accessible seed and venture capital from multiple sources has been the hallmark of these successful parks and their associated incubator programs. In the U.S., private investors or "angels" have often been described as the best source for early seed capital for emerging technology companies. Most tenant firms in these facilities have ample opportunities to pursue private risk capital. However, the venture capitalists make highly selective investments in young companies they perceive as having a high growth potential. Moreover, a host of state and federal grant programs are available for which ample guidance and support is provided by the parks to their technology-oriented tenants. As a result, these two parks like all successful parks and incubator programs in the country have a significant percentage of tenants supported through external funds.

Operational policies of the parks essentially include tenant leasing, and allowance of R&D and manufacturing within the park. In the case of incubators operational policies include entry policy, graduation policy, tenant performance review procedures, equity/royalty policy, intellectual property policy and alumni-firm relationship policy. Both facilities have developed elaborate policies and procedures in all of these areas. In case of incubators more stringent selection/entry criteria is applied across the board. Such criteria often include technical and business feasibility assessments combined with the entrepreneur's needs and possible fit with the park/incubator resources. Further, these are often group level admittance decisions. The normal incubation period is three years and is applied with some flexibility, based on each entrepreneur's needs. Tenant performance at incubator is regularly monitored, and mentors from the private sector are encouraged to participate along with the incubator manager to provide necessary feedback to the entrepreneur. Though not widely practiced in the U.S., equity/royalty holdings in client firms by the park/incubator are a growing practice levied in the form of "success fees," etc. for which new procedures are being developed. Well-run incubator facilities not only stay in contact with their alumni firms (tenant firms which have already graduated) but also involve these firms with the current tenants to provide mentoring.

In the provision of services, both facilities like most successful parks and their associated incubators have been responsive to the client needs and perceived usefulness of the gamut of services often provided through these mechanisms — shared space, typical office services, conference room and other maintenance services, etc. Previous research shows that technology-based client firms have consistently given higher ranks to the university-related services/benefits, such as university image; use of student employees and faculty consultants; and access to libraries and laboratories (Mian 1996a, 1994a). Therefore, both cases provide these services/ benefits, depending upon their overall reputation and commitment to technology incubation. Research results on the value-added contribution and, hence, desirability of typical park/incubator services is mixed. However, most of the typical incubator services, including facilitating networking, business and legal consulting, are available in one form or another to most incubator clients.

Conclusion

This chapter is intended to educate the reader about business incubation and incubator mechanisms as modern entrepreneurship tools employed for supporting the development of new firms throughout the world. The research shows that over the past half century, during which the concept of business incubation has taken root in the United States and then in Europe and elsewhere, their use has grown rapidly. The incubator industry has attained maturity and recognition in this early part of the 21st century.

A closer look at the past three decades of business incubation literature shows that it mostly comprises studies covering (a) incubation perspective including the concept, facility design and models (b) incubator performance assessment and benchmarking the best practices. What is lacking is any substantive work on understanding the incubation process itself. Therefore, the state of the extant business incubation literature may be characterized as "varied, spanning across various disciplines, is fragmented and largely anecdotal, focusing on still a limited number of (incubator) success stories. The research lacks unified basis (use of theories, units of analysis, use of comparison groups), yet it continues to grow, broaden, and refine" (Mian, 2011). Assessing incubators is another controversial and complex task, which warrants longitudinal data. However, with continuous efforts successful facilities have evolved adequate benchmarking procedures that help them maintain sustainable operations.

In term of economic development policy, incubating innovative firms with the involvement of research universities continues to be a favored policy option for those interested in stimulating knowledge-based entrepreneurial growth. However, despite several decades of progress, it is believed that technology business incubation is complex and multi-faceted and there are still numerous unanswered questions and gaps in understanding the process. With the research university assuming the entrepreneurial role of piloting the knowledge economy, well-thought-out and properly planned business incubation programs and the academic-regional policies that shape their performance, provide an attractive option for developing our future knowledge regions. A sustained creation and growth of innovative firms and new products in a region can be better focused by providing enabling institutional platforms in the form of modern incubation mechanisms. Though no single model fits all situations, the incubation strategy has some elements in common that include a cautious approach emphasizing better feasibility studies, phased development, effective regional partnerships, and operating efficient and sustainable programs that are integrated with the regional goals (Mian, *et al.*, 2012).

It may be noted here that in a number of countries such as China and France where government continues to be a major source of incubation funds. While governmental bodies have never been known to be efficient in the allocation of resources, at the same time, market forces and private institutions cannot be relied upon to solve the vicious cycle problems (Venkataraman, 2004), which highlights the key role of regionally led partnerships in the development of future incubation programs (Mian, 2011). Finally, though there are numerous research challenges, which require an ambitious incubation research agenda, sharing the results of our intellectual endeavors supported by the experiential evidence gained from actual case studies will enable us to better serve our communities in the planning and execution of these novel experiments in entrepreneurial economic development.

References

Abetti, P. A. (2004). Government-supported incubators in the Helsinki region, Finland: Infrastructure, results, and best practices. *Journal of Technology Transfer*, 29(1): 19–40.

Aerts, K., Matthyssens, P., and Vandenbempt, K. (2007). Critical role and screening practices of european business incubators. *Technovation*, 27(5): 254–267.

Akçomak, İ. S. (2009). *Incubators as tools for entreprenurship promotion in developing countries.* UNU Wider, Helsinki, Finland, Research Paper No. 2009/52.

Akçomak, İ. S. and Taymaz, E. (2007). Assessing the Effectiveness of Incubators: The Case of Turkey. In Ramani, V. V. and Bala Krishna, A. V. (Eds.), *Business Incubation: An Introduction.* Icfai University Press, Hyderabad, pp. 234–264.

Allen, D. (1985). *Small business incubators and enterprise development, report prepared for the US Department of Commerce.* Pennsylvania State University, University Park, PA.

Allen, D. and McCluskey, R. (1990). Structure, policy, services, and performance in the business incubator industry. *Entrepreneurship Theory and Practice*, 15(2): 61–77.

Allen, D. and Levine, V. (1986). *Nurturing Advanced Technology Enterprises: Emerging Issues in State and Local Economic Development Policy.* Prager, New York.

Autio, E. and Klofsten, M. (1998). A comparative study of two european business incubators'. *Journal of Small Business Management,* 36: 30–43.

Bearse, P. (1998). A question of evaluation: NBIA's impact assessment of business incubators, *Economic Development Quarterly,* 12(4): 327.

Birch, D. (1979). *The Job Generation Process* (unpublished manuscript), MIT Program on Neighborhood and Regional Change, Cambridge MA.

Bollingtoft, A. and Ulhoi, J. P. (2005). The networked business incubator-leveraging entrepreneurial agency? *Journal of Business Venturing,* 20: 265–290.

Campbell, C., Berge, D., Janus, J., and Olsen, K. (1988). *Change Agents in the New Economy: Business Incubators and Economic Development.* University of Minnesota, Minneapolis, MN.

Chan, K. F. and Lau, T. (2005). Assessing technology incubator programs in the science park: The good, the bad and the ugly. *Technovation,* 25: 1215–1228.

Chandra, A. (2007). Approaches to business incubation: A comparative study of the United States, China and Brazil. Working Paper 2007-WP-29, Networks Financial Institute, Indianapolis.

Colombo, M. G. and Delmastro, M. (2002). How effective are technology business incubators: evidence from Italy. *Research Policy,* 31: 1103–1122.

Doutriaux, J. (2001). Business Incubators, current research activities, presentation made at the 2001 Incubation and New Ventures Conference, January 24–25. The Conference Board of Canada, Toronto.

Etzkowitz, H., Carvalho de Mello, J. M., and Almeida, M. (2005). Towards "Meta-innovation" in Brazil: The evolution of the incubator and the emergence of a triple helix. *Research Policy,* 34(4): 411–424.

EU (2002). Benchmarking of Business Incubators. Kent: Center for Strategy and Evaluation Services.

Frenkel, A., Shefer, D., and Miller, M. (2008). Public versus private technological incubator programmes: Privatizing the technological incubators in Israel. *European Planning Studies,* 16(2): 189–210.

Gassmann, O. and Becker, B. (2006). Towards a resource-based view of corporate incubators. *International Journal of Innovation Management,* 10(1): 19–45.

Hackett, S. M. and Dilts, D. M. (2004a). A real options-driven theory of business incubation. *Journal of Technology Transfer,* 29(1): 41–54.

Hackett, S. M. and Dilts, D. M. (2004b). A systematic review of business incubation research. *Journal of Technology Transfer*, 29(1): 55–82.

Hansen, M. T., Chesbrough, H. W., Nohria, N., and Sull, D. N. (2000). Networked incubators, hothouses of the new economy, *Harvard Business Review*, 78(5), 74–84.

Hsu, P. H., Shyu, J. Z., Yu, H. C., You, C. C., and Lo, T. S. (2003). Exploring the interaction between incubators and industrial clusters: The case of the ITRI incubator in Taiwan. *R&D Management*, 33(1): 79–90.

Hytti, U. and Maki, K. (2007). Which firms benefit most from the incubators. *International Journal of Entrepreneurship and Innovation Management*, 7(6): 506–523.

Ketchen, D., Thomas, J., and Snow, C. (1993). Organizational configuration and performance: A comparison of theoretical approaches. *Academy of Management Journal*, 36(6): 1278–1313.

Kim, H. and Ames, M. (2006). Business incubators as economic development tools: Rethinking models based on the Korea experience. *International Journal of Technology Management*, 33(1): 1–24.

Lee, S. S. and Osteryoung, J. S. (2004). A comparison of critical success factors for effective operations of university business incubators in the United States and Korea. *Journal of Small Business Management*, 42(4): 418–426.

Lofsten, H. and Lindelof, P. (2002). Science parks and the growth of new technology based firms — Academic industry links, innovation and markets. *Research Policy*, 31: 859–876.

M'Chirgui, Z., Mian, S., Fayolle, A., and Lamine, W. (2011). Performance determinants of technology business incubators: A resource-based View. Paper presented in the Babson College Entrepreneurship Research Conference, Jume 8–11. Syracuse, New York.

McAdam, M. and McAdam, R. (2008). High tech startups in university science parks and incubators: the relationship between the startup's life cycle progression and the use of the incubator resources, *Technovation*, 28(5), 277–290.

Mian, S. (1991). *An assessment of university-sponsored business incubators in supporting the development of new technology-based firms*, unpublished doctoral dissertation. The George Washington University, Washington, DC.

Mian, S. (1994a). U.S. university-sponsored technology incubators: An overview of management, policies and performance. *Technovation*, 14(8): 515–528.

Mian, S. (1994b). Are university technology incubators providing a milieu for technology-based entrepreneurship? *Technology Management*, 1: 86–93.

Mian, S. (1996a). Assessing the value-added contributions of university technology business incubators to tenant firms. *Research Policy*, 25: 325–335.

Mian, S. (1996b). The university business incubator: A strategy for developing new research/technology-based firms. *The Journal of High Technology Management Research*, 7: 191–208.

Mian, S. (1997). Assessing and managing the university technology business incubator: An integrative framework. *Journal of Business Venturing*, 12: 251–285.

Mian, S. (2011). University's involvement in technology business incubation: What theory and practice tell us? *International Journal of Entrepreneurship and Innovation Management*, 13(2): 113–121.

Mian, S. and Hulsink, W. (2009). Building knowledge ecosystems through science and technology parks. *Proceedings of the 26th IASP World Conference*, 1–4 June. Research Triangle Park, North Carolina.

Mian, S., Fayolle, A., and Lamine, W. (2012). Building sustainable regional platforms for incubating S&T businesses: evidence from the US and French science and technology parks. *International Journal of Entrepreneurship and Innovation*, 13(4): 235–248.

NBIA (1990). The case of oldest incubators, *NBIA Review*, 6(3), 2–4.

NBIA (2001). Summary of the US incubator industry and prospects for incubator model globalization. Report for Japan Association of New Business Organizations, Prepared by D. Adkins.

NBIA (2012). www.NBIA.org/Resources-FAQ (Accessed 30 September 2012).

OECD (1999). Business incubation. *International Case Studies*, p. 176.

OECD (1997). Technology Incubators, Nurturing Small Firms, OCED/GD(97) 202.

OED (1993). The Oxford English Dictionary, Oxford, Clarendon Press.

Peters, L., Rice, M., and Sundararajan, M. (2004). The role of incubators in the entrepreneurial process. *Journal of Technology Transfer*, 29(1): 83–91.

Plosila, W. and Allen, D. (1985). Small business incubators and public policy: Implications for states and local development strategies. *Policy Studies Journal*, 13: 729–734.

Rice, M. (1993). *Intervention mechanisms used to influence the critical success of new ventures: An exploratory study*. Unpublished doctoral dissertation, School of Management, Renssalaer Poly-technic Institute, NY.

Rothaermel, F. T. and Thursby M. (2005). Incubator firm failure or graduation? the role of university linkages. *Research Policy*, 34(7): 1076–1090.

Rothaermel, F., Agung, S. and Jiang, L. (2007). University entrepreneurship: A taxonomy of the literature. *Industrial and Corporate Change*, 16(4): 691–791.

Said, M. F., Adham, K. A., Abdullah, N. A., Hänninen, S. and Walsh, S. (2012). Incubators and government policy for developing it industry and region in emerging economies. *Asian Academy of Management Journal*, 17(1): 65–96.

Schwartz, M. and Hornych, C. (2008). Specialization as strategy for business incubators: An assessment of the central german multimedia center. *Technovation*, 28: 436–449.

Sherman, H. and Chappell, D. (1998). Methodological challenges in evaluating business incubator outcomes. *Economic Development Quarterly*, 12(4): 313–321.

Smilor, R. and Gill, M. (1986). The new business incubator: Linking talent, technology and know-how. Lexington Books, Lexington, MA.

Studdard, N. L. (2006). The effectiveness of entrepreneurial firm's knowledge acquisition from a business incubator. *International Entrepreneurship and Management Journal*, 2: 211–225.

Thierstein, A. and Wilhelm, B. (2001). Incubator, technology and innovation centres in Switzerland: Features and policy implications. *Entrepreneurship and Regional Development*, 13(4): 315–331.

Tornatzky, L., Batts, Y., McCrea, N., Lewis, M., and Quittman, L. (1996). The art & craft of technology business incubation: Best practices, strategies and tools from 50 programs. *NBIA*, Athens, OH.

UKBI (2012). Available at: www.UKBI.co.uk [Accessed 30 September, 2012].

Venkataraman, S. (2004). Regional transformation through technological entrepreneurship. *Journal of Business Venturing*, 19: 153–167.

Von Zedtwitz, M. and Grimaldi, R. (2006). Are service profiles incubator-specific? results from an empirical investigation in Italy. *Journal of Technology Transfer*, 31(4): 459–468.

Westhead, P. (1997). R&D inputs and outputs of technology-based firms located on and off science parks. *R&D Management*, 27: 45–62.

Wynarczyk, P. and Raine, A. (2005). The performance of business incubators and their potential development in the north east region of England. *Local Economy*, 20(2): 205–220.

Zhang, Y. (2004). Critical factors for science park management: The North American and European experience. *International Journal of Entrepreneurship and Innovation Management*, 4(6): 575–586.

Chapter 2

Success Factors of Business Accelerators in Three European Cities: Paris, London, Berlin

Ayna Yusubova and Bart Clarysse

Introduction

Fostering startup development and identifying the main characteristics, factors and conditions that contribute to new ventures success have been the focus of considerable research effort (Bruneel *et al.*, 2012; Bergek and Norrman, 2008; Grimaldi and Grandi, 2005; Hackett and Dilts, 2004b). In the last decade, a variety of business accelerator programs have emerged as a new tool to support startups ecosystems and offer a wide range of opportunities for innovation in the market (Miller and Bound, 2011). The first accelerator Y-Combinator was pioneered by Paul Graham in 2005 in the US. Subsequently, in 2007, David Cohen and Brad Feld founded TechStars with the idea of transforming new venture ecosystems through the accelerator model. In recent years, a number of programs have significantly grown based on the model of these two programs. This has led to the development of strong replication in Europe. There are 57 business accelerators in the European countries, 738 startups graduate from the accelerators, and 3500–4500 new jobs have been created by startups from the accelerator programs (Christiansen, 2009).[1]

Business accelerators are 3–6 month duration programs that help new ventures in early stages of development by providing support services such as office spaces, coaching and mentoring, small amount of financial support and a set of education programs. One of the most crucial elements of business accelerators and the main reason why startup team participates in the accelerator is the mentorship provided by high-quality mentors. Accelerators also provide a networking opportunity that consists of different events, such as "Demo Day", designed to connect startups with investors. Another characteristic of accelerators is that a cohort of companies is supported at the same time. Business accelerators have a positive impact on startup teams by assisting them learn rapidly to become successful entrepreneurs and create valuable networks (Miller and Bound, 2011).

Initially, the existing literature on business incubators operation has also highlighted several key success factors (Bruneel *et al.*, 2012; Bergek and Norrman, 2008; Ratinho and Henriques, 2010; Hackett and Dilts, 2004b; Rice, 2002; Lumpkin and Ireland, 1988). Among them, selection process, services available and networking opportunities appear to be the most influential. Regarding the selection process, the literature review concludes that, in order to succeed, a rational selection process of startup companies must be developed (Gibson and Wiggins, 2003; Bergek and Norrman, 2008; Hackett and Dilts, 2004b; Lumpkin and Ireland, 1988). Similarly, new ventures would benefit from services available as they often lack business skills (Allen and Rahman, 1985) and usually face problems because of the liabilities associated with being new and small (Soetanto and Jack, 2013; Bruneel *et al.*, 2012). Providing business assistance would foster success of new ventures. Networking opportunities are a valuable aspect for startups to build up strategic partnership with external actors such as potential investors, customers and partners as well as an internal network between startups (Soetanto and Jack, 2013).

---

[1] Data were collected from http://files.basekit.com/live229668_euacceleratorsassembly-seedaccelerators-evidencedata.pdf [Accessed August 28, 2014].

Having identified the key success factors of business incubators, the current chapter also attempts to fill the gap in the literature by developing propositions concerning the business accelerators phenomenon. The research found that business accelerators share similar success factors but also have some unique features. Thereby, under the lens of institutional theory (Zucker, 1987; DiMaggio and Powell, 1983; Kondra and Hinings, 1998), the research also proposed that success factors promote legitimacy in the eyes of stakeholders. And the existence of different types of business accelerators is driven by stakeholders' needs and requirements of which in turn encourage accelerators to improve in order to differentiate themselves. Following this, this research emphasizes the different types of business accelerators such as Generic, Specific, Private and Public.

As the business accelerator phenomenon is quite recent, there is a lack of studies that evaluate accelerator program success factors and their impact on new venture development. In order to respond to the research interest, empirical evidence from a total of 13 case studies of business accelerators from London, Berlin and Paris was provided. Data collection involved formal structured interviews with accelerator managers. The repertory grid method was used to encourage the interviewees to describe the similarities and differences between theirs and other well-known accelerators in some respect to activity features such as selection, business supports and networking as well as accelerator strategies and goals. The findings discuss the success factors and different types of business accelerators.

This chapter is organized as follows. The following section guides the readers through the literature review. Then, we explain the operation of business accelerators within institutional theory. Afterwards, we present the methodological framework and describe the findings. The final section provides a discussion of the implications of our findings for policy makers and startup companies, and suggests some potential avenues for future research.

Literature review

New ventures are fundamental mechanisms in economic policies: however, the presence of new innovative startups is critical and needs support.

Table 1.　Differences Between Incubators and Accelerators

	Accelerators	Incubators
Duration	3–6 months	1–5 years
Cohorts of companies	Yes	No
Selection frequency and criteria	Competitive, team focus	Non-competitive, individual entrepreneurs
Mentorship	Intense	Minimal

Business incubators and accelerators are business service providers which have made a significant contribution supporting new ventures in early stages of development around the world. The new emerging literature (Cohen, 2013) states the similarities of accelerators with incubators. While business accelerators are quite a new phenomenon, business incubators have been a crucial tool for regional economic development for several decades now. Table 1 provides the summary of differences between incubators and accelerators.

Business incubators

Business incubators have been established throughout the world to spur economic growth. According to Phan *et al.* (2005), business incubators are property-based organizations focused on the mission of business acceleration through knowledge agglomeration and resource sharing. In other words, they provide a variety of support services such as shared office space, business assistance and access to networks (Bøllingtoft, 2012; Bergek and Norrman, 2008; Grimaldi and Grandi, 2005; Hackett and Dilts, 2004a; Lyons, 2000; Allen and Rahman, 1985). In this way, they facilitate the early stage of development of venture's life and increase their rates of success (Markley and McNamara, 1994; Brooks, 1986).

A number of researches have also been conducted to identify key elements of business incubator success (Soetanto and Jack, 2013; Bruneel *et al.*, 2012; Bergek and Norrman, 2008; Ratinho and Henriques, 2010; Peters *et al.*, 2004; Hackett and Dilts, 2004a; Rice, 2002; Markley and McNamara, 1994; Allen and Rahman, 1985). Critical success factors are defined as dimensions of organization's operations such as events, circumstances, activities that are vital to its success (Soetanto and Jack, 2013; Bruneel *et al.*, 2012; Lumpkin and Ireland, 1988; Dickinson *et al.*, 1984). For instance, the role of a competent and experienced manager in attracting right ventures through selection process, and assisting new startup companies in business development process are critical factors for the successful operation of business incubators. Hence, selection, business and network support are considered key to the success of incubators (Soetanto and Jack, 2013; Bruneel *et al.*, 2012; Bergek and Norrman, 2008; Ratinho and Henriques, 2010; Peters *et al.*, 2004; Hackett and Dilts, 2004a; Rice, 2002; Markley and McNamara, 1994; Lumpkin and Ireland, 1988; Allen and Rahman, 1985).

Selection includes some criteria to accept or reject new venture for entry, and in order to succeed, an appropriate selection process must be carried out (Gibson and Wiggins, 2003; Bergek and Norrman, 2008; Lumpkin and Ireland, 1988). Selection criteria of new ventures consist of different characteristics such as previous employment experience and founders or team members technical expertize, or new ventures' product, market and financial characteristics. Focusing on certain characteristics when selecting startup teams for admission contributes to the success of incubators (Hackett and Dilts, 2004a; Lumpkin and Ireland, 1988). Selection is also crucial for recourse allocation with respect to both startup accelerations (Lumpkin and Ireland, 1988; Cohen and Hochberg, 2014) and to general economy (Hackett and Dilts, 2004a).

The next important component of success of business incubators is business support services. Business support services are associated with training seminars, workshops, coaching and mentoring as well as services such as developing business and marketing plans, building management teams, obtaining capital and access to a range of other more specialized professional and administrative services. New entrepreneurs often lack a full array of business skills (Bruneel *et al.*, 2012; Allen and Rahman, 1985) and probably face problems because of the liabilities associated with being new and small (Soetanto and Jack, 2013). This is when the incubator plays a key role by providing assistance to fill these gaps.

The network is a tremendous value for startup teams to build up crucial strategic partnership with potential customers, field experts and financiers (Soetanto and Jack, 2013). Network opportunity also helps startup companies obtain important information, knowledge and expertize in the areas where startups have gaps (Soetanto and Jack, 2013; Bøllingtoft and Ulhoi, 2005; Rice, 2002).

A variety of business incubators have been driven by the evolution of startup companies' needs and requirements. This encouraged business incubators to diversify and improve their offers and services. Accordingly, there have been different models of business incubators: public and private, networked and university-based incubators (Soetanto and Jack, 2013; Bøllingtoft, 2012; Clarysse *et al.*, 2005; Phan *et al.*, 2005; Bøllingtoft and Ulhøi, 2005; Grimaldi and Grandi, 2005; Mian, 1996b; Cooper, 1985).

Business accelerators

Business accelerators help nascent firms, and particularly high-tech startups succeed in the early stages of development by providing services such as office spaces, mentoring, networking and a variety of educational programs (Cohen, 2013; Hoffman and Kelley, 2012; Miller and Bound, 2011).

The model of accelerators became globally famous with Y-Combinator and TechStars in US, which are also perceived as the most successful accelerators. The main characteristics of accelerators involve a small amount of financial support, usually between 10,000 and 500,000€ for 5–7% equity, the limited duration that usually ranges between 3 and 6 months with the focus on intensive mentoring, a cohort of companies supported at the same time rather than individual companies, a focus on a small team rather than individual entrepreneurs, and finally an application process open to all, yet highly competitive (Cohen, 2013; Miller and Bound, 2011).

Business accelerators are quite a new phenomenon; therefore, little research has been done on accelerators. The purpose of this study is to contribute to business accelerator success factors discussion in European countries. The chapter provides a first attempt to assess business accelerator operation.

Institutional theory

Institutional theory has proven to be an important useful theoretical lens for exploring a wide range of topics in different fields (DiMaggio and

Powell, 1983). The impact of institutional theory especially on organizational success and performance has been widely explored in the organization and strategy literature (Volberda *et al.*, 2012; Shane and Foo, 1999; Kondra and Hinings, 1998).

Institutional theory explains the effect of the institutional context on an organization survival and legitimacy (Zucker, 1987; DiMaggio and Powell, 1983; Oliver, 1991; Kondra and Hinings, 1998). Consequently, the legitimacy is playing a fundamental role in organization survival, success and development. Researchers (Volberda *et al.*, 2012; Levitt and March, 1988) also state that institutional fit increases organization legitimacy which in turn increases performance. Over the years, researchers have offered a number of definitions for the term legitimacy; for instance, according to Suchman (1995, p. 574), *legitimacy involves the assumption that organizational activities are desirable, proper or appropriate within some socially constructed systems of norms, values, beliefs and definitions.* Zimmerman and Zeitz (2002) claim that *legitimacy is a social judgment of acceptance, appropriateness and desirability that enables organizations to access other resources needed to survive and grow.*

DiMaggio and Powell (1983) describe three mechanisms, namely coercive, normative and mimetic through which institutional forces occur. First, coercive isomorphism results from the pressure the government or other organizations exert on an organization in order to affect many aspects of an organization's structure or behavior. Second, normative isomorphism stems from the professionalization that influences organizational characteristics. Third, mimetic isomorphism is a pressure to emulate or model other organization's activities and structure, when goals are ambiguous, or when the environments creates symbolic uncertainty.

Most of the time, stakeholders do not have clear and complete evidence that a given action is the best way to accomplish a certain goal. And organizations also lack legitimacy because of their newness. An organization with available resources, whose performance is below institutional norms, rules, values and models may undertake the institutional processes to bring it in line with the institutional norms. This way, stakeholders will accept it as legitimate (i.e. acceptable and appropriate) because it is within the "normal" range of performance, thus will reduce stakeholders' uncertainty (DiMaggio and Powell, 1983; Oliver, 1991; Kondra and Hinings, 1998). Zimmerman and Zeitz (2002) state that when faced with uncertainty, stakeholders refer back to this stock of norms, rules, values and models in order to proceed. Legitimacy assures stakeholders that the organization is properly constituted, which concurrently improves the chances that the organization acquires all the strategic resources needed to succeed (Zimmerman and Zeitz, 2002).

Accordingly, business accelerators may lack legitimacy due to their newness. Following Suchman (1995, p. 574), legitimacy here is defined as a generalized perception where the operations such as events and activities are desirable and appropriate. This forces accelerators to improve their operations to make them desirable and appropriate for key stakeholders. To establish their legitimacy, business accelerators resort to the three success factors (coercive legitimacy).

In sum, business accelerators build their level of legitimacy by adopting or creating successful operational models. For example, successful accelerators are those with selection processes that attract promising startup teams for admission. Consequently, well-developed structures and activities such as business assistance and network opportunities attract startup teams, investors, corporate companies, governments, policy makers and more different strategic stakeholders to business accelerators.

In addition, business accelerators are perceived as an institution by their stakeholders, for instance, because of their impact on startup development. From the institutional theory point of view (DiMaggio and Powell, 1983), interests and requirements of stakeholders can affect accelerators' actions, structure, activity and strategy that at the same time can enhance success (coercive mechanism). And vice versa, success enhances legitimacy and signals cultural acceptance and the ability to deliver on commitment (Deephouse and Suchman, 2008). Accordingly, there are different models of business accelerators: generic and specific. Generic accelerators focus on different kinds of startups from low-tech to no-tech including manufacturing and service. On the other hand, specific accelerators are industry-focused programs, where Healthbox Europe focuses on digital healthcare related startups, and Climate-KIC Europe focuses on climate impact startups.

Data collection and methods

Using the definition of business accelerators and based on the characteristics mentioned above: financial support (£10k–£50k) usually in exchange for 5–7% equity; limited duration (3–6 months); a cohort of startup teams is supported at the same time; focused on small teams rather than individual entrepreneurs; an application process that is open to all, yet highly competitive (Miller and Bound, 2011), 41 accelerators were identified in three large ecosystems in Europe: London, Berlin and Paris. Europe creates dynamic and healthy conditions for startup programs, hence the existence of approximately 260 startup programs. Particularly, London, Berlin and Paris offer sufficient capital alternatives (Salido *et al.*, 2013). The managing directors of 13 accelerators out of 41 agreed to participate in this research and were interviewed at the end of 2013 and beginning of 2014. Table 2 provides the general characteristics of the 13 accelerators. Multiple case studies (Yin, 2012; Eisenhardt, 1989a) were conducted to investigate deeper the topic of the new business accelerator phenomena and to analyze the success factors that stimulate the development of nascent ventures. Each case serves in a manner similar to multiple experiments — that is, following "replication" logic (Yin, 2012). Data collection involved formal, semi-structured interviews and informal conversations with managers of accelerator programs. The interviews focused on three goals: (1) to gain insight about business accelerators characteristics, strategy and interaction with stakeholders; (2) to gain insight about selection process and criteria of business accelerators and (3) to map the value-added mechanisms offered to startups in terms of business support services and network opportunities.

Utilizing the repertory grid method encouraged the interviewees to describe similarities and differences between theirs and other well-known accelerators. The repertory grid technique offers insight to a rich source of data and enables the researcher to challenge and clarify their own views and gain understanding of the situation as described by the interviewee (Cassell and Walsh, 2004). The duration of the interviews was typically between 60 and 90 minutes. All interviews were recorded and transcribed. The transcriptions served as a main source of data analysis.

Table 2. Accelerator Programs from Europe: Paris, London, Berlin

	Founded year	Location	Funding	Industrial sectors of investment/program focus	Investment/equity	Duration of the program (months)	# selected companies for each cohort
Bethnal Green ventures	2011	London	Public	Generic	1500£ — 6%	3	10
Fintech Innovation Lab	2012	London and New York	Private	Specific (high-tech/bank related)	none	3	6
Techstars London	2013	London	Private	Generic	12,500£ — 6%	3	10
Climate-KIC Europe	2010	Europe	Public	Specific (Climate-impact startups)	95,000€ — none	12–18	20
Healthbox Europe	2012	London and USA	Private	Specific (Digital Healthcare)	50,000£ — 10%	4	7
Axel Springer Plug & Play Accelerator	2013	Berlin	Private	Generic	25,000€ — 5%	3	15
Microsoft Ventures Accelerator	2012	Worldwide	Private	Specific (IT startups)	None/none	4	9
Prosiebensat.1	2013	Berlin	Private	Generic	25,000€ — 5%	3	6/7
Startupbootcamp SBC2go	2013	Berlin	Private	Generic	15,000€ — 8%	6	10
L'Accelerateur	2012	Paris	Private	Generic	5000–15,000€ — 7–12%	3	10
Le Camping	2010	Paris	Public/Private	Specific (web startups)	4000€ — none	6	12
The Family	2013	Paris	Private	Generic	None — 1%	18	93
Scientipole Initiative and Croissance	2002	Paris	Public/Private	Generic	60,000–90,000€ — none	6	120

In order to note the different points, the materials were read by different researchers. In this case, the credibility of findings did not rely solely on the interpretations of single analysis. The researchers divided the analysis into several dimensions and combined with existing literature to identify differences and similarities between the cases. This research consists the dimensions such as selection process and criteria (Bergek and Norrman, 2008; Hackett and Dilts, 2004b; Gibson and Wiggins, 2003; Lumpkin and Ireland, 1988), services and network offered (Soetanto and Jack, 2013; Bruneel *et al.*, 2012; Bøllingtoft and Ulhoi, 2005; Hackett and Dilts, 2004b; Rice, 2002; Allen and Rahman, 1985), strategic focus (generic or specific) and source of funding (Private and Public) (Mian, 1996a; Soetanto and Jack, 2013; Bøllingtoft, 2012; Bøllingtoft and Ulhøi, 2005; Grimaldi and Grandi, 2005; Cooper, 1985). The findings are discussed in the next section.

Findings

Accelerator managers indicated their priorities in starting an accelerator. The main priorities are contributions to startup development and earning profit. The goal achievement is linked with the success of the programs. In this regard, appropriate selection process, business support services and network opportunities are critical to accomplish the key objectives. The purpose of this chapter was to develop an understanding of the business accelerator phenomenon and to identify the key components of success. The findings presented as follows are an integration of 13 business accelerators of case studies found in Europe.

Selection process and criteria

Successful business accelerators have a well-structured selection process that consists of an online application via software platform. (Table 3 provides the detailed selection process of accelerators.) Firstly, the received application is usually reviewed by the internal team and the external partners such as mentors, investors, partners and alumni in order to make a short list of 20–70 promising candidates. The following stage is an interview with the selection committee to select the final 6–20

Table 3.   The Selection Process

Accelerator	Selection process
Bethnal green ventures	Online application via f6s application software/shortlist of startups/face-to-face interview/final 10 startups
Fintech innovation lab	Online application via own software platform/shortlist of 15 startups/Dragons' Den in front of sponsors from banks/ final 6 startups
Techstars London	Online application via f6s application software/shortlist of 75 startups/interview to select between 20 to 30/ face-to-face interview/final 10 startups
Climate-KIC Europe	Online application via own software platform/an internal panel shortlist the applicant/ interview/final 20 startups per annum
Healthbox Europe	Online application via own software platform/2 round of selection for shortlist/ face-to-face interview/
Axel springer plug & play accelerator	Online application via own software platform/shortlist of 30 startups/face-to-face interview/final 15 startups
Microsoft ventures accelerator	Online application via f6s application software/shortlist of 70 startups/first interview-shortlist of 20 startups/ second interview/final 9 startups
Prosiebensat.1 accelerator	Online application via own software platform/shortlist of 20 startups/interview/final 6/7 startups
Startupbootcamp SBC2go	Online application-scouting events/ shortlist/Skype interview with 20 startups/selection day/final 10 startups
L'Accelerateur	Online application via own software platform/shortlist of 50 startups/interview/final 10 startups
Le camping	Online application/shortlist of 50 teams/face-to-face interview — 25 startups/second interview — final 12 startups
The Family	Contacting via email/face-to-face interview
Scientipole Initiative (and Croissance)	Online application via own software platform/ face-to-face interview

best startups. Research shows that the main selection approach of all business accelerators is to focus on venture team and team diversity. The accelerators mainly describe criteria related to the characteristics of the team. The personal characteristics of the team members consist of management skills, technical skills, previous working experience and expertise. Accordingly, the team criteria are emphasized by accelerators as a good indicator to the success of the companies.

Business support services

Accelerator programs provide startup companies with a combination of assistance services. Business accelerators are more oriented towards the intangible services that involve a significant amount of education, high-quality mentorship, coaching, workshops, weekly evaluation during the program period, financial and legal support and tangible services such as office spaces. Table 4 shows the benefits are provided by accelerators.

Mentorship: As explained earlier, the most valuable aspects of accelerator programs and the main reason why startup companies participate in accelerators is the mentorship opportunity. Mentors work with startup teams throughout the duration of the program; they provide valuable advice and feedback based on personal experience on a voluntary basis. For instance, Axel Springer P&P Accelerator (Berlin) schedules meetings with around 90 mentors, and provides mentorship in three directions: business intelligence, online marketing and technical development. Each startup interacts with each type of mentor. Another example is Bethnal Green Venture Accelerator (London) where some 60 mentors are involved. Usually, all mentors are selected though recommendations from mentor networks. Fintech Innovation Lab (London) mentors are executives from the bank industry who are also future customers for the ventures. The accelerator companies select mentors through recommendations, personal network and mentor networks based on their level of expertise, experience and desire to help new entrepreneurs. The majority of the accelerator companies highlighted the mentorship as the most essential element of business support services.

Networking

Accelerator programs offer an external and internal network opportunity for new ventures through a variety of events. As explained above, "Demo Day" is a valuable feature of business accelerators, organized to connect

Table 4.   Provided Benefits of Accelerator Programs

Accelerator	Benefits
Bethnal green ventures	Mentorship, Workshop, Coaching, Weekly evaluation, Co-working space, Variety of events, Demo Day, Networking, Financial and legal support
Fintech innovation lab	Mentorship, Workshop, Coaching, Weekly evaluation, Co-working space, Variety of events, Demo Day, Networking
Techstars London	Mentorship, Workshop, Coaching, Weekly evaluation, Co-working space, Variety of events, Demo Day, Networking, Financial and legal support, Hosting services
Climate-KIC Europe	Coaching, Co-working space, Networking
Healthbox Europe	Mentorship, Workshop, Coaching, Weekly evaluation, Co-working space, Variety of events, Demo Day, Networking, Financial and legal support
Axel springer plug & play accelerator	Mentorship, Workshop, Coaching, Co-working space, Variety of events, Networking
Microsoft ventures accelerator	Mentorship, Workshop, Coaching, Co-working spaceVariety of events, Demo Day, Networking, Financial and legal, BizSpark support
Prosiebensat.1 accelerator	Mentorship, Workshop, Coaching, Co-working space, Variety of events, Demo Day, Networking, Financial and legal
Startupbootcamp SBC2go	Mentorship, Workshop, Coaching, Co-working space, Variety of events, Demo Day, Networking, Financial and legal
L'Accelerateur	Mentorship, Workshop, Coaching, Variety of events, Demo Day, Networking, Financial and legal
Le camping	Mentorship, Workshop, Coaching, Variety of events, Demo Day, Networking Financial and legal, Amazon web services
The Family	Variety of events, Workshop
Scientipole Initiative (and Croissance)	Workshop, Coaching

startups with high quality groups of investors and customers. For example, Microsoft Venture Accelerator connects startups with its biggest customers such as Shell, Siemens and BMW around the world. Fintech organizes events in order to build up a network with executives from bank startups.

Proposition 1. *Success components of business accelerators help gain institutional legitimacy in the eyes of stakeholders and enhance access to the strategic resources that are crucial for survival and growth.*

Different types of accelerators

The focus of accelerators is associated with stakeholders' needs and requirements, which are corporate, business angels, investors and public authorities. Research also highlighted the different types of business accelerators. For instance, based on the focus of accelerators, two types of programs can be distinguished: specific and generic. Generic accelerators offer services to all kinds of startups from low-tech, to no-tech including manufacturing and services. Specific accelerators focus on specific industrial and technology domains such as digital healthcare, information technology, biotechnology, bank industry, environmental technology. The example of specific accelerator is Healthbox Europe which aims to connect healthcare organizations with startups and help them work together. Fintech Innovation Lab, Climate-KIC Europe, Microsoft Ventures Accelerator, Le Camping are also specific accelerators that focus on specific domains (the summary of the main characteristics of each accelerator is provided in Table 2). The main characterizing aspect that differentiates specific accelerators from generic is that, in addition to other services, specific accelerators provide specialized mentoring with highly capable mentors from new venture's core activity, which helps in the development of core aspects of specific products. The mentor of a specific accelerator often invests in startups as business angels. The aim of specific accelerators is also to connect startups with the industry, which in turn gives startups access to real customers and network to the investor community. Accordingly, specific accelerators can be highlighted as a best practice.

Two other types of accelerators, private and public, can also be distinguished based on the source of revenue. The expenses of public accelerators are usually covered by non-profit organizations. For instance, Climate-KIC Europe is supported by European Commission; Bethnal Green Ventures is funded by Cabinet Office and foundations such as Nesta, Nominet Trust. The objective of the public accelerators is to stimulate startup ecosystem within the region or the technology. Private accelerators benefit from corporate and private investors. Fintech Innovation Lab is supported by Accenture and 12 investment and retail banks; likewise, Techstars London is funded by Venture capital and business angels; Healthbox Europe is founded by Healthcare corporate, VC's and business angels; finally, Microsoft Ventures Accelerator obtains funding from Microsoft. There are also mixed type of accelerators — private and public funded, for instance, Le Camping is founded by private funds such as, Google, BNP Paribas, Orange and SNCF and public institution such as Ile de France. The objective of private accelerators is to bridge the gap between new ventures and investors.

Proposition 2. *Stakeholders' different needs and requirements promote different accelerator models.*

Discussion and Conclusion

By focusing on how business accelerators operate, the main purpose of this chapter was first to investigate the success factors of business accelerators. To achieve the research's objective, multiple case studies were used to examine the operation of 13 accelerator programs from Europe: Paris, London, Berlin (Table 2 provides the main characteristics of accelerators). The findings have offered a clear contribution to policy and future research.

Existing literature has examined critical success factors of business incubators (Soetanto and Jack, 2013; Bruneel *et al.*, 2012; Bergek and Norrman, 2008; Ratinho and Henriques, 2010; Peters *et al.*, 2004; Hackett and Dilts, 2004a; Rice, 2002; Markley and McNamara, 1994; Lumpkin and Ireland, 1988; Allen and Rahman, 1985). Like others, this research emphasizes three success factors: selection process and criteria, business support services and networks. This study suggests that business accelerators have well-structured selection process that consists of an online application via software platform and that the main selection approach of all business accelerators is to focus on venture team and team diversity. Accelerator programs provide startup companies with the combination of assistance services such as a significant amount of education, high-quality mentorship, coaching, workshops, weekly evaluation during the program period, financial and legal support and office spaces. The most valuable aspect of all accelerators' support services is the mentorship opportunity whereby startups obtain advice and feedback on product development. Network opportunities provide matchmaking between startups and external actors such as potential investors, customers and partners and internal network between tenants. Accelerator programs offer external and internal network opportunities for new ventures through a variety of events. As mentioned, "Demo Day" is a valuable feature of business accelerators, which is organized to connect startups with a high quality group of investors and customers.

Second, the theoretical part of this research lies in the fact that it enhances the understanding about the success factors of business accelerators. Researchers (Zucker, 1987; DiMaggio and Powell, 1983; Kondra and Hinings, 1998) claim that institutional fit increases organization survival and legitimacy. Legitimacy is playing an important role in organization success and assures stakeholders that the organization is properly constituted (Deephouse and Suchman, 2008; Zimmerman and Zeitz, 2002; Kondra and Hinings, 1998). The organizations also lack the legitimacy because of their newness. Consequently, through success factors business accelerators acquire legitimacy in the eyes of stakeholders. Well-organized and developed success factors are selection process and criteria, business support services and networks signal to stakeholders that the accelerator is properly constituted.

From the institutional theory point of view (DiMaggio and Powell, 1983), stakeholders' interests and requirements can affect the accelerators' actions, structure, activity and strategy that can in turn enhance success. However, as long as the stakeholders' needs are varied, there will be a space for differed models of business accelerators. This study highlights different types of business accelerators: general, specific, private and public that serve the different stakeholders' needs.

Concerning further research, this study shows that there is still much work to be done to improve the understanding of the business accelerators phenomenon and how they impact startup companies. Large-scale studies from other geographical regions should be used to identify the best model of accelerator to achieve certain goals. In addition, research should be conducted to examine how the success factors of this model affect the performance of business accelerators. The results can help policy makers choose which accelerators to support and it can also be the startups' interest in applying to different accelerators, depending on their preferences. Business accelerators represent an interesting area for further deeper qualitative and quantitative analysis.

References

Allen, D. N. and Rahman, S. (1985). Small business incubators: a positive environment for entrepreneurship. *Journal of Small Business Management (pre-1986)*, 23(000003): 12.

Bergek, A. and Norrman, C. (2008). Incubator best practice: A framework. *Technovation*, 28(1–2): 20–28.

Bøllingtoft, A. (2012). The bottom-up business incubator: Leverage to networking and cooperation practices in a self-generated, entrepreneurial-enabled environment. *Technovation*, 32(5): 304–315.

Bøllingtoft, A. and Ulhøi, J. P. (2005). The networked business incubator — leveraging entrepreneurial agency? *Journal of Business Venturing*, 20(2): 265–290.

Brooks, O. J. (1986). Economic development through entrepreneurship: incubators and the incubation process. *Economic Development Review*, 4(2): 24–29.

Bruneel, J., Ratinho, T., Clarysse, B., and Groen, A. (2012). The evolution of business incubators: Comparing demand and supply of business incubation services across different incubator generations. *Technovation*, 32(2): 110–121.

Bruton, G. D., Ahlstrom, D., and Li, H. L. (2010). Institutional theory and entrepreneurship: where are we now and where do we need to move in the future? *Entrepreneurship: Theory and Practice*, 34(3): 421–440.

Caley, E. and Kula, H. (2013). *Seeding Success: Canadian Startup Accelerators — MaRS Data Catalyst*. Available at: https://www.marsdd.com/wp-content/uploads/2013/07/Seeding-Success_v94.pdf

Campbell, C. and Allen, D. N. (1987). The small business incubator industry: Microlevel economic development. *Economic Development Quarterly*, 1(2): 178–191.

Campbell, C., Kendrick, R. C., and Samuelson, D. S. (1985). Stalking the latent entrepreneur: Business incubators and economic development. *Economic Development Review*, 3(2): 43–49.

Carayannis, E. G. and Von Zedtwitz, M. (2005). Architecting gloCal (global–local), real-virtual incubator networks (G-RVINs) as catalysts and accelerators of entrepreneurship in transitioning and developing economies: Lessons learned and best practices from current development and business incubation practices. *Technovation*, 25(2): 95–110.

Cassell, C. and Symon, G. (Eds.). (2004). *Essential Guide to Qualitative Methods in Organizational Research*. Sage, Newbury Park, CA.

Cassell, C. and Walsh, S. (2004). 'Repertory grids', in C. Cassell and G. Symon (eds.), Essential guide to qualitative methods in organizational research (pp. 61–72). Sage Publications Ltd., London.

Christiansen, J. (2009). *Copying Y Combinator, A framework for developing Seed Accelerator Programmes*. Cambridge, University of Cambridge.

Clarkson, M. E. (1995). A stakeholder framework for analyzing and evaluating corporate social performance. *Academy of Management Review*, 20(1): 92–117.

Clarysse, B. and Bruneel, J. (2007). Nurturing and growing innovative startups: The role of policy as integrator. *R & D Management*, 37(2): 139–149.

Clarysse, B., Wright, M., Lockett, A., Mustar, P. and Knockaert, M. (2007). Academic spin-offs, formal technology transfer and capital raising. *Industrial and Corporate Change*, 16(4): 609–640.

Clarysse, B., Wright, M., Lockett, A., Van de Velde, E. and Vohora, A. (2005). Spinning out new ventures: A typology of incubation strategies from European research institutions. *Journal of Business Venturing*, 20(2): 183–216.

Cohen, S. (2013). What do acelerators do? Insights from incubators and angels. *Innovations*, 8(3–4): 19–25.

Cohen, S. and Hochberg, Y. V. (2014). Accelerating startups: The Seed Accelerator Phenomenon. Available at SSRN2418000.

Cooper, A. C. (1985). The role of incubator organizations in the founding of growth-oriented firms. *Journal of Business Venturing*, 1(1): 75–86.

Deephouse, D. L. and Suchman, M. (2008). Legitimacy in organizational institutionalism. *The Sage handbook of organizational institutionalism*, 49: 77.

Dickinson, R. A., Ferguson, C. R., and Sircar, S. (1984). Critical success factors and small business. *American Journal of Small Business*, 8(3): 49–57.

DiMaggio, P. J. and Powell, W. W. (1983). The iron cage revisited: Institutional isomorphism and collective rationality in organizational fields. *American Sociological Review*, 48:147–160.

Eisenhardt, K. M. (1989a). Building theories from case study research. *Academy of Management Review*, 14(4): 532–550.

Eisenhardt, K. M. (1989b). Making fast strategic decisions in high-velocity environments. *The Academy of Management Journal*, 32(3): 543–576.

Gibson, D. V. and Wiggins, J. (2003). Overview of US incubators and the case of the Austin Technology Incubator. *International Journal of Entrepreneurship and Innovation Management*, 3(1): 56–66.

Grimaldi, R. and Grandi, A. (2005). Business incubators and new venture creation: An assessment of incubating models. *Technovation*, 25(2): 111–121.

Hackett, S. M. and Dilts, D. M. (2004a). A real options-driven theory of business incubation. *Journal of Technology Transfer*, 29(1): 41–54.

Hackett, S. M. and Dilts, D. M. (2004b). A systematic review of business incubation research. *Journal of Technology Transfer*, 29(1): 55–82.

Hoffman, D. L. and Radojevich-Kelley, N. (2012). Analysis of accelerator companies: An exploratory case study of their programs, processes, and early results. *Small Business Institute Journal*, 8(2): 54–70

Kondra, A. Z. and Hinings, C. R. (1998). Organizational diversity and change in institutional theory. *Organization Studies*, 19(5): 743–767.

Levitt, B. and March, J. (1988). Organizational learning. *Annual Review of Sociology*, 14: 319–340.

Lumpkin, J. R. and Ireland, R. D. (1988). Screening practices of new business incubators: the evaluation or critical success factors. *American Journal of Small Business*, 12(4): 59–81.

Lyons, T. S., 2000. Building Social Capital for Sustainable Enterprise Development in Country Towns and Regions: Successful Practices from the United States. Paper presented at the First National Conference on the Future of Australia's Country Towns, LaTrobe University, Center for Sustainable Regional Communities, Australia. June 29–30.

Markley, D. M. and McNamara, K. T. (1994). A Business Incubator: Operating Environment and Measurement of Economic and Fiscal Impacts. Center for Rural Development.

Mian, S. A. (1996a). Assessing value-added contributions of university technology business incubators to tenant firms. *Research Policy*, 25(3): 325–335.

Mian, S. A. (1996b). The university business incubator: A strategy for developing new research/technology-based firms. *The Journal of High Technology Management Research*, 7(2): 191–208.

Miller, P. and Bound, K. (2011). *The Startup Factories. The rise of accelerator programmes to support new technologies.* NEST, London, UK.

Oliver, C. (1991). Strategic responses to institutional processes. *Academy of Management Review*, 16(1): 145–179.

Pauwels, C., Clarysse, B., Wright, M., and VanHove, J., (2016). Understanding accelerators in Europe: The "Match-Maker", the "Investor-Led" and the "Ecosystem-Builder" archetype. *Technovation*, 50: 13–24.

Peters, L., Rice, M., and Sundararajan, M. (2004). The role of incubators in the entrepreneurial process. *Journal of Technology Transfer*, 29(1): 83–91.

Phan, P. H., Siegel, D. S., and Wright, M. (2005). Science parks and incubators: Observations, synthesis and future research. *Journal of Business Venturing*, 20(2): 165–182.

Ratinho, T. and Henriques, E. (2010). The role of science parks and business incubators in converging countries: Evidence from Portugal. *Technovation*, 30(4): 278–290.

Rice, M.P. (2002). Co-production of business assistance in business incubators: An exploratory study. *Journal of Business Venturing*, 17(2): 163–187.

Sal ido, E., Sabas, M., and Freixas, P. (2013). The accelerator and incubator ecosystem in Europe. *Telefonica*, 24: 1–20.

Shane, S. and Foo, M. D. (1999). New firm survival: Institutional explanations for new franchisor mortality. *Management Science*, 45(2): 142–159.

Soetanto, D. P. and Jack, S. L. (2013). Business incubators and the networks of technology-based firms. *The Journal of Technology Transfer*, 38(4): 432–453.

Suchman, M. C. (1995). Managing legitimacy: Strategic and institutional approaches. *Academy of Management Review*, 20(3): 571–610.

Volberda, H. W., van der Weerdt, N., Verwaal, E., Stienstra, M., and Verdu, A. J. (2012). Contingency fit, institutional fit, and firm performance: A metafit approach to organization–environment relationships. *Organization Science*, 23(4): 1040–1054.

Wiggins, J. and Gibson, D. V. (2003). Overview of US incubators and the case of the Austin Technology Incubator. *International Journal of Entrepreneurship and Innovation Management*, 3(1): 56–66.

Yin, R. K. (2009). *Case Study Research: Design and Methods*, Vol. 5. Sage, Newbury Park, CA.

Zimmerman, M. A. and Zeitz, G. J. (2002). Beyond survival: Achieving new venture growth by building legitimacy. *Academy of Management Review*, 27(3): 414–431.

Zucker, L. G. (1986). Production of trust: Institutional sources of economic structure, 1840–1920. *Research in Organizational Behavior*, 8, 53–111.

Zucker, L. G. (1987). Institutional theories of organization. *Annual Review of Sociology*, 13: 443–464.

Chapter 3

A Look Inside Accelerators in the United Kingdom: Building Technology Businesses

Bart Clarysse, Mike Wright and Jonas Van Hove

Introduction

Over the last decade, accelerator programs have continued to spread globally as a popular form of support for early-stage ventures. Funded by a mix of investors, public bodies or large corporates, these programs typically provide space, money, mentoring and guidance to batches of entrepreneurs to help them rapidly grow and scale their business idea. However, despite their growing popularity, there is little known, documented literature on the different models and methods that have emerged as the field has continued to adapt and grow. While most accelerators draw on the pioneering models of Y-Combinator and Techstars to some extent, we are increasingly seeing variety in the way new accelerators structure and fund their programs of support.

This research sets out to explore how different accelerators operate, how they differentiate themselves from each other and why. The aim of this work is to build on the early body of research on accelerators such as Nesta's Startup Factories, the Seed Accelerators Ranking Project by Yael Hochberg and Susan Cohen, Telefonica's Accelerator and Incubator Ecosystem in Europe, and the lessons shared by networks such as the

Accelerator Assembly and Global Accelerator Network, in order to demystify accelerator programs for practitioners, funders and policy makers.

Background

We believe that ambitious, innovative startups are a key source of economic growth for the UK. Previous Nesta research shows that just 6% of fast-growing UK businesses generate the lion's share of employment growth in the UK. While these high-growth businesses can be found across all sectors and in all stages of the business lifecycle, new ventures are a significant part of this group.

From the existing body of research, we know that new ventures often face a number of challenges or major hurdling blocks when they start out. For example, startups might struggle because of limited financial resources (Smilor, 1987), a lack of startup experience in the founding team (Gruber *et al.*, 2008), a lack of legitimacy to attract good employees (Zott and Huy, 2007) or a lack of knowledge or understanding of how to seize certain opportunities (Ambos and Birkinshaw, 2010).

Over the decades, a range of investment vehicles, business support services and incubator facilities have evolved to meet these needs, backed by policy makers, private investors, universities and corporates. Incubators became widespread in the early 90s (Hackett and Dilts, 2004), providing support for small ventures, mainly with physical and financial resources (Smilor and Gill, 1986; Allen and McCluskey, 1990). However, the incubator model has been criticized over the years for its lack of exit policy (Bruneel *et al.*, 2012) and its reliance on long-term public funding to be sustainable.

When incubators emerged, many of the innovative new ventures were active in sectors such as biotechnology, micro-electronics and electrical equipment which are typically capital intensive (Wright *et al.*, 2007). Since then, advances in technology and the rise of the digital economy has changed the landscape in which many startups operate, rapidly reducing the costs and time taken to bring a product or service to market.

Accelerators were specifically set up to assist these new digital ventures early in their lifecycle (Birdsall *et al.*, 2013), using a lean startup approach. They differ substantially from typical incubators that were designed for capital-intensive startups or formal IP-based technology spin-offs. First, they are primarily not designed to provide physical resources or office support services, and second, they are less focused on venture capitalists as a next step of finance, but are more closely connected to business angels and small-scale individual investors.

To our knowledge, the first accelerator, Y-Combinator, was established in 2005 in Cambridge, Massachusetts, and has been a source of inspiration for many accelerators to follow. Four years later in 2009, the Difference Engine kick-started the European accelerator sector. In 2013, Seed-DB reported over 213 accelerators worldwide, which have supported approximately 3800 new ventures.

Building on Miller and Bound (2011), we define accelerators as having the following six characteristics:

1. Possible offer of upfront investment (on average between £10k and £50k), usually in exchange for equity (~5–10%).
2. Time-limited support (approximately 3–6 months) comprising programed events and intensive mentoring.
3. An application process that is 'in principle' open to all, yet highly competitive.
4. Cohorts or classes of startups rather than individual companies.
5. Mostly, a focus on small teams, not individual founders.
6. Periodic graduation with a Demo Day/Investor Day.

Most accelerator programs are modeled on the format of Y-Combinator (founded 2005) or Techstars (founded 2006). Y-Combinator funds two batches of entrepreneurs a year and the program runs for three months at a time. Startups are asked to move to the Bay Area, but they primarily work out of their own offices or houses. The cohort meets together for weekly speaker dinners and startups have regular office hours with the Y-Combinator team and mentors. Techstars also runs for three months, but in contrast to Y-Combinator, it offers a more structured program where startups physically move into the accelerator's co-working space for the duration of the program, the cohorts tends to be smaller (around 12 startups compared with around 50 in Y-Combinator), and there is a more regular and intensive approach to mentoring (Christiansen, 2009).

An archetype is a pattern of mutually supporting organizational elements (Ambos and Birkinshaw, 2010). While these two accelerator programs could be viewed as 'archetypes', we know very little about how new models of accelerators have emerged in different political, economic and technological contexts. This is what we aim to investigate in our research.

The research

We set out to interview a range of different types of accelerators. Given the newness of the phenomena, this research is fit to answer the question: what do accelerators do?

Using the 6 accelerator characteristics outlined above (Table 1), we identified 34 accelerators in London. In the UK, there are approximately 40+ accelerators. The distribution of accelerators is thus heavily distorted due to the extreme number of programs in London alone.

Entrepreneurial success in London and in cities such as Edinburgh, Bristol and Manchester is in stark contrast to other parts of the country. In other words, the UK's startup culture is dynamic but unevenly distributed.

Based on the categorization and with a focus on London (total of 34 accelerators), we identified different types of accelerators:

- 8 investor-led accelerators;
- 9 matchmakers;
- 7 ecosystem builders;
- 10 hybrid programs.

The majority of accelerators (~60%) are specialized. Based on our qualitative research, we can state that the design choice of accelerators (specialized or industry agnostic) is influenced by the preferences of the accelerator's founders rather than the industrial strengths in the region. We then categorized these programs by:

- Funding model (public, private, hybrid).
- Sector focus (vertical, horizontal).
- Type of investment (equity, convertible loan).

The remainder of this chapter unfolds along the following lines: first, we present our framework for understanding the internal functions of each accelerator — we call this the building blocks of an accelerator. Then, we explore the three emerging archetypes that we distinguished based on the strategic focus of the accelerator: ecosystem builders, investor-led and matchmakers.

Finally, we explore the practice and policy implications of our research. We identified five important components that shape the structure and design of an accelerator. Each accelerator varied widely in their model, depending on their approach to each of these components.

Table 1.   Examples of UK-based Accelerators

Accelerator	Date created	Length of program (months)	Investment size	Equity stake taken (%)
Techstars London	2013	3	12.500£ + option conv. loan	6
Fintech Innovation Lab	2012	3	/	/
Bethnal Green Ventures	2011	3	15.000£	6
Climate-Knowledge and Innovation Community (KIC) UK	2010	12–18	Max. of 95.000€	/
Microsoft Ventures Acc	2013	4	/	/
Startupbootcamp	2012	3	15.000€	8

N.B. These data should be treated with caution as it is largely self-reported. It should not be considered complete or up-to-date.

Unpacking the Accelerator Model

1. Strategic Focus	2. Programme package	3. Funding	4. Selection process	5. Alumni service
• Key objectives	• Standardized curriculum	• Funding of the accelerator	• Screening criteria	• Alumni interaction
• Sector focus (diversified vs specialization)	• Mentoring package	• Funding of startups	• Selection processes	
• Geographic focus (local vs global)				

Strategic focus

The first core component is the strategic focus of an accelerator. The types of funders or stakeholders supporting the program can shape this. For instance, an accelerator will have different key objectives depending on whether it is backed predominantly by private investors, large corporates or public funders. In Part III, we analyze this further and describe the three emerging archetypes that we distinguished, based on the strategic focus of the accelerator.

Sector/Industry focus is another important strategic choice. This can range from being very generic (no vertical focus at all) to very specific (specialized in a specific industry or technology domain). For example, Fintech Innovation Lab focuses exclusively on the financial sector, Truestart Accelerator is retail-oriented, while Velocity has a health-tech focus.

The founder of Startupbootcamp told us that they are focusing their programs more and more on certain themes, for example, financial technology and insurance in London: We think it makes a lot of sense to group mentors and teams on focused themes and aim to be world class in one thing as opposed to generic.

The geographic focus of accelerators also varies. They can be focused on a specific local area or very international in their activities. Techstars is an example of a program that has spread within the US and now internationally. While the local programs, each operate autonomously, Techstars as a whole aims to share best practice across accelerators.

Program package

The second component we call 'program package'. The program package consists of a standardized curriculum and a mentoring package. This usually includes:

- A 'curriculum' or 'training program' that new ventures go through. This can cover a variety of topics, for instance, finance, user design, PR, marketing and legal aspects.
- A program of events, such as expert workshops and inspiring talks.

- Regular counselling, often in the form of weekly 'office hours'. These regular meetings with the accelerator management team generate mutual trust, and provide the founding teams with business assistance and enable a 'weekly' review of their progress.
- Investor Demo Days. These can be focused as much on customers as on investors; for example, Health Social Innovators focus their Demo Day on getting customers in the room for their startups.
- Co-location in a shared open office space, which encourages peer-to-peer learning and collaboration.

The standardized service package is complemented with a carefully planned mentoring package. Mentors are typically experienced entrepreneurs and they are heavily vetted before being included in the program. They can be matched to specific ventures through speed dating or matchmaking events. One accelerator we interviewed described their 'matchmaking' process as follows:

> "The only method that we found that works is: rent a room in a restaurant, bring in food, a lot of alcohol, close the doors, and in four hours the magic happens".

Mentors can help ventures to define their business model, and to connect with customers and investors. Although there are variations in how the mentoring model is applied, there is evidence of a formal program of mentoring across all accelerators.

Funding structure

There are two important elements to the funding structure of an accelerator: the funding of the accelerator itself, and the funding available to startups. When looking at the funding of the accelerator, we found that most programs received the major part of their working capital from shareholders, such as investors, corporates and public authorities. Few of the programs we interviewed are able to get revenue from investments in the startups that they support, but this could be because these programs are still relatively new and it will take some time before they have noticeable exits in their portfolio companies.

Similar to the findings of Nesta's Good Incubation report, some accelerators were diversifying their model in order to source alternative revenue through the organization of events and workshops. With the funding of startups, we found that most programs followed the traditional accelerator model of offering a small amount of funding in exchange for equity (amounts contributed typically are about a few £10,000).

The equity stakes were typically made on a dilutable basis with pro-rata investments in ensuing rounds being optional case-by-case with only a small handful of accelerators offering them on a non-dilutable basis. Some accelerators also offered some form of follow-on funding for their startups, which reflects the challenges that startups face in securing investment directly after an accelerator.

Selection process and criteria

The design of the screening and selection process is the fourth core component. Entrepreneurial teams are typically selected in batches, but 'how' and 'why' they are selected differs among the accelerators. The method of screening can range from a simple two-staged process to a rigorous multi-staged process. Usually, an open call is organized during a period of time where portfolio companies can register and apply online, often on a software platform such as F6S.com, Fundacity and Angel.co.

Some programs, like Startupbootcamp and Climate-KIC, go a step further and actively scout startup events before the application period. Then, a standardized screening process is organized in which external stakeholders tend to participate. For example, Bethnal Green Ventures use a selection committee, comprising mentors, investors and alumni, to help shortlist companies in its program. The portfolio companies are expected to present their ideas and they are screened in person.

Single founders are selected by exception, but some accelerators will help founders with matchmaking and team formation, which is also of benefit to teams missing a specific skill set. Other accelerator programs such as Startupbootcamp and Climate-KIC UK have entrepreneurs in residence. These entrepreneurs with a specific skill could join entrepreneurial teams, become co-founders, or build their own companies. They give more than advice (compared to mentors) by working together with the teams. Some are paid; others are in a program for the opportunity and personal growth.

Alumni service

The last core component we identified was the alumni service. The accelerators in the study put a lot of emphasis on keeping close and active relations with the companies that graduated from their programs. Most accelerators run regular events for alumni and invite them back into the program to share their experiences where possible. Accelerators that take equity in their startups have an added incentive for providing continued support to help their alumni succeed. Once an accelerator has developed over a number of years, the alumni network can be an important source for mentors and investors, as successful graduates are more likely to invest back into the community that supported them in the first place.

Accelerator archetypes

There were remarkable differences in the accelerators in our study based on their approach to these five core components. However, we were able to distinguish three broad groups of accelerators, based on their strategic focus (Table 2):

1. The investor-led archetype;
2. The matchmaker archetype;
3. The ecosystem archetype.

The 'investor-led accelerator'

The investor-led archetype of accelerators receives funding from investors such as business angels, venture capital funds or corporate venture capital. This accelerator type resembles most of the original concepts of Y-Combinator and Techstars developed in the US. Its objective is to bridge the equity gap between very early-stage projects and investable businesses. Hence, the screening criteria in these programs tend to favor ventures that will take on follow-on capital and become attractive investment propositions. These accelerators typically provide some form of seed financing to startups in exchange for equity.

Often, we see that these accelerators begin to focus on startups that are in the later stages of development. They tend to select ventures that already have some proven record of accomplishment, and in some cases have already raised pre-seed finance. For example, the Managing Director of Techstars London said that because they get such a high number of competitive applications that they are able to pick more developed startups to work with:

> *"We have a team from Estonia that has raised over a million dollars which is just about to start. We have a team from California that has raised one million dollars. They are all seed funded teams".*

As mentioned previously, one of the strategic decisions of an accelerator is whether to be generic or industry specific. Investor-led accelerators often choose to specialize within a specific industry. By concentrating on one specific sector, the accelerator management team can develop the necessary sector-specific knowledge and expertise to identify and exploit the economic potential of entrepreneurial teams. The mentors used in these accelerators are often active business angels themselves and play a further role in follow-up investments. One accelerator director described their mentors as 'investors in disguise'.

The 'matchmaker accelerator'

This type of accelerator has typically been set up by corporates who want to provide a service to their own customers or stakeholders. An example is FinTech Innovation Lab in London, which is run by Accenture; its focus is to create a platform for the financial services industry to collaborate on innovation with early-stage ventures and in the process, Accenture can strengthen its relationship with its banking clients. Similarly, one of the motivations behind the Microsoft Ventures accelerator is to support startups whose solutions will benefit Microsoft's vast SME customer base across Europe.

These accelerators actively involve their corporate stakeholders in the selection process of their ventures. For instance, senior executives of large financial banks sit in on the selection process of FinTech Innovation Lab. Hence, only those ventures are selected which attract the attention of highly placed individuals in these corporates. Mentors are often selected from within the corporates, and they play an important role in helping the startups find their way through the internal decision-making system of the corporate.

Interestingly, there is often no-profit orientation among these accelerators, and they offer no finance to the startups that participate on the program. Instead, these accelerators add value by helping the startups to connect with potential customers. Their network is therefore almost exclusively oriented towards the potential customer base. They are financed on a yearly basis by the corporate and often adopt soft performance measures or engage in symbolic actions (Zott and Huy, 2007) such as broadcasting, newsletters and highlight events to illustrate their legitimacy in the absence of hard key performance indicators.

The 'ecosystem accelerator'

These accelerators typically have government agencies as a main stakeholder. The government agencies are interested in stimulating startup activity, either within a specific region or within a specific technological domain. For instance, the European Commission stimulates the establishment of accelerators within the major technological programs (KICs), which it finances.

The ultimate objective of these programs is to develop an ecosystem of startups within the region or the technology. Hence, selection criteria and processes in these accelerators are organized to attract companies that fit within that vision. For example, Climate KIC[1] UK organizes specific calls focused on 'smart grid' technologies within the research institutes that have activities in that domain.

These accelerators typically select ventures in a very early stage in the lifecycle. Often, a value proposition is not clear, and sometimes it is just an individual with an idea. The ecosystem accelerators have the most in-depth

---

[1] Number 1 Cleantech accelerator worldwide; 2nd in the world overall [by follow-on funding], Seed Accelerator Rankings Project (SARP), [see Hochberg and Kamath (2012)].

Table 2.   Summary of Key Elements from Archetypes in Accelerators

	Investor-led	Matchmaker	Ecosystem
Program package (~mentoring package)	Mentoring involvement: serial entrepreneurs and business angels	Mentoring involvement: internal coaches from corporates	Mentoring involvement: serial entrepreneurs and business developers; most developed curriculum
Accelerator strategy (~stakeholder objectives)	Key stakeholders are investors; goal is to look for investment opportunities	Key stakeholders are corporates; goal is to provide a service for the customer base 'matching potential customers with startups' (NO-profit orientation)	Key stakeholders are government agencies; goal is to stimulate startup activity and create an ecosystem
Screening process and criteria (~screening criteria)	Open application; cohort-based system; favor new ventures in later stages with some proven track record	Open application; cohort-based system; Favor new ventures in later stages with some proven track record	Open application; cohort-based system; Favor new ventures in very early stages
Funding structure (~shareholders and revenue model)	Funding from private investors (business angels, venture capital funds and/or corporate venture capital); standard seed investment and equity engagement	Funding from corporates; no seed investment or equity engagement	Funding from local, national and international schemes; experimenting with funding structure and revenue model (search for sustainability)
Examples	Techstars, Startupbootcamp	Fintech Innovation lab, Microsoft Ventures Accelerator	Climate-KIC, Bethnal Green Ventures

developed curriculum among the three archetypes. They typically organize training sessions, workshops and practical learning-oriented events to help the ventures develop their idea and value proposition. In some cases, mentors can also be consultants or business developers, who — often on a paid basis, as with Climate-KIC UK — help to commercialize the technology or sell the product/service idea. Their involvement with the ventures is much more hands on than the typical mentors or internal coaches that are predominantly present in the two previous examples.

For most ecosystem accelerators, the business model is rather unclear. Typically, their operations are developed to satisfy the needs of the government stakeholder. However, at the same time, most public sponsors require some form of revenue model after an initial financing period. Although most accelerators present the typical investment model as a potential, some experiment with other forms of revenues like asking for payment of tuition fees for the training courses.

Another interesting example is the social impact accelerator Bethnal Green Ventures, based in London. They receive funding from the UK Cabinet Office, Nominet Trust and Nesta, and in many respects, they run like a traditional tech accelerator, investing 15,000£ in exchange for 6% equity in tech startups. However, they focus exclusively on technology-based ventures that leverage products and services for social good. They are strong advocates of 'Tech for Good' and play a role in hosting meetups and events in order to foster the community around this.

Discussion and implications

Our research has uncovered some of the different ways in which the accelerator model has developed in Europe. The three archetypes, investor-led, matchmaker and ecosystem developer, demonstrate how accelerator programs adopt different ways of structuring and running their programs depending on the objectives of their key stakeholders. For instance, the investor-led model focuses heavily on mentoring by serial entrepreneurs and business angels who know-how to create legitimacy for follow-up investments. The matchmaking model is focused on helping ventures through the complex decision-making structures in corporate customers. Instead of mentors, internal coaches in these corporates tend to guide the entrepreneurs to the right decision makers. Finally, the ecosystem builders tend to be more program-led and develop intensive workshops and training sessions to help the ventures finding their way to applications or first customers. Often, the accelerator team is complemented with commercial skills such as business developers that test the idea on the market.

Hybrid archetypes

Within our sample, we note that a number of accelerators have hybrid elements. These hybrid elements can be explained by the differences between the benchmark, which is used as a source of inspiration (e.g. Y-Combinator), and the emerging stakeholder realities within the context in which these accelerators are funded. For instance, one of our accelerator cases, Bethnal Green Ventures, has a clear ecosystem focus and is financed by public sources, but copies the mentorship model typically found in the investor model. In another example, an accelerator we interviewed had a clear matchmaking focus, but it also provided some capital to the startups. Hence, the objective becomes hybrid: does it want to realize returns while keeping the corporates' customers happy? It is questionable whether these different elements will hold over the long term.

The situation becomes particularly difficult when different types of stakeholders are involved. For instance, in some cases, public sponsors require the attraction of private funds (e.g. investor funds) or corporate involvement alongside their funding. For example, the UK Cabinet Office's £10 million Social Incubator Fund requires accelerator programs to match their grant with external funds (which can come from corporates, investors or other public funders). However, these private funds come with their own expectations and hence dual objectives have to be managed by these accelerators. Since these accelerators are extremely small organizations, often with only two or three employees, it is questionable whether this is possible.

We observe in our data, traditional ways to deal with different stakeholders such as 'decoupling' (Meyer and Rowan, 1977). An example of 'decoupling' would be when an accelerator with a clear ecosystem focus takes small slices of equity in its early-stage ventures and places a relatively large potential valuation on that equity in the future. They do so because the public authority expects that after, say, five years the accelerator might become self-sustainable. Decoupling enables the accelerator to maintain its formal structure as ecosystem builder while its activities and communication vary in response to practical considerations. However, public funders and accelerators need to be aware of the potential conflict between objectives and reality.

Practice and policy implications

1. Entrepreneurs need to choose the right type of program for themselves

The three archetypes we have developed can be used to position different accelerators within the overall ecosystem. We suggest that initial advisors to early-stage ventures (e.g. government support agencies, university student and alumni entrepreneurship offices) should consider this framework, and the underlying objectives of different programs, in order to orient nascent entrepreneurs towards particular types of accelerators that may best meet their needs.

2. Different objectives require different metrics

The diversity of archetypes we have identified has implications for policy makers in evaluating the role of these accelerators and supporting them. Rather than evaluating the effectiveness of all accelerators using the same criteria, there is a need to develop measures that take into account the different objectives of different types of accelerator. Policy makers typically have regional development and employment as an objective. This is fine, but they then have to realize that the accelerators they finance cannot be profitable in the short or even medium term. The ventures they invest in, the program they have to develop in order to be successful in their objectives and their strategic focus on the local environment do not allow this. The systematic research evidence is sparse, but only investor-led accelerators in very dense ecosystems such as Silicon Valley appear to have a proven business model. Unfortunately, we often see that policy makers expect ecosystem accelerators to have similar outputs as investor-led ones.

3. Corporate accelerator programs need to balance dual objectives

Not only policy makers but also corporates play an active role in setting up accelerators. Looking at the accelerator scene in Europe, it is remarkable how much interest large corporates show in setting up accelerator programs. In this case, we observe that investor-led accelerators are often a source of inspiration. However, it is unlikely that these accelerator forms can be fully adopted by corporates. Their success is based upon the ability to track deal flow and spot early opportunities that need follow-up investment. In contrast, corporates often have dual objectives and see these accelerators as technology-scouting opportunities. Well-known examples such as Telefonica's Wayra accelerator offer their support to the ventures to further develop their technology and test it as an operator. This means that the corporate accelerator also has a 'matchmaking' objective, which implies the need for a different structure from the investor-led accelerator. The latter type deploys mentors to evaluate the ventures and assist them in making the business plan ready for the next capital round, while the former makes use of internal coaches to integrate the new venture's sales process into the corporates decision-making structure. Since 'investor-led' and 'matchmaker' objectives do not entirely match, it will be interesting to see which objectives dominate as these programs evolve over the next few years.

4. Successful accelerators require clear vision and objectives

As accelerators have grown in popularity, many nascent entrepreneurs and organizations such as universities, companies and regional development agencies feel attracted to the idea of starting an accelerator. Universities see it as a way to promote student entrepreneurship, companies as a way to tap into startup innovation and talent, and development agencies as a way to create employment. Examples of university-led accelerators include 'Beta Foundry' at Oxford University, InnovationRCA at the Royal College of Art and the pre-accelerator 'Imperial Create Lab' at Imperial College, London.

Our research shows that starting such an accelerator needs a very clear vision and strategy about the objectives that it wants to achieve. Given the results so far, it seems unlikely these accelerators will be profitable or even sustainable without continued financial support for a number of years.

Although they fill an important role, the need for this type of support needs to be legitimate. If not, the accelerator initiatives will disappear as soon as the financial support for them decreases.

5. Accelerator support needs to be time-limited to avoid the 'life support' incubation trap

Finally, our findings suggest that accelerators may help solve some of the problems noted earlier that are associated with traditional incubators. In the past, some incubators have been accused of merely acting as life support and keeping tenants alive in order to secure rent and fill their incubation space. As most accelerators invest in their startups in contrast to some traditional incubators, they have an added incentive to make sure that the selected startups survive and scale. Accelerators are a way to shorten the journey of startups, resulting in either quicker growth or quicker failure. However, some accelerators do allow alumni to remain in the space after the program has ended and there is the potential that this may create adverse consequences if it is not time limited.

Future research

As spatial context may have an important influence on entrepreneurial and innovation ecosystems (Levie *et al.*, 2014), further research is needed both to compare similar regions in other countries and to compare our findings with different environments, for example regions outside major metropolises.

As accelerator programs develop, our framework, comprising the three accelerator models, can serve as a basis for more rigorous evaluations of accelerator performance and can be used to define suitable success metrics in achieving certain objectives. Although we have identified three archetypes, subsequent analyses might also usefully examine the challenges faced by particular accelerators as they attempt to evolve over time into different models, depending on the success or otherwise of their initial configuration.

Although beyond the scope of this chapter, which has focused on the accelerators themselves, an interesting avenue is to study the impact accelerators have on the trajectory of the new ventures that participate in these programs. The type and phase of the entrepreneurial journey of startups is likely to have an important impact on the approach used by the accelerator and on the value they would add. Further research on the entrepreneurial process can offer interesting insights on the relative influence of accelerators on that process. This would enable identification of best practices with the aim of implementing a customized acceleration strategy to propel startups.

Importantly, in order to truly gauge the effectiveness of different models there is a need for studies that compare accelerated ventures to a control group of non-accelerated ventures in order to provide robust insights into the contribution of accelerators. Furthermore, explicitly focusing solely on one sector or technology is perceived as an interesting strategic option by decision makers. Assessment of differences in effectiveness and value-added contributions to the startups can improve our understanding of the possible benefits of specialized accelerators.

Conclusion

This qualitative research extends Miller and Bound (2011) study about accelerators and their implications for the entrepreneurial ecosystem. Their study has provided a wealth of insights regarding the categorization of accelerators. However, many questions remain outstanding due to the paucity of data. We, therefore, followed the call for more in-depth research on the origins and features of accelerator models and the heterogeneity of their strategies and operations.

Against a background of sparse research prior to this, our study has produced several interesting results that have novel implications for the incubator and entrepreneurship literatures and practice. First, in order to categorize accelerators and to avoid confusion, we have slightly adapted the definition of Miller and Bound (2011). Second, the report provides a comprehensive set of diverse features to describe the architectural blueprint of an accelerator. Third, we can draw from the results that accelerators can fit into at least three different configurations, some with more than one variant. Each of the different archetypes has its own actionable principles, depending heavily on the affiliated strategic partners (investors, corporates, government agencies, etc.). The model of the accelerator and its services is often dictated by or related to, the capital structure i.e. the type of funding it receives. As each stakeholder strives to invest in something they believe in to generate the right output, we also remain cautious of whether hybrid archetypes have the ability to meet the different expectations of their stakeholders.

Of course, because the phenomenon is so new, uncertainty still exists about the future success of accelerators. What is undeniable, though, is the compelling economic logic of such organizations. We hope that the findings of our study will open the way for further systematic analyses of the processes and impacts of accelerator programs.

References

Allen, D. N. and McCluskey, R. (1990). Structure, policy, services, and performance in the business incubator industry. *Entrepreneurship, Theory and Practice*, 15(2): 61–77.

Ambos, T. C. and Birkinshaw, J. (2010). How do new ventures evolve? An inductive Study of archetype changes in science-based ventures. *Organization Science*, 21(6): 1125–1140.

Birdsall, M., Jones, C., Lee, C., Somerset, C., and Takaki, S. (2013). *Business Accelerators: The Evolution of a Rapidly Growing Industry*. MBA, University of Cambridge.

Bruneel, J., Ratinho, T., Clarysse, B., and Groen, A. (2012). The evolution of business incubators: Comparing demand and supply of business incubation services across different incubator generations. *Technovation*, 32(2): 110–121.

Christiansen, J. (2009). Copying Y Combinator, A framework for developing Seed Accelerator Programmes. MBA dissertation, University of Cambridge, United Kingdom. Retrieved June, 5, 2014.

Gruber, M., MacMillan, I. C., and Thompson, J. D. (2008). Look before you leap: Market opportunity identification in emerging technology firms. *Management Science*, 54(9): 1652–1665

Hackett, S.M. and Dilts, D.M. (2004). A systematic review of business incubation research. *Journal of Technology Transfer*, 29(1): 55–82.

Hochberg, Yael V. and Kamath, Kristen (2012). U.S. Seed Accelerator Rankings. Kellogg School of Management, Northwestern University: Evanston, IL, USA

Levie, J., Autio, E., Acs, Z., and Hart, M. (2014). Global entrepreneurship and institutions: An introduction. *Small Business Economics*, 42(3): 437–444.

Meyer, J. W. and Rowan, B. (1977). Institutionalized organizations: Formal structure as myth and ceremony. *American Journal of Sociology*, 83(2): 340.

Miller, P. and Bound, K. (2011). *The Startup Factories: The rise of accelerator programs to support new technologies*, Discussion Paper, NESTA, London, UK.

Smilor, R. W. (1987). Commercializing technology through new business incubators. *Research Management*, 30(5): 36–41.

Smilor, R. and Gill, M. (1986). *The New Business Incubator: Linking Talent, Technology and Know-How.* Lexington Books, Lexington, MA.

Wright, M., Clarysse, B., Mustar, P., and Lockett, A. (2007). *Academic entrepreneurship in Europe.* Edward Elgar Publishing, London, UK.

Zott, C. and Huy, Q. N. (2007). How entrepreneurs use symbolic management to acquire resources. *Administrative Science Quarterly*, 52(1): 70–105.

Appendix A

Some detailed overviews of accelerator programs based in UK can be found in the following sections.

A.1. Bethnal Green Ventures (BGV)

Backers: Public funding (Cabinet Office) and foundations (Nesta, Nominet Trust).

Investment → equity taken: £15K à 6% (standard offer).

Program focus: social for-profit startups (health, education and sustainability).

Unique value proposition: a founder-friendly model fitted for the needs of social profit startups with a focus on searching customers through their broad network of experts and mentors.

A.1.1. *Selection process & criteria*

Process:

Online application via f6s application software platform asking for a description of the business

↓

Applicants are shortlisted down to 30 candidates by the selection committee made up of the accelerator's core team, representatives of investors, alumni and mentors

↓

Face-to-face interview (30 minutes, pressure-like testing) with the accelerator's core team, which then selects the final 10 startups

Criteria: BGV's selection and criteria procedure is not a customer-led model, it is an **entrepreneurial-driven** model. According to Paul Miller, they think about it in terms of the demand side as being the startups (more a philosophical decision). The following points are taken into account: full-time founding team; team focus; ideas can be accepted; social impact and ambition (no little lifestyle businesses); team background & dynamic; incorporation of the business is not required.

For the duration of the program, entrepreneurs set up a simple company limited by shares (for-profit). After developing the business model, entrepreneurs have the choice of whether they are going down the non-profit route.

A.1.2. *Summary of operations and services*

The program has evolved out of the Social Innovation Camp, which was funded by Nesta. It holds a broad 'horizontal' focus that includes three main topics: health and ageing, education and employability, sustainability (~Nesta's investment themes). Subsequently, they position themselves as a social impact accelerator where financial return is not the main objective. They are about open source working and social innovations in the three months intensive program.

Like most accelerators the general value proposition consists of workshops; coaching; weekly evaluation; co-working space; various of events; Demo Day; networking; financial and legal support. To a certain extent, BGV is a blueprint of the traditional tech accelerator program (Techstars model). In other words, they impose entry and exit conditions and offer services and support activities that should lead to a market-ready business. The program relies on their network of mentors to bring in industry expertize and the team focuses on the basics of starting and running a business. The approach is a reflection of the 'Lean Startup' trend by focusing on talking to prospective customers, developing and iterating the product/service and searching for investment.

Mentoring: Mentorship is the great value driver for most of the accelerator programs. This is also the case for BGV (mentor-led program). The program starts with an intensive speed dating between the mentors and founders. The mentors will look at how the startups generate value and where improvements can be made. Around 60 mentors are involved; some have been specifically recruited according to their individual expertize that can be matched with the participating startups. Some are ad hoc mentors, and some more long-term. Selection of mentors happens through referral and recommendations of other mentors or people that they trust. No strict selection process is in place but an informal interview is required. By differentiating the participating startups into three archetypes, different mentors are assigned for each archetype. They have created groups of startups based on the startup's main objective:

(1) 'Proposition seekers' are startups still developing their business proposition, mainly in finding out the combination of the problem, the solution and the customers;
(2) 'Customer hunters' have basically a proposition but have not identified the customer yet and
(3) 'Scalers' have figured out the two other aspects but have difficulty with scaling up.

A.1.3. *Funding structure*

BGV has a limited liability partnership (LLP) structure with a for-profit part and a not-for-profit part. The former can take external investment and is the investment vehicle for investing in the startups. The latter, which owns the majority of the LLP, is used to cover the operational costs and can accept grants. Funding for investment, and to deliver the program comes from Nesta, The Nominet Trust and the Cabinet Office. Standard investment is £15K for 6% equity (ordinary shares) in return and the term of being kept up-to-date after graduation. No structure for any follow-on investment is in place. However, BGV do provide post-program support by offering three extra months of free office space and letting the alumni use their network and resources after graduation.

A.1.4. *The results*

Their biggest financial success until now is the alumni startup Fairphone that is building the world's first "ethical" mobile phone. They have a strong and lively community, sold already +25,000 Fairphones and a team that has grown from 5 people to around 20 people today.

A.2. Fintech innovation lab

Backers: Privately funded (Accenture), supported by 12 Investment and retail banks, with the backing of several public sector bodies.

Investment → equity taken: none à none.

Program focus: Fintech startups.

Unique value proposition: a goodwill model that provides senior level mentoring and connect the startups with potential customers at top institutions, hereby helping the startups be more investable for B2B sales in the financial services sector.

A.2.1. *Selection process & criteria*

Process:

Online application via own software platform

Applications are reviewed by the senior executives of the partner banks themselves and are shortlisted down to 15 startups

'Boot camp (1 half-day)' for the top 15 shortlisted candidates who will get to meet the key financial services executives and trial-run their pitch

Selected applicants go to the 'Dragon's Den (two half-days)' where they pitch in front of senior sponsors from the banks (CIO, CTO). The best six startups get selected

Criteria: open to all early-stage startups that can take value out of the program and not already established tech businesses in the financial services; B2B technologies (also B2C focus); full-time founding team; beta-prototype required; team background.

The key areas in where banks want to innovate: big data, analytics, security, mobile, and operational technology. Startups are three-years old, generate some revenue and are looking to diversify into other industries.

A.2.2. *Summary of operations and services*

Accenture puts innovation in the spotlight through its accelerator program. The program is driven by a growth motive, not a profit motive, and proved highly successful in helping startups. Accenture covers the program operating costs, including paying for office space for the startups at a shared-workspace during the three months of the program. In its first two years, the program was based at Level39, as shared workspace in Canary Wharf. The intensive three-month program begins with a series of training and mentoring sessions to help prepare the startups to best position their technology proposition to the banks. This includes training on understanding the banking industry, and the different strategic drivers of each of the banks. It also involves corporate etiquette training and some pitch coaching. Following this is the "meat" of the program that is the 12 "Speed-Dating" events run by each bank on the program. Here the startups get to meet and pitch to a wide range of senior executives from within each of the banks. Following this, the "chaperones" from each of the banks work with the startups to help them follow-up on the discussions they started in the speed dating.

Accenture's objectives from the accelerator program are as follows:

- Create a platform for the financial services industry to collaborate on innovation with startups and early-stage companies — in the process, strengthening its relationships with its bank clients.
- Invest in the future of London's economy by supporting entrepreneurs.
- Support London as the leader in financial services technology.
- Identify interesting new technology innovations that could be applied to the financial services sector.

Mentorship: Each startup is supported by 'a chaperone' which are leading executives from the banks providing startups with senior-level guidance. This creates a strong interaction between the startups and the banks (potential customer). There is a very intensive speed dating during the first two weeks of the program with a series of different executives. It gives the startups and their chaperone a few leads (lead generation). Independent mentors are also involved but more on an as-needed basis.

This type of accelerator has an Investor Day. Before Investor Day takes place, the core team of the accelerator and the senior executives from the banks that participate, gathers for what is called the 'chaperone review'. Here is where the chaperones report to these senior executives what they have done and how the startups has evolved. The aim of this meeting is to educate the banks to make informed investment decisions.

A.2.3. *Funding structure*

Accenture covers the operational costs of running the program.

A.2.4. *The results*

Data from the first batch of companies show that the startups have an increase of 41% in full-time employees. Notable is that revenues of the startups have gone up by 140% and they have raised a total of £10 million in follow-on investment to date.

A.3. Techstars London

Backers: Private funding (VC's and business angels).

Investment → equity taken: £12.5K + optional £60K convertible debt note à 6% (standard offer).

Program focus: generic.

Unique value proposition: the first mentor-led training program with a global network and numerous support structures beyond the original program. It has been replicated over 1000× globally.

A.3.1. *Selection process & criteria*

Process:

Online application via f6s application software platform asking for a description of the business + by referral through affiliated investors.

↓

The applications are reviewed by the core team accelerator to select the 75+ most promising startups.

↓

A series of interviews with the accelerator's core team and external experts to reduce the selection to 20–30 teams for final selection.

↓

Face-to-face interview with a selection committee made up of the accelerator's core team, which then selects the top 10 startups.

Criteria: Highly focused on team and opportunity; full-time founding team; team focus; team background and dynamics; prototype required.

Techstars select the top 10 startups out of more than 1000+ applications. There is a broad spectrum of teams selected including repeat entrepeneurs and seed funded teams.

A.3.2. *Summary of operations and services*

The origin of Techstars can be found in Colorado, Boulder. Its impetus was 2006 and from then on, they have been expanding steadily, running a total of 12 programs today. Every program of Techstars is managed by an experienced entrepreneur with empathy towards the startups ('founder-friendly'). In 2013, the tech-accelerator has launched its first program outside the US by merging with the UK-based accelerator Springboard. Techstars offers a structured program where startups move to the accelerator for the duration of the program to benefit from the creation of a peer-to-peer environment and the intensive mentoring.

The support consists of the following elements: workshops; coaching; Demo Day; networking; legal and banking support; hosting services

(Amazon web services, Windows, Rackspace startup program), free co-working space. They are accredited by UKTI as a seed investment competition to make it for foreign entrepreneurs easier to gain a visa. In addition "Hackstars and associates" are available to assist the startups in every possible way. They are perceived as consultants to the Techstars ventures. A small allowance is paid to cover some of their expenses. Post-program support is provided in terms of free desk space after graduation. Monthly alumni events are organized to keep the alumni structure and network active.

Mentorship: The Techstars' model is to bring in mentors to help its startups. It has a 10:1 mentor to startup ratio to make sure each venture gets undivided attention. All mentors get to meet each startup by starting the program with a mentoring marathon i.e. 10 days of intensive speed dating between the mentors and founders.

A.3.3. *Funding structure*

Techstars London LLP is a for-profit company. The ventures accepted into the program are offered around £20K in seed funding. In addition, they are offered a £100K convertible debt note. In return for the seed investment, they take 6% ordinary shares. The program is privately funded by business angels and VC's. It can also offer follow-on investment through an additional investment (match-funding vehicle). Furthermore, we can notice in the past years a vertical integration into seed funds. Techstars added seed-staged VC funds to their portfolio, more precisely Techstars Ventures runs a seed and Series A stage fund to invest in Techstars graduates and in companies started by Techstars alumni and mentors.

A.3.4. *The results*

This elite accelerator has gone on to launch 292 startups worldwide of which 231 are still active. Techstars' ventures have collectively raised over £500M worth of investment and created 2458 jobs to date.

A.4. Climate-KIC UK

Backers: Public funding (European Commission, EIT).

Investment → equity taken: €95K → none (standard offer).

Program focus: Climate impact startups (climate change mitigation and adaptation).

Unique value proposition: non-profit organization that is prepared to take the risk and come in at the early idea stage. It is positioned as funding for the feasibility of commercialization of a concept and steps leading to investor readiness.

A.4.1. *Selection process & criteria*

Process:
Online application via own software platform + selection events (mainly business plan competitions where Climate-KIC sponsors prizes and grants wildcards to the winners)

↓

Applications are reviewed by an internal panel (~team accelerator) and an external panel (entrepreneurs/mentors) for feedback + scoring

↓

An internal panel shortlists the applicants

↓

Interview with the internal panel, which then selects the best startups (20 per annum)

Three standard questions are asked during the interview: (1) tell about yourselves, your background and passion, (2) describe your idea simply and (3) your appetite and plan for success.

Criteria: Climate impact + chances of success; news value, strength of IP or differentiation; scalability; quality or potential of entrepreneurs (however matchmaking possible if it is a good idea but entrepreneurial skills are lacking).

A.4.2. *Summary of operations and services*

Climate-KIC is one of three KICs set up by the European Institute of Innovation and Technology (EIT), an EU body charged with generating economic growth through innovation. It is a basic program that is harmonized across Europe (France, Germany, UK, Switzerland, Netherland and Denmark) however each 'innovation factory' has its local differences in terms of selection criteria, etc. Also a node just opened in Copenhagen and several pre-acceleration programs in Valencia, Bologna, Budapest, Wroclaw, Birmingham and Frankfurt. The objectives are to prove the feasibility of concepts and transform ideas moving into their startup phase. The Climate-KIC accelerator program, based in UK, has 75% of businesses in the later stages of the pipeline that attracted at least €1 million from external sources.

The Climate-KIC model is inspired by Y-Combinator fitted to the needs of research-driven startups through tailored coaching by the core team, support from expert commercial advisers and an Entrepreneur-in-Residence. In addition it offers a startup curriculum through master classes and video-based learning, free office-space, a tour to Silicon Valley, pitch coaching, creative design support, pan-European events and a huge global network. Science, Technology and Engineering support is available via vouchers from some of the world's leading scientific research institutions and laboratories. A community Hub has been installed for networking and connecting with corporate partners. There is up to 95,000€ grant funding available, awarded over three stages:

(1) Period of 3–6 months for drafting the initial business model and market prioritization hypothesis (~20,000€).
(2) Period of 3 to 6 months to verify assumptions (Lean Launchpad method) and get customer feedback to validate the business model (~25,000€).
(3) Period of 3 to 6 months to gain market traction i.e. customer-and investor wise (~50,000€).

Each period is marked by an evaluation of the achievements. Progress to the next stage is thus only possible when specific milestones are reached.

Startups are initially assessed by an internal and external panel however at the transition of stage 1 to stage 2 to stage 3, the panel is internal. In stage 3, the startup will get vouchers to go to pitching road shows and access to a network of partners and investors to try to look for investment. Startups are able to receive even more grant funding through entering the national (~20,000€) and pan-European Venture Competition (~40,000€). Technology startups from academic institutions represent a major part of the deal flow.

A.4.3. *Funding structure*

Climate-KIC is Europe's largest Public–Private innovation partnership i.e. it has an integrated community of partners of which 47% are from business, 32% are from world class academia, and 21% are public bodies. It can be seen as a funding vehicle from out the European Commission that grants funding of up to 95,000€ to high impact startups. There is an annual budget of approximately €15 million for 2014 for Climate-KIC Entrepreneurship activities (2013 €10 million). Tenants sign a grant agreement saying what the program consists of and in turn are obliged to give yearly reports with evidence of their achievement and expenses. As there is the expectancy to be sustainable in the mid-term, the model may evolve in the future to an equity-taking investment scheme (upfront or after the startups go through the accelerator).

A.4.4. *The results*

Already 16 ventures have proven their market potential. Of those 16 start-ups, 11 have raised more than €1 million in follow-up funding.

Chapter 4

Inter-Incubator Relationships and New Venture Performance in China's Technology Business Incubators between 2008 and 2012

Yunhao Zhu

Introduction

There is no doubt of the important role that new ventures play in the development of economies; they are a major source of sales, new jobs and innovation in most economies (Rice, 1995; Peña, 2004; Colombo and Delmastro, 2002; Siegel *et al.*, 2003c; Phan *et al.*, 2005; Chen, 2009). However, lives of these small and new firms are very tough and fraught with difficulties. Not surprisingly many do not survive beyond their early, critical years (Peña, 2004; Colombo and Delmastro, 2002; Bøllingtoft and Ulhøi, 2005; Hackett and Dilts, 2004a). For example, on average one out of three new companies in Europe fails before the second year of its existence, and 50–60% of them do not survive the seventh year (Aerts *et al.*, 2007). In China, this problem is especially severe: the estimated failure rate for an initial entrepreneurial attempt is as high as 90% in 2010 (Song *et al.*, 2013).

In many cases, to survive, new ventures have to overcome several barriers due to liability of newness (Stinchcombe, 1965; Zhang and Li, 2010;

Li *et al.*, 2012), including small size, insufficient financial capital, poor management, high overhead and so on (Siegel *et al.*, 2003c; Hackett and Dilts, 2004b; Chan and Lau, 2005; Begerk and Norrman, 2008; Colombo and Delmastro, 2002; Chen, 2009; Bøllingtoft and Ulhøi, 2005). This is especially true for new technology-based firms (NTBFs) which will face a highly dynamic market driven by unanticipated, sharp technology changes (Kirwan *et al.*, 2006).

Business incubators (BIs) are adopted in many countries as politically attractive and widely accepted tools to ameliorate the above-mentioned problems by compensating for new ventures' gaps in knowledge, competence and resources (Rice, 2002; Scillitoe and Chakrabarti, 2005; Schwartz and Hornych, 2010; Grimaldi and Grandi, 2005). The last two decades witnessed the rapid growth of BIs all over the world (Phan *et al.*, 2005; Aerts *et al.*, 2007), particularly in developing countries such as China, Brazil, Turkey, etc. (Lalkaka and Shaffer, 1999; Vanderstraeten and Matthyssens, 2012). Researchers and practitioners have paid increasing attention to the emergence and growth of BIs (Hackett and Dilts, 2004a; Ratinho and Henriques, 2010). It has been argued that the creation of BIs is a vehicle for facilitating the survival and growth of new ventures and promoting job and wealth creation at the nation, state, and city levels (Bruneel *et al.*, 2012). Some countries have placed the development of BIs at the center of their national and/or local development programs (Peña, 2004; Ratinho and Henriques, 2010). Considering the economic and political significance for BIs, what factors can affect their performance?

Past literature on BIs has focused either on the importance of endogenous factors within the incubators, e.g. incubator–incubatee interactions, inter-firm interactions, etc. (Allen and McCluskey, 1990; Scillitoe and Chakrabarti, 2009, 2010; Chan and Lau, 2005; Mian, 1996; Begerk and Norrman, 2008; Haapasalo and Ekholm, 2004) or the importance of linkages with prominent external organizations (Hansen *et al.*, 2000; Sa and Lee, 2012; Colombo and Delmastro, 2002; Rothschild and Darr, 2005), especially university–industry linkages (Westhead and Storey, 1995; Thursby *et al.*, 2001; Thursby and Kemp, 2002; Thursby and Thursby, 2002; Siegel *et al.*, 2003a, 2003b, 2003c). While these studies have contributed substantially to our nascent understanding of incubation performance, there are gaps in the literature. These studies have implicitly treated BIs as if they are independent of one another. However, in case of multiple BIs, it is likely that inter-incubator relationships will have important impacts on incubator and affiliated new-venture performance. For example, Porter (1998a) argued that an industrial cluster could affect the productivity of other clusters.

According to Barnett and Carroll (1987), despite the fact that most studies have focused on interdependence between organizations, interdependence can exist between the communities which contain several populations of organizations. Thus, it is reasonable to argue that the boundaries of BIs are open and porous and do not prevent knowledge and resources from flowing from one incubator to another. In this study, we adopt an ecological view (Freeman and Audia, 2006; Hannan and Freeman, 1977, 1989; Zhang *et al.*, 2009) to explore how inter-incubator relationships will affect a focal BI's new-venture performance. Furthermore, the interdependence of BIs has two forms: mutualism and competition, which will jointly affect BIs' new-venture performance. To be more specific, we delineate two dimensions of inter-incubator relationships: regional incubator density and geographic proximity to the nearest incubator, and propose that each dimension will have an inverted U-shaped relationship with a focal BI's new-venture performance due to the joint effects of mutualism and competition.

More importantly, the linkage between inter-incubator relationships and BIs' new-venture performance is not universal but rather could be context specific. The underlying logic indicates that the effects of inter-incubator relationships on a focal BI's new-venture performance will depend on the extent to which the BI's ability to acquire additional resources in the situation of limited region's carrying capacity. When a BI has alternative and more convenient channels to acquire additional resources, the BI may become less passionate to interact with other BIs, and the effectiveness of inter-incubator relationships for the BI and affiliated new ventures may be mitigated. Based on this argument, we try to examine the moderating role of two institutional contexts: government ownership (with strong political networking) and specialization strategy (with strong peer networking). We propose that the substitution effects may occur between different types of networks. More specifically, BIs' political networking and peer networking may mitigate the effectiveness of inter-incubator relationships in terms of both mutualism and competition.

In summary, we will address two research questions: (1) How do inter-incubator relationships (i.e. regional density and geographic proximity) related to a focal BI's new-venture performance? (2) How do institutional contexts (i.e. government ownership and specialization strategy) moderate the links between inter-incubator relationships and new-venture performance? We examine these ideas in the context of Chinese national technology business incubators (TBIs) from 2008 to 2012. What makes a China study of inter-incubator relationships intriguing is in the vast and differentiated geographical distribution of TBIs. TBIs are a specific type of BIs focusing exclusively on promoting NTBFs. Despite the wide ranging research conducted on BIs, few studies have focused on TBIs (Phillips, 2002). In addition, recent literature clearly emphasized the potential for enhancing the effectiveness of TBIs. However, there is little systematic, empirical evidence utilizing published data on the effectiveness of the TBIs in the performance of their underlying functions. This may be partly due to the fact that TBIs are not as clearly defined in the world and gaining the requisite institutional knowledge about multiple populations of TBIs poses a formidable empirical challenge (Phillips, 2002). In this study, Chinese TBIs were chosen because there is a clearly defined set of published statistics. In addition, according to the Chinese Ministry of Science and Technology (MST), a government department in charge of BIs, China is ranked second only to the United States in the number of TBIs by the end of 2006 (MST, 2007).

The remainder of the chapter is organized as follows. In the following section, we describe the context of the study by presenting some stylized facts about Chinese TBIs. The next section begins with a discussion of theory and hypotheses. I then present the empirical results followed by the implications. The last section describes the main conclusions and limitations.

Context of the study

In an attempt to duplicate the success the U.S.'s Silicon Valley in developing NTBFs, the Chinese central government embarked on a series of science and technology initiatives at the beginning of the reform era. One of the most important programs, the Torch Program, was put in place in

1988 with the main objective: '*to develop high- and new-technology products, establish technology-oriented enterprises, and pave the way for the commercialization of innovations that will come out of major national science and technology programs*' (Hu, 2007).

A major ingredient of the Torch Program was the establishment of TBIs in the whole country to foster the development of NTBFs. Figure 1 shows the evolution over time of the number of TBIs. In China, the unimpaired enthusiasm of national and local government agencies has led to the current number of over 1200 TBIs — by far the largest and one of the densest populations in Asia. In comparison with developed countries, China has been a laggard in the development of such initiatives.

The first Chinese TBI, Wuhan Eastlake Hi-tech Innovation Center, was established in 1987. According to Figure 1, the TBI movement did not really take off until the early 2000s. Between 1999 and 2012, the number of TBIs skyrocketed from a mere 110 to 1239. In general, the size of TBIs in China is relatively large when compared with their US and European counterparts. In 2012 alone, Chinese TBIs provided a rental space of 43 million m^2 and such a size supported some 70,000 new ventures. The affiliated incubatees with an average of 20 employees created a total of 1.2 million jobs and generating annual revenue of more than 490 billion yuan. By the end of 2012, the accumulated number of graduates incubated by TBIs had reached 45,000.

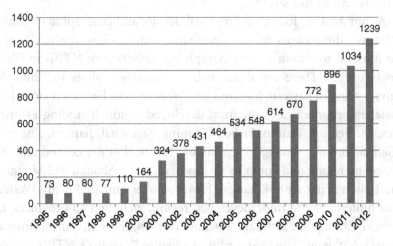

Figure 1. The Number of TBIs in China from 1995 to 2012

Most of the Chinese TBIs are initiated by national or local government or its agencies. As such, the purchases of land and initial investments in infrastructure for TBIs are partially financed by these official institutions. Cities and municipalities, in particular, show a high commitment to establishing these property-based initiatives. To regulate the development of TBIs, MST has enacted a regulation specifying a range of standards. TBIs meeting these standards are given the title of 'NTBIs' which can enjoy favorable publicity and benefit from financial support, preferential policies and other governmental resources. For example, the regulation stipulates that the number of incubatees located in any one NTBI must surpass 80. Within the pool of incubatees in NTBI the proportion with intellectual property must beyond 30%. With respect to selection criteria, the applying firm's age at entry must be less than 24 months. To qualify as a graduate, the incubatees must meet at least two of the following three criteria: (a) it has at least one intellectual property; (b) its annual revenue exceeded 10 million yuan for two consecutive years; (c) it is merged or acquired, or goes public and becomes a listed company at home or abroad. Such a national level status assessment is performed on an annual basis, and if the TBIs fail to meet the standards for two continuous years, the qualification of 'NTBIs' will be revoked. Because the general TBIs do not usually employ the same relatively stringent criteria as the NTBIs do and the detailed data of general TBIs is missing, we focus only on the NTBIs in this study.

As our analysis focuses on regional density and geographic proximity as the two dimensions of inter-incubator relationships, the reader may find it useful to visualize the geographic distribution of NTBIs in China (see Figure 2). There are three main contrasting regions in China for analysis: namely, Eastern, Midland and Western. The Eastern region is the coastal and economically, the most developed region, including 11 provinces, i.e. Beijing, Tianjin, Hebei, Liaoning, Shanghai, Jiangsu, Zhejiang, Fujian, Shandong, Guangdong, Hainan. Midland is the central and still developing region and contains nine provinces, i.e. Shanxi, Nei Monggol, Jilin, Heilongjiang, Anhui, Jiangxi, Henan, Hubei, Hunan. Finally, Western is the hinterland and underdeveloped region, including 10 provinces, i.e. Guangxi, Chongqing, Sichuan, Guizhou, Yunnan, Shaanxi, Gansu, Qinghai, Ningxia, Sinkiang, Tibet. According to Figure 2, China's NTBIs are not

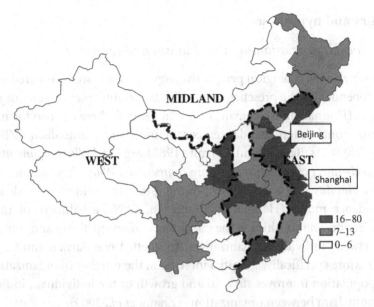

Figure 2.   The Geographic Distribution of Chinese NTBIs in 2012

evenly distributed throughout the country. For example, there are 435 NTBIs in 2012, and most NTBIs inhabit China's Eastern and coast region, where most of the technological and educational resources and industrial capability are located (Hu, 2007). While 292 NTBIs are on the Eastern region of China, the Midland and Western region only have 84 and 59 NTBIs, respectively. More specifically, the top seven provinces with the largest number of NTBIs are all located in Eastern areas, such as Jiangsu, Shandong, Zhejiang, Beijing, Liaoning, Guangdong and Shanghai, while within the Western region, Gansu, Qinghai, Ningxia, Sinkiang, Xizang, Guizhou have no more than three NTBIs in each province. Additionally, it is obvious that some NTBIs are in close proximity to others, whereas others are relatively distant from the nearest NTBI. Thus, the variable regional incubator density and geographic proximity to the nearest incubator in a specific province provide an opportunity to examine how inter-incubator relationships affect BIs' new-venture performance. In the next section, we draw upon an ecological perspective to develop theory and research hypotheses.

Theory and hypotheses

Inter-incubator relationships: mutualism and competition

According to the ecological perspective, organizations are considered to be interdependent if the presence of one affects the outcomes of other organizations (Hannan and Freeman, 1977). In general, there are two forms of organizational interdependence: competition and mutualism (Zhang *et al.*, 2009). As Barnett and Carroll (1987) argued, '*When organizations negatively affect one another, they are competitive. When they enhance each other's viability, organizations are mutualistic*'. According to the density dependence model (Hannan and Freeman, 1989), a hallmark of inter-organization relationships is the coexistence of competition and mutualism between individual organizations (Barnett, 1990; Barnett and Caroll, 1987). More specifically, an initial increase in the number of organizations in a population improves survival and growth of the individuals, indicating mutualism between organizations (Zhang *et al.*, 2009).

Mutualism occurs because organizations '*making similar demands on the environment combine their efforts, intentionally or otherwise*' to improve their position in the population (Aldrich, 1999). However, as the number of organizations further increases and exceeds a certain point, competition between organizations dominates and increases mortality of the individuals, indicating the competition stage of inter-organization relationships. Competition occurs because the joint resource requirements of multiple organizations approach an environment's carrying capacity. Thus, '*The mutualistic benefits of an initial increase in density, combined with the competitive effects of further increases, create an inverted U-shaped effect of population density on organizational outcomes*' (Zhang *et al.*, 2009). Based on past studies on interdependence between organizations, it is reasonable to propose that interdependence between BIs has two forms: mutualism and competition.

In the business incubation context, mutualism between BIs derives from the greater and more generalized attention that multiple related BIs can attract from external actors to their locations (Romanelli and Khessina, 2005). More specifically, when the important external actors such as venture capitalists, angel investors, entrepreneurs and customers interact with incubatees in one BI, they are more likely to become aware of incubatees in other BIs if these BIs are located in a proximate network of cross-incubator exchanges (Zhang *et al.*, 2009). As a result, the presence of multiple BIs within a specific region can enhance the region and BIs' capability for entrepreneurship development. This can affect external actors' decisions about where to commercialize research, transfer technologies and locate businesses, and decisions about where to invest financial capital, which in turn can lead to mutual benefits for these BIs and affiliated new ventures.

Competition among BIs generally arises from the joint dependence of multiple BIs on the same set of finite resources in a specific region (Hannan and Freeman, 1989). As key resources sought by BIs such as tenants, technology entrepreneurs, scientists, venture capitalists and angel investors are in short supply in a specific region at a particular point of time, BIs are in a state of competitive interdependence. Ruef (2000) defined carrying capacity as '*the maximum number of organizations having some identify (potential or realized) that can be supported by the environment at a particular point of time*'. Thus, when the region's carrying capacity is greater than that required, the surplus can support greater demand (Zhang *et al.*, 2009) and one can anticipate increased BI and new-venture growth. However, when BIs' size and joint resource requirements reach the region's carrying capacity, increased competition will likely occur and decrease BIs and affiliated-ventures' development.

In summary, we propose that the interdependence between BIs has two forms: mutualism and competition, which will jointly affect the focal BI and affiliated new-venture performance. In this study, we focus on two dimensions of inter-incubator relationships: regional incubator density and a focal BI's geographic proximity to the nearest incubator. Regional incubator density is defined as the number of BIs in a specific region, while geographic proximity captures the spatial distance between a focal BI and the nearest neighboring BI. By systematically examining the effects of the two dimensions, we are able to offer a more complete picture of the role of inter-incubator relationships in BIs' new-venture performance.

Following Zhang *et al.* (2009)'s logic, we argue that each of the two dimensions will affect the levels of mutualism and competition between BIs. The functional form of mutualism and competition between BIs that we expect draws upon the view of density dependence model of the population ecology literature (Barron *et al.*, 1994; Hannan and Freeman, 1977, 1989; Haveman, 1993). The density dependence model assumes that mutualism grows with density at a decreasing rate, while competition grows with density at an increasing rate (Haveman, 1993). Similarly, we propose that mutualism between BIs' new-venture performance with regional incubator density and geographic proximity at a decreasing rate, while competition between BIs grows with these dimensions at an increasing rate.

Regional incubator density and new-venture performance

The impact of density on organizational survival and growth has been widely discussed in the density dependence model of the population ecology literature (Carroll and Hannan, 2000; Zhang *et al.*, 2009). Considering the consistency of many empirical results supporting an inverted U-shaped relationship between density and organizational performance, it is reasonable to propose that regional incubator density may have a similar effect on BIs and affiliated new-venture performance. The reason is that the number of BIs in a specific region will not only provide opportunities for knowledge spillover across incubator boundaries but also reflect the competition among the incubators for the similar and limited resources (Tallman and Phene, 2007; Zhang *et al.*, 2009). More specifically, when the number of BIs in a specific region is low, increases in incubator density will enhance recognition that a given region and BI location is appropriate for technology and entrepreneurship development, which Romanelli and Khessina (2005) termed as region's 'industrial identity'. Consequently, the important external actors such as venture capitalists, angel investors, talents, and scientists will increasingly consider the region and BIs as a fertile location for entrepreneurship and direct their investment decisions toward the region and BIs accordingly, which will mutually benefit the BIs and hence affiliated new ventures. However, as regional-incubator density continues to increase, competition between BIs in the region will increase, which will gradually erode the benefits of mutualism (Zhang *et al.*, 2009). As BIs and ventures are located in the same region, they often draw upon and compete for a common resource pool. As a result, competition with other BIs is likely to undermine a focal BI and its incubatees' survival and growth. For example, in our Chinese research context, it is common that BIs in a specific region compete for resources and support from central and local government agencies. In addition, these BIs tend to attract resources from a limited set of labor resources, raw materials and financial institutions (Zhang *et al.*, 2009). Thus, as the number of BIs in a region further increases, combined resource requirements of these incubators and incubatees are more likely to reach the region's carrying capacity (Ruef, 2000). When the resources required in common become scarce, it will impede the growth of BIs and affiliated new ventures located in the region. In summary, the mutualistic benefits of increased numbers when regional incubator density is low combine with the competitive pressures placed on BIs, when density increases beyond a certain point it will jointly create an inverted U-shaped relationship between regional incubator density and the focal BI's new-venture performance. Thus, we propose

Hypothesis 1. *Regional incubator density will have an inverted U-shaped relationship with the focal BI's new-venture performance.*

Geographic proximity and new-venture performance

Geographic proximity was one of the most important dimensions of inter-organization and inter-community relationships in the past literature (Zhang *et al.*, 2009). The importance of geographic proximity between communities has been discussed by many scholars (Porter, 1998a, 1998b). For example, Tallman and Phene (2007) argued that geographic proximity played an important role in facilitating knowledge spillover across geographic boundaries of industry clusters. Herein, we try to investigate how spatial heterogeneity affects a focal BI's new-venture performance by directly measuring geographic proximity between adjacent BIs (Zhang *et al.*, 2009). According to the ecological theory, at low levels of geographic proximity between a focal BI and the nearest BI, increases in geographic proximity can produce mutualistic benefits. That is because increases in geographic proximity between adjacent BIs increase the chance of inter-incubator learning. According to Porter (1998a), industry clusters located in close geographic proximity to others are more likely to learn about and share the latest information and knowledge about markets and technologies than more isolated clusters.

In addition, increases in geographic proximity between adjacent BIs can enable BIs to draw greater attention to themselves from external actors due to reduced search cost for external actors. According to Romanelli and Khessina (2005), when external actors interact with new ventures in one BI, they are more likely to learn about ventures in another BI if these BIs are located proximately. However, as a focal BI's geographic proximity to the nearest BI further increases and exceeds a certain point, competition between these BIs is likely to increase, which will gradually erode the benefits of mutualism. Closely located BIs will draw upon and compete for a common resource pool, thus creating greater competition for limited resources (Zhang *et al.*, 2009).

According to Ruef (2000), as geographic proximity between adjacent BIs further increase, combined resource requirements of these incubators and incubatees are more likely to reach the region's carrying capacity, which will make it difficult for these BIs and ventures to continuously grow. In summary, the net effect produces mutualism at low levels of geographic proximity and the effect shifts to competition at high levels of geographic proximity. Accordingly, we propose

Hypothesis 2. *Geographic proximity to the nearest incubator will have an inverted U-shaped relationship with the focal BI's new-venture performance.*

Moderating role of institutional contexts

The logic underlying above-mentioned hypotheses suggests that the effects of inter-incubator relationships on a focal BI's new-venture performance will depend on the extent to which the BI's ability to acquire additional resources in the context of limited region's carrying capacity. When the focal BI has alternative and convenient channels to acquire even more resources, the BI may be less than fully committed to the knowledge and resources flows across different BIs. As a result, the effectiveness of inter-incubator relationships for the BI and its new ventures may be mitigated. Thus, we try to investigate the moderating effects of two conceptual variables: government ownership with stronger political networking and specialization strategy with stronger peer networking.

Government ownership

Unlike well-established enterprises, BIs are deeply embedded in the political system (Phan *et al.*, 2005). BIs as examined in this study are considered strategically important programs in many countries (Peña, 2004), and they are often publicly funded (Hackett and Dilts, 2004b; Phillips, 2002). For example, most TBIs in the U.S. were supported by public funds, and incubator managers claimed that it would be impossible to provide services without this government support (Aernoudt, 2004). According to Child and Markoczy (1993), national and local governments still control significant portions of strategic factor resources and have considerable power to approve projects and allocate resources. As a result, entrepreneurs of new firms tend to maintain a 'disproportionately greater contact' with government agencies.

Many scholars have found that firms' linkages with government agencies, i.e. their political networking, are positively related to firm performance (Nee, 1992; Peng and Luo, 2000; Chen *et al.*, 2004). This is particularly the case when we consider China's transition economy (Li and Zhang, 2007), which is experiencing significant institutional change in moving from central planning to market competition. Xin and Pearce (1996) argue that in transition economies, firms' political networking can substitute for the insufficient formal infrastructure (i.e. *guanxi* in Chinese). It is therefore reasonable to propose that BIs' linkage with government agencies, i.e. BIs' political networking, represents a unique type of managerial resource that may help BIs deal with the redistributive power.

In this study, the inverted U-shaped relationships between inter-incubator relationships and a focal BI's new-venture performance may become weaker if the BI is owned by national or local government agencies. Compared with non-government-owned BIs, government-owned BIs are founded by national or local government or its agencies, and these BIs naturally have legitimacy and receive support or even protection from the government agencies that have found them (Li and Atuahene-Gima, 2001; Li and Zhang, 2007; Li *et al.*, 2012). Government agencies will provide additional support in terms of financing, information and technology for these BIs, which can alleviate risks and resource constraints for BIs and their new ventures. Furthermore, the government ownership can create or enhance a favorable public image and reputation for government-owned BIs and hence their new ventures. This legitimacy can enable these BIs and affiliated ventures to acquire other resources more easily. In a word, government ownership provides an entry ticket for government-owned BIs to join the rich political networking, and these BIs can rely on such channel to obtain more resources.

In contrast, for non-government-owned BIs, the region's carrying capacity and the channels of access to more resources are still limited, and therefore facilitating inter-incubator interactions to acquire resources from other BIs is attractive. In summary, the government-owned BIs' strong political networking can extend their resource channels, and acquiring resources from other BIs in the region will become less urgent for them. In other words, the effects of inter-incubator relationships on new-venture performance will be mitigated in the case of government-owned BIs. Thus, we propose the following hypothesis:

Hypothesis 3. *The inverted U-shaped relationship between inter-incubator relationships and affiliated new-venture performance will be weaker in government-owned BIs than in non-government-owned BIs.*

Specialization strategy

As incubatees are all physically located under the same roof, it makes collaboration among the new ventures, i.e. peer networking, much more likely (Lyons, 2000). Indeed, an important aspect of the value-added contributions of a BI location to affiliated ventures is seen in its potential to foster internal networks and synergies between the firms 'in-house', i.e. circulating useful information, acquiring certain projects jointly and establishing mutual contract agreements (Schwartz and Hornych, 2008, 2010; Lyons, 2000). Thus, BIs try to fulfill an essential bridging function, bringing together their incubatees through shared offices, meeting rooms, copy shops, dining halls and so on (Schwartz and Hornych, 2010). McAdam and McAdam (2008) find that geographical proximity within the BI can influence the frequency of contacts and thus the development of peer networking. In other words, geography proximity between incubatees facilitates ongoing interactions and development of personal relationships, and accelerates the transfer of valuable knowledge and information and the exchange of experience (Schwartz and Hornych, 2010; Bøllingtoft and Ulhøi, 2005).

A common feature of BIs is the coexistence of specialized business incubators (SBIs) and diversified business incubators (DBIs), which differ in their specialization strategy. Indeed, the vast majority of BIs in the world belong to DBIs which are characterized by a wide range of sectors or technology fields, resulting in a highly diversified tenant structure (Von Zedtwitz, 2003; Schwartz and Hornych, 2008). Compared with DBIs, SBIs are able to concentrate on one specific sector or technology field and thus can build stronger peer networking and exploiting more social capitals.

According to the theory of Marshall–Arrow–Romer externalities, the geographical clustering of firms in the same industry is likely to generate knowledge spillover that leads to dynamic externalities (Hu, 2007). Applied in the situation of BIs, the decisive key factor in inducing and establishing peer networking is some overlap of the core competence, knowledge, and marker focus (Schwartz and Hornych, 2008, 2010; Hansen *et al.*, 2000). Chan and Lau (2005) argued that incubatees must be clustered in the same sector for sharing of knowledge, information and experience take place. Totterman and Sten (2005) found that too much diversification will impede the transfer of valuable knowledge and the exchange of experience among tenants. Thus, SBIs have stronger peer networking, and the affiliated new ventures can rely on such internal networks to obtain more resources than their DBI counterparts. In addition, for incubatees located in SBIs, the different competitive scope with firms located in other BIs will inhibit knowledge spillover across BI boundaries. For example, the different technology will restrain mobility opportunities for employees to move from SBIs to other BIs. Moreover, given the high performance often claimed by researchers and practitioners for SBIs (Schwartz and Hornych, 2008, 2010), the specialization strategy can also enhance a favorable image and reputation for SBIs and their new ventures, which can enable these BIs to acquire other resources more easily. Finally, specialization strategy allows for service rationalization and allows incubator management of SBIs to provide high quality and sufficient complementary resources (von Zedtwitz and Grimaldi, 2006; Vanderstraeten and Matthyssens, 2012; Wolpert, 2002).

In contrast, due to weaker peer networking and less resource pool, new ventures of DBIs are more likely to engage in cross-incubator communication, resource flows and information exchange to facilitate firm survival and growth. Also, because of the heterogeneity of tenant structure, the incubator management of DBIs often cannot provide sufficient services and resources (Westhead and Batstone, 1998; Chan and Lau, 2005). In summary, the SBIs' strong peer networking can extend their resource channels, and acquiring resources from other BIs in the region will become less urgent for them. In other words, the effects of inter-incubator relationships on new-venture performance will be mitigated in the case of SBIs. Thus, we propose

Hypothesis 4. *The inverted U-shaped relationship between inter-incubator relationships and affiliated new-venture performance will be weaker in SBIs than in DBIs.*

Methods

Data

Our data include all NTBIs from 2008 to 2012. Data were collected from several sources. One is 2009–2013 'China Torch Statistical Yearbooks' provided by the Chinese MST, which provides data on each NTBI's annual sales revenue, employment size, number of graduates, incubator size, the education of incubator management and employees of incubatees, etc. These data are collected by incubator management from the resident ventures; then, they are aggregated to the incubator level and reported annually to the MST, which publishes the data. We collected additional information from the website of the national and local business incubation association and from the individual NTBI's websites and brochures. We also telephoned some incubator top managers and entrepreneurs of incubatees to verify the data. To develop a better understanding of the China's TBI programs, we embarked on in-depth interviews with the incubator top managers and a range of entrepreneurs in Hefei Science Park, one of the most successful NTBIs in Anhui Province. Furthermore, we studied China's economic growth programs and policies in recent years to distinguish additional variables that might influence incubator and affiliated new-venture performance. Relying on data from China and City Statistical Yearbooks which conducted by the national and local statistics bureaus, we identified longitudinal data on each host city's GDP, FDI and the number of universities and colleges. We did not use data prior to 2008 because those data were sparse and the yearbooks used different formats, which made comparison difficult. Because our data were a yearly time series, we lagged the independent variables by one year in our models. As a result, NTBIs with only one year observation were dropped and finally, we got 1945 observations.

Measures

Dependent, independent and control variables used in this study are as follows. To enhance the robustness of the study, we examined three performance dimensions of new ventures: survival, sales and employment (Barbero *et al.*, 2012; Bruneel *et al.*, 2012; Campbell, 1987). As noted earlier, these data are collected by incubator managers from the resident tenants; then they are aggregated to the incubator level. These data were updated annually and corrected for inflation (using RMB value in 1990). More specifically, we measured *survival (D1)* as the natural logarithm of the total number of graduates of each NTBI in a year (in unit); *sales (D2)* as the natural logarithm of the total sales revenue of each NTBI in a year (in 1000 RMB); and *employment size (D3)* as the natural logarithm of the total number of employees of each NTBI in a year (in person). We run separate multivariate linear regressions for each dependent variable.

For the independent variables, we examined two dimensions of inter-incubator relationships: *regional incubator density* and *geographic proximity to the nearest incubator*. Following Barnett's (1990) measure of local population density, we calculated regional incubator density separately for each incubator for each year by using the number of NTBIs within a focal NTBI's provincial location. We focused on the province level to measure regional incubator density because NTBIs located in the same province are subject to the provincial government's administration and support. Thus, all NTBIs in a given province share common rules and regulations that govern their operations (Zhang *et al.*, 2009). Empirically, a province may have multiple NTBIs, while a city can have only one or two NTBIs, and thus only the specialization of a region at the provincial level provides variation in regional incubator density. In regard to geographic proximity variable, consistent with previous studies (Baum and Haveman, 1997; Zhang *et al.*, 2009), we measured geographic proximity of a NTBI to the nearest NTBI as follows. We first measured the geographic distance between NTBIs as the natural log of the distance in kilometers using the Baidu Map, the largest search engine in China. To transform geographic proximity, we subtracted the values of geographic distance from the maximum value in the data to obtain the values of geographic proximity. The (logged) values of geographic proximity ranged from 0 to 10.99. For moderator variables, we created a dummy variable — *government ownership* — coded as '1' if an NTBI was owned by national and local government agencies, and '0' otherwise. Similarly, *specialization strategy* was coded as '1' if an NTBI was defined as an SBI, and '0' otherwise. As an agreed definition for SBIs has yet to be found (Schwartz and Hornych, 2008), we adopt Schwartz and Hornych's (2010) method to define SBIs: '*Business incubators are defined here as specialized if support elements and processes, as well as the selection criteria applied by the incubator management, focus on firms from solely one sector*'.

Estimation model

To test the hypotheses, we controlled for alternative explanations for incubation performance. First, at the region level, we control for attributes of the host city in which a NTBIs is located, including the *city's GDP*, *FDI* and *number of universities and colleges*. Local city GDP was controlled because it indicates the size of the local economy, the growth of which could in turn influence growth of the local NTBIs and affiliated new ventures (Hu, 2007; Zhang *et al.*, 2009). The measure was corrected for inflation and log transformed in the prior year. We controlled for city FDI, measured as capital invested in a city by sources not from China but rather from a company headquartered outside of China. FDI includes all foreign capital invested in a given city in the prior year (Hu, 2007; Zhang *et al.*, 2010). The measure was further corrected for inflation and finally log transformed.

We also controlled for the number of higher education institutions (universities and colleges) in a city, which could influence a focal BI's new-venture performance by providing educated workers for the NTBI (Hu, 2007; Zhang *et al.*, 2009). Second, at the incubator level, we control for *incubator age*, *incubator size* and *education of incubator management*. As the newly established BIs have better incubation performance than do the older ones (Bruneel *et al.*, 2012), incubator age is incorporated and calculated as the logarithmic form of the number of years from the NTBI's establishment (Schwartz and Hornych, 2010). Next, the firm size is a well-known factor that will affect firm performance. Incubator size is therefore included as the logarithmic form of the total number of personnel recruited in the NTBI (Scillitoe and Chakrabarti, 2010).

In addition, many studies on entrepreneurship have confirmed that the education of managers have important impacts on firm performance (Li *et al.*, 2012). It is reasonable to argue that a focal BI's new-venture performance may be influenced by the education level of the incubator management. We used the proportion of personnel who have tertiary education out of the incubator management as the measure.

Third, according to the co-production theory, the achievement of incubation outputs is not only determined by the incubator itself, but also by the active involvement of the incubatees (Rice, 2002). Thus, at the incubatee level, we created the proportion of employees who have tertiary education out of total employees in all incubatees as a proxy for ventures' absorptive capacity (Cohen and Levinthal, 1990; Rothaermel and Thursby, 2005b; Berchicci *et al.*, 2013). Finally, to account for the possibility that the growth of NTBIs may vary systematically over years, our models controlled for calendar year dummy variables (Podolny *et al.*, 1996; Zhang *et al.*, 2009). The inclusion of the calendar year dummy variables can also distinguish the effects of incubator age from the effects of calendar time.

Results

Recall that the study sets out to examine the effects of inter-incubator relationships upon a focal BI's new-venture performance, as well as the moderating effects of government ownership and specialization strategy on these relationships. Before we examine the results from the regression analysis, the simple descriptive statistics of all variables are presented in Table 1.

Unsurprisingly, the dependent variables, i.e. *survival, sales, and employment size*, are positively correlated with each other ($r = 0.85, 0.62$ and *0.61*). The positive, yet modest correlations among the three performance dimensions suggest that they capture related yet distinct aspects of

Table 1.   Means, Standard Deviations and Correlations of all Variables in Analyses

	Mean (log)	S.D. (log)	1	2	3	4	5	6	7	8	9	10	11	12	13
Survival	1.85	0.95													
Sales	9.82	3.52	0.85**												
Employment size	6.76	2.38	0.62**	0.61**											
GDP	7.39	2.67	0.61**	0.89**	0.90**										
FDI	10.83	3.98	0.10	0.30*	0.15	0.41*									
NO. of Universities	2.69	1.44	0.08	0.12	0.19+	0.40*	0.54**								
Incubator age	2.23	0.59	-0.03	-0.04	-0.05	-0.05	-0.05	-0.04							
Incubator size	6.74	2.37	-0.02	0.02	0.04	0.04	0.04	0.05	0.00						
Education of incubator management	0.82	0.30	0.61**	0.67**	0.68**	0.05	0.06	0.09	-0.04	0.05					
Education of incubatees	0.68	0.28	0.15	0.20	0.20	0.19	0.21	0.63**	-0.04	0.04	0.38*				
Government ownership (GO)	0.64	0.48	-0.06	-0.11	-0.20	0.13	0.12	0.09	-0.03	0.04	0.18	0.18			
Specialization strategy (SS)	0.39	0.48	0.53**	0.31**	0.22**	0.20	0.20	0.11	-0.00	-0.03	0.19	0.17	-0.61**		
Regional density (RD)	2.55	1.20	0.65**	0.68**	0.66**	0.64**	0.63**	0.35*	-0.03	0.02	0.15	0.10	0.20	0.14	
Geographic proximity	5.59	3.56	0.30**	0.33**	0.47**	0.51**	0.52**	0.40*	0.00	0.03	0.38*	0.47*	0.07	0.11	0.40**

+ $p < 0.10$; * $p < 0.05$; ** $p < 0.01$; stand and errors in parentheses.

new-venture performance, thus allowing us to validate our findings and extend the insights of our study. Also, the significant and negative correlation between *government ownership* and *specialization strategy* ($r = -0.61$) reveals that most government-owned BIs are belonging to DBIs. Moreover, the positive and modest correlation between *regional density* and *geographic proximity* ($r = 0.40$) indicates that they capture related yet distinct dimensions of inter-incubator relationships, which allow us to validate our study.

Using the EVIEWS 6.0 statistical software, we examined the regression results for the two dimensions respectively. Table 2 presents the regression results in terms of regional incubator density, while Table 3 presents the regression results on geographic proximity. For each dimension, we estimated three models. Model 1 (1a, 1b and 1c) is the base model consists of the dependent variables regressed against the control variables. Model 2 (2a, 2b and 2c) adds the effects of regional density/geographic proximity and its squared term to test whether inter-incubator relationships have a non-linear effect on a focal BI's new-venture performance. Model 3 (3a, 3b and 3c) illustrates the moderating effects of government ownership and specialization strategy. To create the interaction terms, both independent and moderator variables were mean centered to reduce the potential problem of multicollinearity (Aiken *et al.*, 1991). According to the results, the lagged dependent variables (*lagged Di, I* = 1, 2, 3), host city's GDP, and the education of incubator management positively affect the focal BI's new-venture performance. Turning to the moderate variables, the coefficient for specialization strategy is positive and significant. This finding suggests that SBIs perform better and DBIs in terms of assisting new ventures. However, the results indicate that government-owned BIs failed to meet their high expectations in terms of facilitating new venture survival and growth (Peters *et al.*, 2004).

Hypothesis 1 proposes that regional incubator density has an inverted U-shaped relationship with the focal BI's new-venture performance. The results show that the coefficient for regional incubator density is positive and significant and the coefficient for its squared term is negative and significant (see Models 2a, 2b and 2c in Table 2). Thus, Hypothesis 1 is supported. An examination of our sample shows that some Western provinces (which are located in the far west of China) only have one or two

Table 2.   Regression Results — Regional Incubator Density

Variables	Survival (D1)			Sales (D2)			Employment size (D3)		
	Model 1a	Model 2a	Model 3a	Model 1b	Model 2b	Model 3b	Model 1c	Model 2c	Model 3c
Constant	0.40(0.23)*	0.40(0.23)**	0.66(0.25)**	0.24(0.38)	0.24(0.38)	0.71(0.41)	0.27(0.20)	0.29(0.20)	0.43(0.21)
Lagged Di	0.08(0.03)**	0.07(0.03)**	0.06(0.03)*	0.15(0.03)**	0.14(0.03)**	0.13(0.02)**	0.29(0.03)**	0.27(0.03)**	0.27(0.03)**
GDP	0.13(0.05)*	0.11(0.06)+	0.08(0.06)+	0.86(0.09)**	0.81(0.10)**	0.77(0.10)**	0.53(0.05)**	0.57(0.05)**	0.56(0.05)**
FDI	-0.00(0.03)	-0.00(0.03)	-0.01(0.03)	0.14(0.05)**	0.13(0.05)*	0.10(0.05)**	0.03(0.02)	0.04(0.02)	0.03(0.02)
No. of universities	0.04(0.05)	0.02(0.05)	0.06(0.05)	-0.24(0.08)**	-0.24(0.09)**	-0.17(0.09)*	-0.09(0.04)*	-0.14(0.04)**	-0.12(0.04)**
Incubator age	0.00(0.03)	0.00(0.03)	0.00(0.03)	0.06(0.05)	0.07(0.05)	0.06(0.05)	-0.03(0.02)	-0.02(0.02)	-0.02(0.02)
Incubator size	-0.04(0.02)+	-0.04(0.02)+	-0.04(0.02)+	-0.02(0.04)	-0.02(0.04)	-0.02(0.04)	-0.00(0.02)	-0.00(0.02)	-0.00(0.02)
Education of incubator management	0.34(0.17)*	0.29(0.17)+	0.33(0.16)*	0.55(0.28)+	0.49(0.28)+	0.55(0.28)*	0.39(0.14)**	0.36(0.14)**	0.37(0.14)**
Education of incubatees	0.50(0.13)	0.09(0.13)	0.10(0.13)	0.29(0.22)	0.34(0.22)	0.35(0.22)	0.16(0.11)+	0.20(0.11)+	0.21(0.11)+
GO	-0.14(0.10)	-0.13(0.10)	-0.07(0.10)	-0.32(0.17)+	-0.32(0.17)+	-0.22(0.17)+	-0.04(0.10)	-0.03(0.09)	-0.00(0.10)
SS	0.35(0.11)**	0.34(0.10)**	0.35(0.10)**	0.63(0.18)**	0.62(0.18)**	0.64(0.18)**	0.03(0.11)	0.02(0.09)	0.03(0.09)
RD		0.43(0.14)**	0.40(0.14)**		0.69(0.23)*	0.64(0.23)**		0.12(0.12)+	0.10(0.12)+
RD²	-0.10(0.02)**	-0.10(0.02)**	-0.09(0.02)**		-0.14(0.04)**	-0.13(0.04)**		-0.05(0.02)**	-0.04(0.02)*
RD × GO			-0.29(0.06)**			-0.47(0.12)**			-0.13(0.06)*
RD × SS			-0.02(0.06)+			-0.08(0.11)+			-0.03(0.06)
Year dummies	Included	Included	Included	Included	Included	Included	Included	Included	Included
Adjusted R-square	0.61	0.63	0.64	0.90	0.91	0.92	0.93	0.95	0.95
Observations	1945	1945	1945	1945	1945	1945	1945	1945	1945

+ $p < 0.10$; * $p < 0.05$; ** $p < 0.01$; stand and errors in parentheses.

Table 3. Regression Results — Geographic Proximity

Variables	Survival (D1)			Sales (D2)			Employment size (D3)		
	Model 1a	Model 2a	Model 3a	Model 1b	Model 2b	Model 3b	Model 1c	Model 2c	Model 3c
Constant	0.40(0.23)*	0.39(0.23)+	0.64(0.23)*	0.24(0.38)	0.25(0.38)	0.79(0.42)	0.27(0.20)	0.21(0.20)	0.37(0.22)
Lagged Di	0.08(0.03)**	0.08(0.03)**	0.08(0.03)**	0.15(0.03)**	0.14(0.03)**	0.13(0.03)**	0.29(0.03)**	0.28(0.03)**	0.28(0.03)**
GDP	0.13(0.05)*	0.13(0.05)*	0.10(0.05)+	0.86(0.09)**	0.86(0.09)**	0.82(0.10)**	0.53(0.05)**	0.50(0.05)**	0.49(0.05)**
FDI	-0.00(0.03)	0.00(0.03)	0.00(0.03)	0.14(0.05)**	0.14(0.05)**	0.14(0.05)**	0.03(0.02)	0.04(0.02)	0.04(0.02)
NO. of universities	0.04(0.05)	0.03(0.05)	0.05(0.05)	-0.24(0.08)**	-0.24(0.08)**	-0.20(0.08)**	-0.09(0.04)*	-0.12(0.04)**	-0.11(0.04)*
Incubator age	0.00(0.03)	-0.00(0.03)	-0.00(0.03)	0.06(0.05)	0.06(0.05)	0.06(0.05)	-0.02(0.02)	-0.03(0.02)	-0.03(0.02)
Incubator size	-0.04(0.02)+	-0.04(0.02)+	-0.04(0.02)+	-0.02(0.04)	-0.02(0.04)	-0.03(0.04)	0.00(0.02)	0.00(0.02)	0.00(0.02)
Education of incubator management	0.34(0.17)*	0.34(0.17)*	0.32(0.17)*	0.55(0.28)+	0.55(0.28)+	0.52(0.28)+	0.39(0.14)**	0.39(0.14)**	0.38(0.14)**
Education of incubatees	0.50(0.13)	0.04(0.13)	0.04(0.13)	0.29(0.22)	0.28(0.22)	0.28(0.22)	0.16(0.11)	0.14(0.11)	0.14(0.11)
GO	-0.14(0.10)	-0.14(0.10)	-0.13(0.10)	-0.32(0.17)+	-0.32(0.17)+	-0.32(0.17)+	-0.04(0.09)	-0.03(0.09)	-0.03(0.09)
SS	0.35(0.11)**	0.35(0.11)**	0.35(0.11)**	0.63(0.18)**	0.61(0.18)**	0.63(0.18)**	0.03(0.09)	0.03(0.09)	0.04(0.09)
RD		0.02(0.03)	0.00(0.03)		0.02(0.05)	0.02(0.05)	0.08(0.02)**	0.08(0.02)**	0.07(0.03)*
Regional density squared		-0.00(0.00)	-0.00(0.00)		-0.00(0.00)	-0.00(0.00)	-0.00(0.00)*	-0.00(0.00)**	-0.00(0.00)*
Regional density × Government ownership			-0.07(0.03)*			-0.14(0.05)**			-0.04(0.02)+
Regional density × Specialization strategy			-0.07(0.03)*			-0.16(0.03)**			-0.05(0.22)+
Year dummies	Included	Included	Included	Included	Included	Included	Included	Included	Included
Adjusted R-square	0.61	0.61	0.62	0.92	0.92	0.92	0.90	0.91	0.92
Observations	1945	1945	1945	1945	1945	1945	1945	1945	1945

+ p < 0.10; * p < 0.05; ** p < 0.01; stand and errors in parentheses.

NTBI. To test the robustness of the findings, we did outlier checks, which may exert an excessive influence on the results. The results indicated that there are three outliers which located in Western region. We dropped the outliers and re-estimated the model, and the results were consistent with the original finding.

Hypothesis 2 predicts that a focal BI's geographic proximity to the nearest incubator has an inverted U-shaped relationship with the focal BI's new-venture performance. The results show that the coefficient for geographic proximity is positive and the coefficient for its squared term is negative (see Model 2c in Table 3), although the results in Models 2a and 2b in Table 3 are not significant. Thus, Hypothesis 2 is partially supported. Similarly, we find that some Western NTBI is exceptionally distant from others. The outlier analysis indicated that there are 10 extreme outliers. We dropped the outliers and re-estimated the model, and obtained similar findings.

Hypothesis 3 argues that the government ownership of BIs will negatively moderate the links between inter-incubator relationships and affiliated new-venture performance. The results show that the interaction terms between regional incubator density/geographic proximity and government ownership are negative and significant (see Models 3a, 3b and 3c in Tables 2 and 3). Thus, Hypothesis 3 is supported. To facilitate interpretation, we plotted the moderating effect of government ownership on the relationship between regional incubator density and incubatees' sales revenue in Figure 3 (the government ownership took the values of one and zero). According to Figure 3, the effect of regional incubator density on new-venture performance becomes less sensitive in government-owned BIs than in non-government-owned BIs. In other words, the substitution effects may occur between BIs' political networking and inter-incubator relationships.

Hypothesis 4 proposes that the specialization strategy of BIs will negatively moderate the links between inter-incubator networking and affiliated new-venture performance. The results show that the interaction terms between regional incubator density/geographic proximity and specialization strategy are negative and significant (see Models 3a, 3b and 3c in Tables 2 and 3). Hypothesis 4 is therefore confirmed. Similarly, we plotted the moderating effect of specialization strategy on the relationship

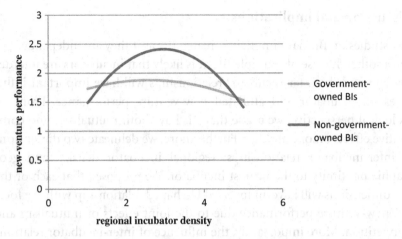

Figure 3. The Moderating Effects of Government Ownership on the Relationship between Regional Incubator Density and Incubatees' Sales Revenue

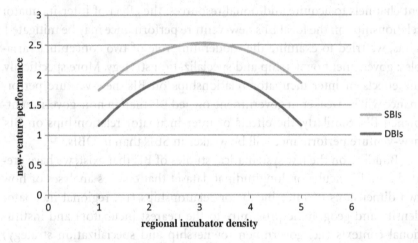

Figure 4. The Moderating Effects of Specialization Strategy on the Relationship between Regional Incubator Density and Incubatees' Sales Revenue

between regional incubator density and affiliated incubatees' sales revenue in Figure 4 (the specialization strategy took the values of one and zero). As shown in Figure 4, the effect of regional incubator density on new-venture performance becomes less sensitive in SBIs than in DBIs. In other words, the substitution effects may occur between BIs' peer networking and inter-incubator relationships.

Discussion and implications

Past studies on BIs have implicitly treated BIs as if they are independent of one another. In case of multiple BIs, it is likely that incubators are interdependent and the inter-incubator relationships will have important influences on incubator and affiliated new-venture performance. From an ecological perspective, we argue that BIs have both mutualistic and competitive effects on one another. Furthermore, we delineate two dimensions of inter-incubator relationships: regional incubator density, and geographic proximity to the nearest incubator. We proposed that each of the two dimensions will have an inverted U-shaped relationship with the focal BI's new-venture performance due to the joint effects of mutualism and competition. More importantly, the influence of inter-incubator relationships on BIs' new-venture performance is not universal but rather could be context specific. When the BIs have alternative and even more convenient channels to acquire additional resources, the effect of inter-incubator relationships on the focal BI's new-venture performance may be mitigated. Thus, we tried to examine the moderating role of two conceptual variables: government ownership and specialization strategy. More specifically, the effects of inter-incubator relationships on BIs' new-venture performance will be weaker in government-owned BIs than in non-government-owned BIs. Similarly, the effects of inter-incubator relationships on BIs' new-venture performance will be weaker in SBIs than in DBIs.

Building on the few systematical studies of BIs that exist, we have created a multi-incubator, longitudinal dataset that enables analyses of how two dimensions of inter-incubator relationships (i.e. regional incubator density and geographic proximity to the nearest incubator) and institutional contexts (i.e. government ownership and specialization strategy) affect the focal BI's new-venture performance over time. With a unique dataset on all TBIs in China from 2008 to 2012, we found that regional incubator density and a focal BI's geographic proximity to the nearest incubator both have an inverted U-shaped relationship with the focal BI's new-venture performance.

The findings support our argument that BIs are interdependent and that interdependence between BIs, which includes both mutualism and competition, has an inverted U-shaped influence on the focal BI's new-venture performance. The results demonstrated that the number of BIs in a specific region not only provides opportunities for resource flow across incubator boundaries, but it also reflects competition among incubators in a specific region with limited environmental carrying ability.

In addition, it suggests that regional incubator density and geographic proximity to the nearest incubator are important dimensions of inter-incubator relationships, and that both mutualistic and competitive forces play out between BIs in ways that jointly affect the focal BI's new-venture performance. While we expected that inter-incubator relationships would have a significant impact on the focal BI's new-venture performance, the magnitude of the effects exceeded our expectations. For example, all else being equal, a NTBI's expected graduates (surviving firms) would be 6.8 times more if regional incubator density was to change from 1 to 20, and the number of graduates would be smaller as regional incubator density further increases. Thus, our findings are especially important considering the expansion of BIs in the world, especially in China.

However, when the BIs have alternative channels to acquire additional resources, the magnitude of the effectiveness of inter-incubation relationships can be mitigated to some extent. As described above, compared with non-government-owned BIs, government-owned BIs have natural linkages with national or local government agencies, and can rely on such political networking to obtain additional resources. The political networking can extend government-owned BIs' source channels, and hence acquiring resources from other BIs in the region becomes less attractive for them. Consequently, the mutualism and competition between BIs are less sensitive in government-owned BIs than in non-government-owned BIs. However, the findings do not support the common view that government-owned BIs performed better than their non-government-owned counterparts in terms of assisting new ventures.

In the context of China which have long been constrained by the legacy of Marxist ideology implemented through central economic planning, the incubator managers (especially top managers) of government-owned-BIs are often selected for their positions primarily due to their political loyalty rather than for their functional experience. As a result, the government-owned BIs become agents of the government, and incubator managers often lack sufficient knowledge and skills to incubate new ventures. In addition, as the governmental resources available are limited and the number of government-owned BIs is still growing, the government-owned BIs must spend much time and money on coordinating, managing and maintaining the linkages with various government agencies.

Finally, as resources are mainly obtained from government agencies for non-commercial purpose, government-owned BIs may spend these resources on incubators' operational issues such as fundraising, hiring staff and marketing to serve government priorities, which will impede the survival and growth of the affiliated new ventures. Indeed, in another work, we tested the impact of incubation fund (a type of investment mainly stemming from government agencies) on incubatee performance; however, the result was not statistically significant.

In regard to specialization strategy, our findings support the proposition that SBIs have stronger peer networking, and can rely on such networking to obtain additional resources by accelerating agglomeration advantages. In addition, the incubator management teams of SBIs are capable of providing complementary services and resources for their new ventures. As a result, the incubatees of SBIs may become reluctant to share knowledge and information with incubatees located in other BIs, and the mutualism and competition between BIs become less urgent for SBIs' ventures.

In summary, although diverse network linkages can enable BIs access to a wide range of valuable information and resources that enhance the survival and growth of affiliated new ventures (Granovetter, 2000; Adler and Kwon, 2002; Katila and Ahuja, 2002), the different types of networks interrelated in complex ways, and not all networks are mutually reinforcing (Nahapiet and Ghoshal, 1998). For example, Ahuja (2000) examined the joint effect of direct ties and indirect ties on firm innovation, and found that the impact of indirect ties on a firm's innovation output was lower when the firm had a greater number of direct ties. Thus, the substitution effect occurs between different types of networks.

This study has contributed to a better understanding of incubation performance in several ways. First, to the best of our knowledge, this study is among the first empirical investigations of the role of inter-incubator relationships in BIs' new-venture performance. While some scholars focused on the importance of the linkages with some prominent external organizations (especially higher education institutions), we contribute to the literature by systematically and empirically examining how the two dimensions of inter-incubator relationships (i.e. regional incubator density and geographic proximity) affect BIs' new-venture performance. As a result, the affiliated incubatee development often becomes vibrant at the intersection of BIs because insights, skills and technologies from different fields and directions merge, thus sparking new businesses and facilitating new venture survival and growth. Furthermore, this study examined the extent to which both mutualistic and competitive forces coexist between BIs.

Our findings that the significant impact of regional incubator density and geographic proximity to the nearest incubator on the focal BI's new-venture performance demonstrated that the number of BIs in a specific region not only provides opportunities for knowledge flows and leveraging across incubator boundaries, but it also reflects competition among BIs for resources in the context of limited region's carrying capacity. Mutualistic benefits occur when multiple BIs have optimal levels of regional incubator density and geographic proximity in a specific region. Vigorous competition occurs when combined resource requirements of BIs reach the region's carrying capacity.

Our findings also contribute to the BI literature by examining how different types of networks may jointly influence BIs' new-venture performance. Since the political networking and peer networking represent important alternative resource channels for inter-incubator networking, they can decrease the effects of inter-incubator relationships on BIs' new-venture performance. Finally, this study advances the literature by applying an ecological perspective to examine the overall economic growth of geographical clusters of numerous interrelated NTBFs in the context of China's TBIs which are often neglected in BI literature.

The results of this study suggest specific implications for government agencies, incubator management, and new ventures. As BIs' political networking has a strong positive influence on affiliated new-venture performance especially in transition economies, government agencies should use the governmental resources effectively and discreetly. In addition, government agencies ought to ensure pre-conditions are satisfied when any BI is been contemplated. Before establishing a new BI, national and/or local policy makers should examine the pre-conditions comprehensively. For example, when a new BI is to be founded, policy makers should consider the new BI's location, i.e. the regional incubator density and its geographic proximity to the nearest incubator and other organizations such as universities, research institutions. They should produce the optimal level of regional incubator density and geographic proximity to maximize the benefits of the BI's external networks.

Our results also point to the functions and responsibilities of the incubator management. The extent of specialization strategy represents a strategic variable for incubator management because they can select and modify an incubator's industry and technology mix by selectively admitting firms in targeted sectors. Additionally, the selection of potential tenants generally requires that the new ventures should exhibit a high degree of cooperation propensity with other firms and external organizations. These choices for BIs can affect the effectiveness of the BI's internal networks and external networks. Hence, the strategic implications of our findings are significant, suggesting that incubator management must attend not only to the internal dynamics within a specific BI but also to the incubator's relationships with other organizations.

For new ventures, the study suggests that the firm-specific determinants may potentially influence the final incubation performance. Phan *et al.* (2005) argue that the nature of entrepreneurs may have a particularly important impact on incubation performance. Thus, entrepreneurs need to learn how to leverage the firms' internal and external resources to produce more outcomes.

Conclusion

Past studies on BIs have implicitly treated BIs as if they are independent of one another. From an ecological perspective, we argue that the interdependence of BIs has two forms: mutualism and competition, which jointly affects BIs' new-venture performance. More importantly, the impact of inter-incubator relationships on BIs' new-venture performance is not universal but rather could be context specific.

To be more specific, when the BIs have alternative and more convenient channels to acquire additional resources, the effects of inter-incubator relationships on new-venture performance will be mitigated in terms of mutualism and competition. We therefore examined the moderating effects of two institutional contexts: government ownership and specialization strategy.

Using a unique dataset on Chinese TBIs national from 2008 to 2012, we found that each of the two dimensions of inter-incubator relationships, regional incubator density and geographic proximity, has an inverted U-shaped relationship with BIs' new-venture performance. In addition, the substitution effect occurs between different types of networks. More specifically, BIs' political networking may mitigate the effectiveness of inter-incubator relationships, and the effects of inter-incubator relationships on the focal BI's new-venture performance are weaker in government-owned BIs than in non-government-owned BIs. Similarly, BIs' peer networking may mitigate the effectiveness of inter-incubator relationships, and the effects of inter-incubator relationships on the focal BI's new-venture performance are weaker in SBIs than in DBIs.

This study has limitations that should be addressed in future research. One is that it was conducted within a single country during a period of economic transition from a planned economy to a market economy. Thus, an extension of this line of research could make cross-country comparisons to enhance variation in national economies (i.e. developing countries and developed countries), and institutional difference in the governance of such countries. For example, Porter (1998b) argued that the depth and breadth of industrial clusters in developed countries are usually greater compared with developing countries.

In addition, replications of our model in different types of BIs are needed for more confident generalization (e.g. University BIs, Science Parks, Social BIs, etc.). Furthermore, there is no evidence in the data considering the different types of networks, such as political networking (e.g. tax reductions, import privileges, facility and land use rights, etc.), peer networking e.g. horizonal cooperation versus vertical cooperation; Bøllingtoft, 2012; Bøllingtoft and Ulhøi, 2005), university networking (e.g. infrastructure services, student employees, faculty involvement, university licenses, university image, etc.; Rothaermel and Thursby, 2005a, 2005b; Siegel *et al.*, 2003a, 2003b) and professional service organizations networking (e.g. technology service firms, accounting and financial service firms, law firms, talent search firms, venture capitalists, etc.; Zhang and Li, 2010). We encourage future research to pay more attention to a deeper and broader set of internal and external networks of BIs.

Acknowledgments

The study was partially supported by the National Social Science Foundation of China (No. 08&ZD043).

References

Adler, H. and Kwon, S. W. (2002). Social capital: Prospects for a new concept. *Academy of Management Review*, 27(1): 17–40.

Aernoudt, R. (2004). Incubators: Tool for entrepreneur? *Small Business Economics*, 23(2): 127–135.

Aerts, K., Matthyssens, P., and Vandenbempt, K. (2007). Critical role and screening practices of European business incubators. *Technovation*, 27(5): 254–267.

Ahuja, G. (2000). Collaboration networks, structural holes, and innovation: A longitudinal study. *Administrative Science Quarterly*, 45: 425–455.

Aiken, L. S., West, S. G., and Reno, R. R. (1991). *Multiple Regression: Testing and Interpreting Interactions*. Sage Publications, Newbury Park, California.

Aldrich, H. E. (1999). *Organizations Evolving*. Sage Publications, Thousand Oaks, CA.

Allen, D. N. and McCluskey, R. (1990). Structure, policy, services, and performance in the business incubator industry. *Entrepreneurship, Theory and Practice*, 15(2): 61–77.

Barbero, J. L., Casillas, J. C., Ramos, A., and Guitar, S. (2012). Revisiting incubation performance how incubator typology affects results. *Technological Forecasting and Social Change*, 79(5): 888–902.

Barnett, W. P. (1990). The organizational ecology of a technological system. *Administrative Science Quarterly*, 35: 31–60.

Barnett, W. P. and Carroll, G. R. (1987). Competition and mutualism among early telephone companies. *Administrative Science Quarterly*, 32(3): 400–421.

Barron, D. N., West, E., and Hannan, M. T. (1994). A time to grow and a time to die: Growth and mortality of credit unions in New York, 1914–1990. *American Journal of Sociology*, 100: 381–421.

Baum, J. A. C. and Haveman, H. A. (1997). Love thy neighbor? Differentiation and agglomeration in the Manhattan hotel industry, 1898–1990. *Administrative Science Quarterly*, 42: 304–338.

Berchicci, L. (2013). Towards an open R&D system: Internal R&D investment, external knowledge acquisition and innovative performance. *Research Policy*, 42(1): 117–127.

Bergek, A. and Norrman, C. (2008). Incubator best practice: A framework. *Technovation*, 28(1–2): 20–28.

Bøllingtoft, A. (2012). The bottom-up business incubator: Leverage to networking and cooperation practices in a self-generated, entrepreneurial-enabled environment. *Technovation*, 32(5): 304–315.

Bøllingtoft, A. and Ulhøi, J. P. (2005). The networked business incubator–leveraging entrepreneurial agency? *Journal of Business Venturing*, 20(2): 265–290.

Bruneel, J., Ratinho, T., Clarysse, B. and Groen, A. (2012). The evolution of business incubators: Comparing demand and supply of business incubation services across different incubator generations. *Technovation*, 32(2): 110–121.

Campbell, C. (1987). *Change agents in the New Economy: Business Incubators and Economic Development*. University of Minnesota Press, Minneapolis, MN.

Carroll, G. R. and Hannan, M. T. (2000). *The Demography of Corporations and Industries*. Princeton University Press, Princeton, NJ.

Chan, K. F. and Lau, T. (2005). Assessing technology incubator programs in the science park: The good, the bad and the ugly. *Technovation*, 25(10): 1215–1228.

Chen, C. C., Chen, Y. R. and Xin, K. (2004). Guanxi practices and trust in management: A procedural justice perspective. *Organization Science*, 15(2): 200–209.

Chen, C. J. (2009). Technology commercialization, incubator and venture capital, and new venture performance. *Journal of Business Research*, 62(1): 9–103

Child, J. and Markoczy, L. (1993). Host country managerial behavior and learning in Chinese and Hungarian joint ventures. *Journal of Management Studies*, 30(4): 611–631.

Cohen, W. M. and Levinthal, D. A. (1990). Absorptive capacity: A new perspective on learning and innovation. *Administration Science Quarterly*, 35(1): 128–152.

Colombo, M. and Delmastro, M. (2002). How effective are technology incubators? Evidence from Italy. *Research Policy*, 31(7): 1103–1122.

Freeman, J. H. and Audia, P. G. (2006). Community ecology and the sociology of organizations. *Annual Review of Sociology*, 32: 145–169.

Granovetter, M. (2000). The Economic Sociology of Firms and Entrepreneurs. In: Swedberg, R. (Ed.), *Entrepreneurship*. Oxford University Press, Oxford, U. K.

Grimaldi, R. and Grandi, A. (2005). Business incubators and new venture creation: An assessment of incubating models. *Technovation*, 25(2): 111–121.

Haapasalo, H. and Ekholm, T. (2004). A profile of European incubators: A framework for commercialising innovations. *International Journal of Entrepreneurship and Innovation Management*, 4: 248–270.

Hackett, S. M. and Dilts, D. M. (2004a). A real options-driven theory of business incubation. *Journal of Technology Transfer*, 29(1): 55–82.

Hackett, S. M. and Dilts, D. M. (2004b). A systematic review of business incubation research. *Journal of Technology Transfer*, 29(1): 55–82.

Hannan, M. T. and Freeman, J. (1977). The population ecology of organizations. *American Journal of Sociology*, 82: 929–964.

Hannan, M. T. and Freeman, J. (1989). *Organizational Ecology*. Harvard University Press: Cambridge, MA.

Hansen, M. T., Chesbrough, H. W., Nohria N., and Sull D. N. (2000). Networked incubators: Hothouses of the new economy. *Harvard Business Review*, 78(5): 74–84.

Haveman, H. A. (1993). Follow the leader: Mimetic isomorphism and entry into new markets. *Administrative Science Quarterly*, 38: 593–627.

Hu, A. (2007). Technology parks and regional economic growth in China. *Research Policy*, 36(1): 76–87.

Katila, R. and Ahuja, G. (2002). Something old, something new: A longitudinal study of search behavior and new product introduction. *Academy of Management Journal* 45: 1183–1194.

Kirwan, P., van der Sijde, P. and Groen, A. (2006). Assessing the needs of new technology based firms (NTBFs): An investigation among spin-off companies from six European Universities. *The International Entrepreneurship and Management Journal*, 2(2): 173–187.

Lalkaka, R. and Shaffer, D. (1999). Nurturing entrepreneurs, creating enterprises and technology business incubation in Brazil', Proceedings of the International Conference on Effective Business Development Services, Rio de Janeiro, Brazil.

Li, H. and Atuahene-Gima, K. (2001). Product innovation strategy and the performance of new technology ventures in China. *Academy of Management Journal*, 44(6): 1123–1134.

Li, H. and Zhang, Y. (2007). The role of managers' political networking and functional experience in new venture performance: Evidence from China's transition economy. *Strategic Management Journal*, 28: 791–804.

Li, H., Zhang, Y., Li, Y., Zhou, L., and Zhang, W. (2012). Returnees versus locals: Who perform better in China's technology entrepreneurship? *Strategic Entrepreneurship Journal*, 6: 257–272.

Lyons, T. S. (2000). Building social capital for sustainable enterprise development in country towns and regions: Successful practices from the United States. Paper presented at the First National Conference on the Future of Australia's Country Towns, June 29–30, LaTrobe University, Australia.

McAdam, M. and McAdam, R. (2008). High tech start-ups in university science park incubators: The relationship between the start-ups's lifecycle progression and the use of the incubator's resources. *Technovation*, 28(5): 277–290.

Mian, S. A. (1996). Assessing value-added contributions of university technology business incubators to tenant firms. *Research Policy*, 25(3): 325–335.

Ministry of Science and Technology (MST) (2007). Available at: http://www.most.gov.cn/kjbgz/200712/t20071224_57980.htm on [Accessed 25 December 2007].

Nahapiet, J. and Ghoshal, S. (1998). Social capital, intellectual capital, and the organizational advantage. *Academy of Management Review*, 23(2): 242–266.

Nee, V. (1992). Organizational dynamics of market transition: Hybrid forms, property rights, and mixed economy in China. *Administrative Science Quarterly*, 37(1): 1–27.

Peña, I. (2004). Business incubation centers and new firm growth in the Basque country. *Small Business Economics*, 22(3–4): 223–236.

Peng, M. W. and Luo, Y. (2000). Managerial ties and firm performance in a transition economy: The nature of a micro-macro link. *Academy of Management Journal*, 43(3): 486–501.

Peters, L., Rice, M., and Sundararajan M. (2004). The role of incubators in the entrepreneurial process. *Journal of Technology Transfer*, 29(1): 83–91.

Phan, P. H., Siegel, D. S., and Wright M. (2005). Science parks and incubators: Observations, synthesis and future research. *Journal of Business Venturing*, 20(2): 165–182.

Phillips, R. G. (2002). Technology business incubators: How effective as technology transfer mechanisms? *Technology in Society*, 24(3): 299–316.

Podolny, J. M., Stuart, T. E., and Hannan, M. T. (1996). Networks, knowledge, and niches: Competition in the worldwide semiconductor industry, 1984–1991. *American Journal of Sociology*, 102: 659–689.

Porter, M. E. (1998a). Clusters and the new economics of competition. *Harvard Business Review*, 76(6): 77–90.

Porter, M. E. (1998b). *On Competition*. Harvard Business School Press, Boston, MA.

Ratinho, T. and Henriques, E. (2010). The role of science parks and business incubators in converging countries: Evidence from Portugal. *Technovation*, 30(4): 278–290.

Rice, Mark P. (2002). Co-production of business assistance in business incubators: An exploratory study. *Journal of Business Venturing*, 17(2): 163–187.

Rice, M. P. and Matthews, J. B. (1995). Growing New Ventures Creating New Jobs.

Romanelli, E. and Khessina, O. M. (2005). Regional industrial identity: Cluster configurations and economic development. *Organization Science*, 16(4): 344–358.

Rothaermel, F. T. and Thursby, M. (2005a). Incubator firm failure or graduation? The role of university linkages. *Research Policy*, 34(7): 1076–1090.

Rothaermel F. T. and Thursby, M. (2005b). University-incubator firm knowledge flows: Assessing their impact on incubation firm performance. *Research Policy*, 34(3): 305–320.

Rothschild, L. and Darr, A. (2005). Technological incubators and the social construction of innovation networks: An Israeli case study. *Technovation*, 25(1): 59–67.

Ruef, M. (2000). The emergence of organizational forms: A community ecology approach. *American Journal of Sociology*, 106(3): 658–714.

Sá, C. and Lee, H. (2012). Science, business, and innovation: Understanding networks in technology-based incubators. *R&D Management*, 42(3): 243–253.

Schwartz, M. and Hornych, C. (2008). Specialization as strategy for business incubators: Assessment of the Central German Multimedia CSenter. *Technovation*, 28(7): 436–449.

Schwartz, M. and Hornych, C. (2010). Cooperation patterns of incubator firms and the impact of incubator specialization: Empirical evidence from Germany. *Technovation*, 30(9–10): 485–495.

Scillitoe, J. L. and Chakrabarti, A. K. (2005). The sources of social capital within technology incubators: The roles of historical ties and organizational facilitation. *International Journal of Learning and Intellectual Capital*, 2(4): 327–345.

Scillitoe, J. L. and Chakrabarti, A. K. (2009). A conceptual model of the incubation of new technology-based ventures: A social capital perspective. *Review of International Comparative Management*, 10(3): 468–482.

Scillitoe, J. L. and Chakrabarti, A. K. (2010). The role of incubator interactions in assisting new ventures. *Technovation*, 30(3): 155–167.

Siegel, D., Waldman, D. and Link, A. (2003a). Assessing the impact of organizational practices on the relative productivity of university technology transfer offices: An exploratory study. *Research Policy*, 32(1): 27–48.

Siegel, D. Westhead, P. and Wright, M. (2003b). Assessing the impact of university science parks on research productivity: Exploratory firm-level evidence from United Kingdom. *International Journal of Industrial Organization*, 21(5): 1357–1369.

Siegel, D., Westhead, P. and Wright, M. (2003c). Science parks and the performance of new technology based firms: A review of recent UK evidence and an agenda for future research. *Small Business Economics*, 20(2): 177–184.

Song, Z. G., Niu, F., and Zhang, Y. (2013). Entrepreneurial situation, critical learning events and stakeholder influence capacity. *Chinese Journal of Management*, 10(4): 558–565.

Stinchcombe, A. L. (1965). Organizations and social structure. In March, J. D. (Ed.). *Handbook of Organizations*. Rand McNally, Chicago, IL, pp. 142–193.

Tallman, S. and Phene, A. (2007). Leveraging knowledge across geographic boundaries. *Organization Science*, 18: 252–260.

Thursby, G. and Kemp, S. (2002). Growth and productive efficiency of university intellectual property licensing. *Research Policy*, 31(1): 109–124.

Thursby, J. G. and Thursby, M. C. (2002). Who is selling the ivory tower? Sources of growth in university licensing. *Management Science*, 48(1): 90–104.

Thursby, J. G., Jensen, R. and Thursby, M. C. (2001). Objectives, characteristics and outcomes of university licensing: A survey of major U.S. universities. *Journal of Technology Transfer*, 26(1–2): 59–72.

Totterman, H. and Sten, L. (2005). Start-ups: Business incubation and social capital. *International Small Business Journal*, 23(5): 487–511.

Vanderstraeten, J. and Matthyssens, P. (2012). Service-based differentiation strategies for business incubators: Exploring external and internal alignment. *Technovation*, 32(12): 656–670.

Von Zedtwitz, M. (2003). Classification and management of incubators: Aligning strategic objectives and competitive scope for new business facilitation. *International Journal of Entrepreneurship and Innovation Management*, 3(1–2): 176–196.

Von Zedtwitz, M. and Grimaldi, R. (2006). Are services profiles incubator-specific? Results from an empirical investigation in Italy. *Journal of Technology Transfer*, 31(4): 459–468.

Westhead, P. and Storey, D. (1995). Links between higher education institutions and high technology firms. *Omega*, 23(4), 345–360.

Westhead, P. and Batstone, S. (1998). Independent technology-based firms: The perceived benefits of a Science Park location. *Urban Studies*, 35(12): 2197–2219.

Wolpert, J. D. (2002). Breaking out of the innovation box. *Harvard Business Review*, 80(8): 77–83.

Xin, K. R. and Pearce, J. L. (1996). Guanxi: Connections as substitutes for formal institutional support. *Academy of Management Journal*, 39(6): 1641–1658.

Zhang, Y. and Li, H. (2010). Innovation search of new ventures in a technology cluster: The role of ties with service intermediaries. *Strategic Management Journal*, 31: 88–109.

Zhang, Y., Li, H., Li, Y., and Zhou L. (2010). FDI spillovers in an emerging market: The role of foreign firms' country origin diversity and domestic firms' absorptive capacity. *Strategic Management Journal*, 31: 969–989.

Zhang, Y., Li, H., and Schoonhoven, C. (2009). Intercommunity relationships and community growth in China's high technology industries 1998–2000. *Strategic Management Journal*, 30: 163–183.

Chapter 5

Innovation Habitats
for Technology Startups in Brazil

Guilherme Ary Plonski

Introduction

The first science park (Stanford Research Park) was established in 1951. Eight years later, the first business incubator (Batavia Incubator) started operations. Neither one of those pioneering innovation niches was intentional, as they resulted from the acumen of entrepreneurial minds that perceived unconventional usages of available real estate. Science parks (*a.k.a.* research parks or technology parks, the latter in Latin America) and incubators have proliferated and now operate in a large number of countries, regardless of their economic level or political ideology.

In contrast to the two pioneering models, business incubators and technology parks were introduced in Brazil as part of an agenda aimed at developing knowledge-based new drivers for economic and social development. Their implementation was intensely based on academic institutions with the support of government and specific private non-profit organizations. Nowadays, there are more than 400 Brazilian innovation habitats that cooperate regionally and nationally, constituting a national innovative entrepreneurship movement (in short, "the Movement"), led by its trade association.

This chapter traces the creation and evolution of business incubators and technology parks in Brazil, and highlights their material and intangible results. It also portrays the entrepreneurial ecosystem that nurtures and is nurtured by these habitats. Finally, it discusses the main challenges and prospects for the Movement.

A brief history

Let us advance a new nation (1984–1993)

The genesis of the Brazilian innovation habitats occurred in the 1980s, a shifting period in the country's political history. The population's resentment against the authoritarian regime had become evident in well attended ceremonies in memory of political prisoners killed during torture sessions by the military authorities, and in mass rallies for free and direct elections. The decline of the regime had been fueled by economic stagnation, as those years became known as "The Lost Decade".[1]

During that unstable period, three planned albeit unrelated events established the earliest innovation habitats in Brazil. The inaugural action was the enactment of Executive Resolution 084/1984 by the National Council for Scientific and Technological Development (CNPq),[2] establishing a "Program to Implement Technology Parks in Brazil". It was the first of its kind in Latin America.

What motivated the Council to propose a novel course of action, which was so distant from its traditional activities of providing grants to support research? The underlying rationale was to establish innovative ways of promoting technology transfer from universities to the business sector. The inspiration came from thriving cases abroad. During the commemorations of the 20th anniversary of that groundbreaking event, the President of the Council that had signed the Executive Act explained: "*We had information regarding the installation of technology parks in France and*

---

[1] Brazil's Gross National Product had a yearly average increase between 6% and 11% in every quinquennium since the end of the Second World War. During 1980–1984, the average yearly growth had drastically been reduced to 1%.

[2] The Conselho Nacional de Desenvolvimento Científico e Tecnológico was headed at the time by Professor Lynaldo Cavalcanti de Albuquerque, a visionary academic leader.

mainly in the United States of America, with the successful cases of Boston and Silicon Valley, and also in England. The initial idea had been not to lag behind them" (Albuquerque, 2004).

The Program, aimed at initially implementing six technology parks, included some original institutional provisions:

1. To locate the parks in cities with a critical mass of technologies ready to be worked out, but necessarily distant from State capitals (with one exception);
2. To encompass four of the five regions in the country, in order not to restrict the Program to the higher-income ones and
3. To use newly ad hoc created private non-profit foundations to implement and manage the parks, instead of benefitting from already existing public organizations.

The last provision raised eyebrows at the time, as it was not common to transfer public funds to private non-philanthropic organizations. Nevertheless, it was a main tenet of the Program, as the proponents had a clear view that public administration's bureaucratic rules were incompatible with the dynamics of implementing and operating the technology parks.

Accordingly, six private foundations were created with the specific purpose of implementing and operating a technology park. The sites were Manaus, in the low-density Northern Region (the only State capital contemplated); Campina Grande, in the low-income Northeastern Region; Petrópolis and São Carlos, in the advanced Southeastern Region; and Joinville and Santa Maria, in the economically balanced Southern Region. In spite of the adversities along the journey, two of the six sites prospered and are currently in full-fledged operation: Campina Grande and São Carlos.[3]

In addition to the CNPq initiative, two local innovation habitats emerged without relation to the national Program. In 1985, the São Paulo State Government decided to create a pioneer business incubator, to serve

---

[3] The two technology parks continue to be operated by the original institutions, respectively, *Fundação Parque Tecnológico da Paraíba* and *Fundação Parque de Alta Tecnologia de São Carlos*.

as a model for other initiatives. Called Nascent Industries' Development Center (CEDIN),[4] it was coincidentally installed in the city of São Carlos, one of the six locations chosen by the national Program. There was a reason for this coincidence. São Carlos, a relatively small city (240,000 inhabitants in 2015), located ca. 250 km from the State capital, already had a strong reputation as a high-technology city.[5]

In 1986, a business incubator emerged in Florianópolis, capital of Santa Catarina State, in the Southern region. It was a rather unexpected event, as the city, located on an island renowned for its beauty, relied economically on the public sector (government and universities) and on the personal services industry. The incubator, named Business Center for Advanced Technology Laboring (CELTA),[6] was created by a private non-profit foundation, established two years earlier by faculty members of the Santa Catarina Federal University's Engineering School, as a means of providing an attractive professional alternative for students who graduated and wanted to stay in the city. At the time, they had to move to other regions to begin their careers, as environmental restrictions prevented industrial activities in Florianópolis.

Florianópolis was added to the six original sites of CNPq's Program to Implement Technology Parks in Brazil, in spite of being a business incubator and not a conventional technology park. The creation of a specific foundation to operate this innovation habitat had not been deemed necessary, as was the case of the six others, since CELTA was under the auspices of an already existing private non-profit organization.

---

[4] The Centro de Desenvolvimento de Indústrias Nascentes, established by the State Government in 1985, underwent several institutional changes, which were reflected in its oscillating performance. Nowadays, it operates under the auspices of the São Carlos municipality, with partial State funding.

[5] São Carlos hosts two top university campuses and other research institutions, which have a tradition of spinning off high-technology companies in advanced areas such as Optoelectronics and Photonics. It was recognized in 2011 as the National Technology Capital by Federal Law 12,504. One of the attributes that qualified São Carlos to earn the title was the highest number of PhD degrees per capita ratio (1:180); as a reference, Brazil had an average of one PhD for each group of 5423 inhabitants.

[6] The Centro Empresarial para Laboração de Tecnologias Avançadas became one of the Brazilian incubators' flagships.

In 1986, the National Innovation Agency (FINEP)[7] and the Organization of American States (OAS) commissioned a study. In Brazil, 13 initiatives were identified and assessed that helped entrepreneurs who originated in universities or research institutes to pursue the transformation of their (research) projects into marketable products.[8] In addition to the eight sites already mentioned (six from the original CNPq Program, São Carlos and Florianópolis), five other initiatives were identified, some of them in unexpected locations. One such case was Santa Rita do Sapucaí, a small city (40,000 inhabitants in 2015). The attempt to install a business incubator was linked to the strategic intention of the local leadership to become the hub of an "Electronic Valley".[9]

This study generated a by-product that became the driving force of what is known as the national innovative entrepreneurship movement, or in short, "the Movement". People affected by the study decided to create an association in order to promote the then exotic idea of creating knowledge-intensive high risk new firms. On October 30, 1987 a small group of 16 people, representing 12 institutions from 5 states, decided to found the National Association of Entities that Promote Advanced Technologies Enterprises (ANPROTEC).[10] The *raison d'être* of the Association was, according to Article 2b of the original bylaws,

> To promote the establishment of new Technology Parks, Technopoles, Business Incubators and other mechanisms aimed at boosting innovative enterprises, enabling them as tools for the economic, social and cultural transformation of the country. (ANPROTEC, 1987)

---

[7] The Financiadora de Estudos e Projetos is a Federal public company that finances and subsidizes technology projects.

[8] ANPROTEC Memory Project. Available at http://www.memoriaanprotec.org.br/a-anprotec/historia/. The study focused on identifying and assessing initiatives in Argentina, Brazil, Colombia, Mexico and Uruguay. The Brazilian section was commissioned to a mixed team from Federal University of Rio de Janeiro (UFRJ) and University of São Paulo (USP).

[9] Santa Rita do Sapucaí has a vibrant entrepreneurial ecosystem that generated circa 150 electronic, information technology and telecommunications firms.

[10] The name was changed in 1999, by substituting 'Advanced Technologies' for 'Innovative.' ANPROTEC adopted a different name in the international arena: Brazilian Association of Science Parks and Business Incubators.

The Movement was up to date with the international trends in the field. Indeed, ANPROTEC was established almost at the same time as the two leading related USA trade organizations: the National Business Incubation Association (NBIA) was founded in 1985, and the Association of University Research Parks (AURP) in 1986. In contrast with what evolved in that country, where innovation habitats unraveled into two associations, ANPROTEC comprised both Business Incubators and Technology Parks since its inception.

The initial path to achieving the knowledge-based new drivers for economic and social development by means of innovation habitats evolved in rough terrain. On one hand, the political environment changed for the better, as the authoritarian regime was superseded by democratically elected governments, under a newly minted constitution. On the other hand, the macroeconomic variables got completely out of control, leading to hyperinflation, *viz.*, a yearly average of about 470% during 1984–1989, the first five years of the Movement. As a consequence of the deterioration of the economy, compounded by the risks inherent to any major pioneering endeavor, CNPq Program's goals were not attained in the short term.

Nevertheless, in spite of technology parks a distant reality at the time, the Program contributed to disseminating another type of innovation habitat — the business incubator. It was simpler to implement and much cheaper than a technology park. It was also more in tandem with the maturity level of the Brazilian innovation system. This proposition was confirmed by facts on the ground. The number of business incubators grew slowly but steadily, reaching 13 on the eve of a second remarkable event in recent Brazilian history — overcoming hyperinflation.

Incubators' florescence (1994–2000)

The inflation spiral had advanced like a tsunami during the early years of the civil regime, overturning all sophisticated governmental attempts to stop the increase. Inflation reached an unbearable 2700% in 1993. Nevertheless, what seemed impossible happened the following year, as a well-engineered economic plan gained public confidence. As a consequence, the inflation rate plummeted to 15% in 1995, maintaining a yearly average of 8.5% during the following 20 years.

Changes in the population's mood and behavior were rapidly noted. Accustomed to very short-term reasoning in terms of investment (basically, trying to find a reliable bank that would at least neutralize the rapid loss of purchasing power of their savings), segments of the Brazilian population gradually decided to unbury the dream of creating a business,[11] a process that requires confidence in the long-term stability of the economic environment and political institutions.

The new atmosphere was also reflected in increased interest in establishing technology firms on the basis of academic knowledge, either as an outcome of general higher education, or as the product of research activities. Some Brazilian universities and research institutes took the forefront and established business incubation processes, in many cases combined with entrepreneurship education programs.

Business incubators attracted the attention of Government officials interested in finding new economic drivers, and drew the curiosity of the more sophisticated general press, always eager to present novelties to their readership. The growing level of interest was obviously supported by narratives of successful graduated companies, enhanced by the receipt of coveted innovation prizes and/or by investments from the then almost inexistent venture capital sector. It has to be mentioned that a success case was not limited to financial results or market share. The capacity to create and market unheard of solutions was a key appeal to public policy makers, academic leadership and society at large.

One of the many illustrative stories is Bematech, a company created by two young electronic engineers on the basis of their Master's degree work on dot matrix printers. The decision to transform their findings into a new enterprise was taken in 1987. Two years later, they were accepted as the first incubatee in the newly established Curitiba Technology Incubator. In 1990, the company was formalized, and during the following year new shareholders were admitted, in order to capitalize the company's growth.

---

[11] In 2000, the first year that Brazil participated in the Global Entrepreneurship Monitor (GEM) study, the country was in the top position with regard to the fraction of the population involved in nascent firms (not necessarily knowledge-intensive). According to GEM terminology, "a person was considered to be involved in a nascent firm if they had engaged in any activity to start the firm in the past 12 months, expected to own all or part of the new firm once it became operational, and the initiative had not paid salaries and wages to anyone, including owner managers, for more than three months" (GEM, 2000).

In 1994 and 1995, Bematech was a recipient of the FINEP National Innovation Prize, the importance of which can be sensed by the fact that the President of Brazil attends the annual ceremony. In 1998, Bematech won the National Innovative Entrepreneurship Prize, in a competition annually organized by ANPROTEC as a means to promote innovation habitats and the firms that benefitted from them.

In 2000, Bematech became a pioneer in the emerging Brazilian commercial automation market. The following year it began exporting. Later on, it established R&D centers and acquired companies abroad, including in the USA. In August 2015, 25 years after creating the company, its founders decided to make Bematech part of Totvs, a multinational Brazilian-based conglomerate of information technology solution providers, in order to become a global player.

Wolney Betiol, Bematech's co-founder, has always been an active promoter of innovative entrepreneurship. In one of his public declarations he states that *"There is an important entrepreneurship movement in Brazil, noticeable through business incubators, which are a form of creating business models and products adjusted to the reality"* (ANPROTEC, 2007).

As mentioned earlier, 13 incubators had been established at the end of the first decade of the introduction of innovation habitats in the Brazilian society, a little more than one per year. The Movement expanded rapidly during the last seven years of the previous century, adding almost 20 new incubators every year. By the end of 2000, the total number of incubators in operation reached 135, more than 10 times as many as in 1993.

In addition to the growth, during 1994–2000, the incubation model expanded geographically, covering most of the 27 states. At the same time, multiple and diverse applications developed, making incubators better understandable as a family with different genera and species. An example of the diversification initiated during that period is the creation of Cooperative Technology Incubators. This locally developed model links and combines academically produced knowledge with popular initiatives, in order to achieve social inclusion. The first of this sort of Incubators was created by the UFRJ, adapting the experience of its successful regular Technology Incubator.

Municipalities and development agencies started business incubators along a similar line. They focused on transforming knowledge into innovative products, but did not have advanced technology as a prerequisite.

Hence, ANPROTEC's membership diversified, bringing new types of members into what had been the turf of academic institutions during the formative years. This motivated the Association to change its name into the more comprehensive denomination National Association of Entities that Promote Innovative Enterprises.

The rapid expansion of the number of incubators and incubatees had only been possible because of the support of several institutional partners, both traditional (CNPq and FINEP) and new ones. Among the latter, the main backer of the movement became the Brazilian Service of Support for Micro and Small Enterprises (SEBRAE).[12]

It is time to innovate (2001–2015)

As the 21st century arrived, a new term entered the Brazilian general vocabulary: 'innovation'. It had obviously been used before, although mainly restricted to the academic community involved in science and technology policy and management studies, and to some business R&D leaders. The turning point was the National Conference on Science, Technology and Innovation, organized in September 2001 by the Ministry of Science and Technology and the Brazilian Academy of Sciences. Attended by 1300 senior representatives of the "triple helix", *viz.* academia, industry and government, far-reaching conclusions and recommendations were agreed upon, aiming at a new developmental pathway for the country, enabled by convergence of knowledge production and the competitive requirements of business.[13]

The innovation mystique was already created in 2000 during the preparation for the Conference, and later reinforced by the subsequent 2004 Innovation Law, generating an influx of technology parks initiatives. A survey by ANPROTEC (2008) indicated 94 projects, mostly still in the conceptual or early implementation phases. The vast majority (85%) of the projects had been initiated in 2000 or later.

---

[12] The *Serviço Brasileiro de Apoio às Micro e Pequenas Empresas* is a private non-profit organization created in 1990, funded by a compulsory contribution from all medium and large companies.

[13] The term 'innovation' percolated in multiple segments of the Brazilian society, and rapidly became a mantra.

In some cases, the connection was explicit, as in the narrative of the creation of TECNOPUC, the technology park of the Rio Grande do Sul Pontifical Catholic University (PUC-RS), one of the flagships of the Movement. In mid-2001, PUC-RS purchased from the Brazilian Army a vacant barrack adjacent to the campus, in order to expand its traditional academic activities. The decision to refocus the use of that valuable space and transform the new area into the first phase of a technology park was triggered by the feedback from a computer sciences Professor who had been sent by the University authorities to follow the 2001 Conference's discussions.[14]

Parallel to the rapid expansion of technology parks initiatives, the number of business incubators also increased during 2001–2015. The last official figures derived from studies commissioned by the Ministry of Science, Technology and Innovation (2012 and 2013) portray the following (CDT/UnB, 2014):

Business Incubators

- Total in operation: 384.
- Number of incubatees and graduated companies: 6255.
- Jobs generated: 45,605.
- Yearly turnover: US$ 2.6 billion.[15]

Technology Parks

- Number of parks in operation: 28.
- Number of enterprises installed: 939.
- Jobs generated: 32,327.

---

[14] Professor Jorge Audy was promoted to Vice-Rector and led PUC-RS's successful effort to implement TECNOPUC, as part of a comprehensive innovation ecosystem. As of January 1, 2016, he became the President of ANPROTEC. TECNOPUC nowadays hosts 120 corporation R&D laboratories (the first were HP's and Dells's facilities), startups and professional organizations, providing 6500 jobs, mostly highly qualified. Through TECNOPUC's active management, the cooperation between the University (both faculty members and students) and industries located in the Technology Park is intense and systematic.

[15] The turnover is usually considered conservative as measured in local currency (R$ 4.6 billion). By way of contrast, the US$ 2.3 billion figure might be overestimated, as the evolution of the exchange rate in 2014–2015 favored the USD.

The main industry focus of the business incubators is Information Technology (40%). The vast majority (80%) of professionals active in the approximately 2500 graduate firms have at least completed higher education programs.[16] This is in sharp contrast with the profile of the economically active population, where the fraction of professionals with higher education is 6.5%.

As Innovation habitats became ubiquitous, two recent developments deserve attention, one external and the other internal to the Movement. On the internal front, there is general recognition that Brazilian business incubators have been generating a substantial number of new innovative ventures, which create job opportunities for highly qualified professionals and help mitigate brain drain. They also contribute to regional development, and to the solution of specific problems that were not resolved by incumbent companies. However, the incubators need to improve their processes in order to be in line with the so-called Third Generation Incubators[17] (Garcia *et al.*, 2015).

Within this context, ANPROTEC and SEBRAE elaborated a new operating model for Brazilian incubators. The platform is called Reference Center for Business Incubation (CERNE). Its central purpose is to induce major improvements in the incubators' effectiveness, by means of model and operation standards. The expected result is an increase in the incubator's capacity to systematically generate successful innovative companies, reducing the prevalent level of variability. A pilot group of 140 incubators was established with the support of SEBRAE, in order to implement the key practices proposed by the CERNE model. A second chance to adhere to CERNE opened, also with SEBRAE's support. Fifty incubators completed the current phase and are awaiting certification, in order to move to the next level of maturity, as follows:

CERNE 1 — Company: in this first level, all the processes and practices are directly related to the development of incubatees. Accordingly, in addition to processes such as planning, qualification, consultancy,

---

[16] Almost a third of the professionals have Doctor's, Master's or specialist degrees.

[17] According to Ryzhonkov (2013), the first generation of incubators (1960–1985) focused on physical space and shared resources; the second generation (1985–1995) concentrated on services to support business development. Finally, the third generation, started in around 1995, refocused their attention on networks.

selection and monitoring, practices directly related to the management of the incubator are also included.

CERNE 2 — Incubator: the focus of this level is to ensure effective management of the incubator as an organization. Therefore, the incubator must implement processes that enable its strategic management; the expansion of services provided and target audience; and the evaluation of its results and impacts.

CERNE 3 — Partners Network: the focus of this level is to consolidate a network of partners to expand an incubator's operations, creating capable and effective tools to meet non-resident companies. Therefore, at this level the incubator strengthens its role as one of the nodes of the networks involved in the process of promoting innovation.

CERNE 4 — International Operations: at this level, the incubator must acquire sufficient maturity to act internationally, and to systematically promote the globalization of incubated companies.

The recommended path is that incubator managers implant maturity levels in the proposed sequence, in order to optimize resources and facilitate the implementation process. SEBRAE invested US$ 28 million in the partial support of CERNE.

The external relevant development is the multiplication of startups, startup promotion programs and accelerators. This segment is akin to the traditional innovation habitats (business incubators and technology parks). However, these new mechanisms and firms did not join the Movement. In fact, a Brazilian Association of Startups (ABStartups) was created, and managed to recruit 200 members in four years, circa 5% of the estimated number of Brazilian startups. A Brazilian Association of Innovation and Investment Accelerators (ABRAII) was also recently established.

This phenomenon, which emerged in 2011–2012, was immediately perceived by the Movement. In the introduction to a concise report published in 2014, on the occasion of the completion of the 30th anniversary of the foundational Executive Resolution passed by CNPq, ANPROTEC's Board stated that

> (...) *assembling circa 300 members, including business incubators, technology parks, educational and research institutions and other entities connected to*

entrepreneurship and innovation, the Association assumes the fundamental role of guaranteeing the continuation and the sustentation of the results constructed over decades.

With this mission we enter a new cycle in our movement, marked not only by the generational transition of its leaders and managers, but also by the emergence of new institutional actors, that now share with technology parks and business incubators the entrepreneurship and innovation scenery. Reaffirming its leadership role, ANPROTEC believes that this is the moment for aggregation, bringing near the movement all those that share our interests and dreams (ANPROTEC, 2014).

The entrepreneurial ecosystem

Background

As seen from the outside, the Brazilian Innovation Framework, which includes the entrepreneurial ecosystem, looks quite intricate. Two facts have to be taken into account, in order to understand the inherent complexity (ANPROTEC, 2015).

The first one is the relative youth of the Brazilian Innovation Framework. Although innovative activities have been present in the Brazilian economic scenery since, at least, the immediate post World War II period, a national framework for innovation began to be established only in 2001, at the already mentioned National Conference of Science, Technology and Innovation. A national Innovation Law, one of the recommendations of the 2001 Conference, was enacted only in December 2004, and needed substantial amendments, sanctioned in January 2016. The Brazilian Innovation Framework is still in construction, often evolving quite slowly, sometimes quite rapidly, but seldom changing along a predictable and smooth path.

The second fact is the multifaceted character of the Brazilian Innovation Framework. To a great extent, this is due to the existence of three spheres of government: Federal, State and Municipal. (This overlapping division of layers of government is, of course, not unique to Brazil.) The role of the state sphere can be quite strong, mainly in those states that have excellent universities, a diversified industry, and a well-funded agency to finance research and development, such as São Paulo. Most states have their own Law to promote Science, Technology and Innovation, albeit inspired by the Federal Law. Progress has been made in terms of coordination among the states, through the National Council of State Secretaries for Science, Technology and Innovation-Related Issues (CONSECTI), and the National Council of the State Foundations that Support Research. Co-financing innovation projects by the Federal and State spheres is a relatively recent occurrence. As for municipalities, this is the level of government that has the least financial resources to support innovation habitats. Therefore, municipalities are often left out of coordination efforts between the State and Federal levels of government.

The fragmentation among governmental organization structures aggravates the situation. This managerial nightmare is powered by the tradition of elected officials to sow alliances by dividing Federal ministries or state secretaries among political parties, so that enough trump cards are available. This leads to a need for investing time and energy, in order to achieve a minimum of consistency in decision making and of synergy in the allocation of resources.

Relevant partners

As the business incubators' outcomes received wider recognition, in 2000 the Federal Government launched the National Program to Support Business Incubators (PNI), led by the Ministry of Science and Technology. This Ministry had absorbed the previously existing two agencies that were at the inception of the Movement — CPNq, which in 1984 introduced innovation habitats in the national agenda, and FINEP, which in 1987 had been one of the signatories of the original ANPROTEC bylaws.

As the entrepreneurship promotion activities grew in scale and scope, and there was a perceived demand to continue its ascendant course, ANPROTEC proposed a reformulation of PNI in order to transform the Program into a consensus building platform among the main backers of the Movement. In March 2009, the Ministry of Science and Technology made a new regulation upgrading PNI for the new requirements. First, the name was changed to National Program to Support Business Incubators and Technology Parks, reflecting the then evident presence of the latter type of innovation habitats. Its object was defined as

Fomenting the consolidation and the emergence of technology parks and business incubators that contribute to stimulate and accelerate the process of creation of micro and small business characterized by the high technology content of its products, processes and services, and also by intense techno-logical innovation activity and by the usage of modern managerial methods (Ministry of Science and Technology, 2009).

The most significant improvement was the formation of an Advisory Council, coordinated by the Ministry of Science and Technology's Secretary for Technological Development, composed by representatives from the following institutions and organizations:

1. CNPq, which is responsible for the promotion and stimulus of the development and maintenance of scientific and technological research, and for the preparation of human resources qualified for research in all areas of knowledge;
2. FINEP, which supports studies, projects and programs relevant to the economic, social, scientific and technological development of the country;
3. Ministry of Development, Industry and Foreign Trade, which is the main element of connection between public policies related to inno-vation and the demands of the production sectors, particularly by its Secretary of Innovation;
4. National Development Bank, which stimulates and supports opera-tions associated to capabilities building and development of innova-tive environments;
5. CONSECTI which represents the subnational public policy makers;
6. SEBRAE which is in charge of implementing the Small Business General Law, enacted in 2006, particularly its Chapter 10, which is dedicated to stimulating innovation in micro and small firms;
7. National Confederation of Industry, which leads the Business Mobilization for Innovation (MEI), a group of circa 100 CEOs of large industries that aims at embodying and improving management of

innovation in the Brazilian firms, and at increasing public instruments focused on innovation and

8. ANPROTEC, which represents the Movement.

A representative of the Municipal Forum of Science, Technology and Innovation Secretaries and Executives was added to the original nine members. Some positive effects of the new PNI are as follows:

1. Greater coordination between the institutions and organizations represented in the Advisory Board in designing competitive programs to support investment in innovation habitats' new projects, for instance, by launching joint requests for proposals;
2. The commissioning of studies to assess the performance of business incubators and technology parks;
3. The proposal of multiparty innovative projects aimed at improving the general conditions of the Movement, such as advanced training for innovation habitats managers and public policy makers related to innovation and entrepreneurship;
4. The creation of a user-friendly platform for information exchange, also serving as a 'clearing house' for issues related to innovative entrepreneurship and
5. Increased visibility of the Movement in the formulation of public policies.

An extensive report recently published shows the positive effects of PNI's competitive programs to the technology parks and business incubators that received the support (Fundação Certi, 2015).

Innovation habitats have been present in most recent guidelines for the country's Science, Technology and Innovation. One example is the so called 'Blue Book', which synthetizes the results of the Fourth National Conference on Science, Technology and Innovation for Sustainable Development. Convened in 2010, with a strong and diversified attendance of most stakeholders, the Conference marked the end of a decade of successful introduction of the concept of innovation in the wider Brazilian public, enabling it to become understood as a systemic component of the national production structure.

Several recommendations of the Conference presented in the Blue Book were particularly pertinent to the Movement: for example, the demand to diversify the methods of financing innovation, by means of synergy among public mechanisms to finance early-stage entrepreneurship; mitigation of the risks inherent to product and process innovations; stimulus to create Risk Funds focused on new ventures; and adoption of a broader concept of innovation by the financing agencies. The plea for achieving synergy among public mechanisms to finance early-stage entrepreneurship reflects PNI's purposes.

Other recommendations related to the Movement were the request to create a network of areas of innovation, mainly science and technology parks, in coordination with clusters and other forms of regional development promotion; and the call to promote the emergence of startups by means of pre-incubators, business incubators and science and technology parks. A more general issue, nevertheless also important for incubatees and graduates alike, was the proposition directed at the need to prepare firms for internationalization and global competitiveness through support and incentives of public and private institutions.

Reinforcement of PNI's initiatives was explicitly mentioned in the National Strategy for Science, Technology and Innovation, both in the 2012–2015 and the 2016–2019 editions (the latter is still under discussion).

ANPROTEC established long-term links with national organizations that are not represented in PNI. Two especially important connections are the Federal Congress and the Brazilian Association of Private Equity & Venture Capital (ABVCAP), represented in the Association's Advisory Board respectively by a Congress member active in Innovation and Entrepreneurship issues,[18] and by the ABVCAP's President or Vice-President.

Internationalization

Brazilian innovation habitats have a tradition of active global presence, coordinated by ANPROTEC.[19] The basic motivation is knowledge exchange

---

[18] The most recent Congress member of ANPROTEC's Advisory Board was the main promoter of the recent changes in the legal framework for innovation.

[19] ANPROTEC adopted Brazilian Association of Science Parks and Business Incubators as its international name.

associated with firsthand acquaintance with good practices of business incubators and technology parks abroad. Organized delegations attend major international trade venues and conferences related to innovation habitats. One emblematic case is the annual IASP World Conference, focused on Science and Technology Parks and Areas of Innovation. The participation is frequently enriched by a one or two week technical mission, consisting of in-depth visits to referential innovation habitats, entrepreneurial ecosystems and people responsible for public policies aimed at promoting innovative entrepreneurship.

The knowledge flow is bidirectional. In 2003, the World Bank Information for Development Program (infoDev) distributed a tool to support incubators known as iDISC, which resulted from a project developed by Anprotec in Brazil. The iDISC tool was conceived as a data and information center to disseminate state-of-the-art knowledge about business incubation, aimed at helping the creation and improvement of business incubators in developing countries. In 2009 the infoDev Global Forum on Innovation and Entrepreneurship was organized in conjunction with the annual Brazilian Nacional Seminar on Technology Parks and Business Incubators, gathering 1000 participants from around 30 countries in Florianópolis. In the same direction, the Movement helped the implementation of incubation processes in Latin American countries and in Angola.

A second major reason for international cooperation is the creation of opportunities for internationalization of incubatees and recently graduated firms. In 2013, the land2land.com.br platform was launched as a means to help entrepreneurs identify innovation habitats in different countries that have programs to support the internationalization of incubatees and other intensive-knowledge small firms. The platform is a result of a joint effort by SEBRAE, the Brazilian Agency for Promoting Exports and Investments (APEX-Brasil)[20] and ANPROTEC. By the end of 2014 the platform integrated 12 Brazilian and 24 foreign innovation habitats.

A convergent action is the Connect Program, an initiative coordinated by the European Business Network (EBN), in partnership with ANPROTEC, to promote reciprocal exchange between Brazilian and European entrepreneurs.

---

[20] APEX-Brasil is supervised by the Ministry of Development, Industry and Foreign Trade, a member of PNI's Advisory Board.

There are strong ties between the Movement and the International Association of Science Parks and Areas of Innovation (IASP). Several Brazilian technology parks are full members of the International Association, and ANPROTEC is an institutional member of IASP. There is a frequent exchange of communications, visitors and speakers. Current or former members of ANPROTEC's Board are often elected to coordinate IASP's Latin American Division or occupy key positions in IASP's governance.[21]

ANPROTEC and IASP are founding members of the World Alliance for Innovation (WAINOVA), which coordinates 27 associations of technology parks and innovation-based business incubators all over the world. Its mission is to contribute to the world's economic and social development by promoting innovation, technology transfer and the establishment of innovation-based companies.

Legal framework

In addition to its intrinsic multifaceted character, and to a certain extent, as a consequence of its youth, the Brazilian Innovation Framework is often affected by inconsistent interpretations of the legal framework by different Government agencies. These discrepancies affect several aspects of the innovation support programs, and also the everyday operation of innovation processes, eroding the innovation animus in both companies and scientific and technological institutions.

Some of the main benefits to industry enabled by the Innovation Law have their effect reduced, as they are often questioned by legal and control agency officers, e.g. with regard to the use of tax incentives and of public direct subsidies by companies for their research and development activities. Among other reasons, the reluctance of several companies is associated with the perception of the risk of being fined by the tax authorities, in case of non-recognition of the legitimacy of expenses attributed by the firm's accountancy to innovative activities.

---

[21] A founder and former president of ANPROTEC was the President of the Executive Board of IASP. Another former President of the Brazilian Association is a member of IASP's Advisory Board.

Various legal aspects of the Innovation Law negatively affected the innovation habitats' operations. One of the copious examples of good intentions with inadequate wording was the permission given by the Law for the use of university-owned public facilities by private companies for R&D purposes. This clause was initially considered a sufficient basis for a public university technology park starting negotiations with private companies. The idea was enticing them to invest in state-of-the art R&D centers in a site nearby a university campus, reaping the benefits of proximity with academic centers of excellence and enhancing its attractiveness in the eyes of brilliant young students.[22] Negotiations were broken up as soon as the corporate law office saw the term "permission" in the Law, as the legal meaning is that the permitter may revoke the permission at any moment without compensation for the investment made by the private company, even in case of early unilateral termination of the contract or agreement. The better alternative would be to use the term "concession", as a unilateral change of mind by the university leadership would still be possible, but contingent on compensation to the private company for early termination of the contract or agreement.

Another related deterrent was the Law's omission of time limits for such deals. In the absence of any specification, public university lawyers adopt the five-year limit applicable to all public contracts, with possible extensions. However, this time period is clearly insufficient for allowing the return of the private investment. The possibility of contract extension is ineffective in practice. Private companies have good reasons to fear academy differences in opinion with regard to public–private partnership, as the governance rules of public universities require electing a new rector every four years, with no successive reelection.

Several initiatives have been attempted, in order to cope with what has been nicknamed the "legal insecurity" of the Brazilian Innovation Framework. The first attempt to identify and tackle this challenge led to a seminar involving representatives of several stakeholders, organized as early as December 2006. The next legislative effort was the enactment

---

[22] Almost all research universities in Brazil are public, either Federal or State.

of a National Code of Science, Technology and Innovation, in 2011. The driving force behind this Bill was to consolidate all the Federal relevant legislation related to innovation, currently dispersed in different laws, decrees and other legal instruments. The main goals were the elimination of contradictions and ambiguities, and at the same time making dramatic improvements, in order to simplify and rationalize the everyday operation of the innovation processes. The Bill was extensively enhanced in 2012, with the contribution of four main entities of the Brazilian Innovation System, one of them ANPROTEC.

After a convoluted process, on February 26, 2015 Constitutional Amendment 85 was unanimously approved by the Federal Congress. The amendment provides for the addition of "science, technology, research and innovation" to the Brazilian constitution. This tenet in the construction of the Brazilian national system for science, technology and innovation is considered an important step for developing public–private partnerships and improving interactions between the scientific/academic spheres. It also regulates the public funding of Brazilian companies, as it provides the legal basis for the use of public resources by the private sector, which has been questioned in some courts.

Constitutional Amendment 85 also explicitly mentions, for the first time, science and technology parks, technology poles and innovation habitats. A key immediate benefit is overcoming opinions of some legal advisors who did not recognize these innovation habitats as legitimate objects of public support. It also opened the way for the Bill to enhance the 2004 Innovation Law.

The Bill, which was first introduced in 2011 and underwent numerous revisions, was finally unanimously approved by Federal Congress in December 2015, and then sanctioned by the President on January 11, 2016, becoming Law 13243. Unexpectedly, nine items included in the Bill approved by the legislature received last minute presidential vetoes. The 30 or so associations and organizations that had coalesced into an alliance during the long process of negotiating the new legal framework are considering another round of the battle in order to reverse these vetoes.

In spite of these unexpected changes, Law 13243 constitutes a great improvement in the legal framework for innovation in general, and for innovation habitats in particular. A few examples of new positive rules follow.

> *The Union, the States, the Federal District, the Municipalities, the respective governmental financing agencies and public science and technology institutions may support the creation, implementation and consolidation of habitats that promote innovation, technology parks and poles and business incubators included, as a form of stimulating technological development, competitiveness, increase and interaction between companies and science and technology institutions.*
>
> *Business incubators, technology parks and poles and other habitats that promote innovation shall establish their own rules to foment, conceive and develop partnership projects, and to select companies to enter those habitats.[23]*
>
> *The Union, the States, the Federal District, the Municipalities, the respective governmental financing agencies and public science and technology institutions may assign the use of real estate for the installation and consolidation of habitats that promote innovation, directly to the interested companies or science and technology institutions or by means of private profit or nonprofit organization (...).*

The enforcement of the innovative provisions of the new Law will demand a patient and persistent effort, as changing a culture is much more challenging than changing laws, as difficult as the latter might have been.

Challenges and prospects

The challenges and prospects of the innovation habitats are partly contingent on manageable factors, and in part affected by situations outside of direct control. The prospects for the foreseeable future of the Movement are naturally dependent on the wisdom and concerted effort to deal with manageable factors. A strategic exercise carried out on the occasion of the

---

[23] This ruling allows innovation habitats to circumvent the more strict interpretation of the former legal framework, which led to the application of the same norms for purchasing lightbulbs or defining new incubatees. Internal rules might establish 20 years as the period of time for a new R&D Center in a technology park installed on public land.

30th anniversary of CNPq's Executive Resolution identified 25 actions, divided in five categories (ANPROTEC, 2014). A sample of the proposed actions, filtered by the dramatic modifications of Brazil during the short time elapsed.

1. Increase the integrated actuation of the Movement's actors in the whole country, in order to develop joint solutions to the bottlenecks that affect technology parks and business incubators;
2. Engage corporations in the Movement, in order to foster partnerships with enterprises nurtured in innovation habitats, enabling technology transfer, investment and cross innovation;
3. Connect the innovation habitats to the Federal Ministry for Cities, so that technology parks and business incubators are identified as strategic platforms for urban development[24];
4. Amplify the dialogue with the National Development Bank, in order to make the Bank an effective partner in financing the infrastructure of Innovation habitats, especially technology parks;
5. Contribute to the creation of high-impact firms, connected both to vocation and to the regional and local needs of society and
6. Prepare the generation that will succeed the pioneer leadership of the Movement.

The situations outside of direct control are stridently present as this chapter is being concluded in January 2016. The period of economic bonanza that enabled a noteworthy improvement in the daily lives of the low-income segments is over, as it was powered by a wave of strong international demand of commodities. The dire economic circumstances of

---

[24] A noteworthy success is Porto Digital (the name means Digital Port), inaugurated in 2000, with the goal of creating a pole of development based on world class software industry in a historic albeit deteriorated and depressed area of Recife, a large city in the Northeastern region. The completely degraded urban area is now revitalized, both in physical and sociocultural dimensions, as a result of the actions of Porto Digital. The strategy of installing a brownfield technology park allowed the requalification of the historical space, and provided a new economic reality to the city. Porto Digital's contribution peaked 3.5% of the Pernambuco State Gross Product in just 15 years of operation (Zouain and Plonski, 2015).

Brazil (production reduction combined with a significant increase in inflation) are compounded by a deep political and ethical crisis. The net result is the loss of credibility by large segments of society in the strategic acumen and managerial capacity of the country's public leadership.

The Movement has the capability of not being paralyzed by uncertainty, as it was born three decades ago, amidst an analogous conjunction of stagflation and political turmoil. It learned how to swim against the flow of bad news and worse omens, envisioning and promoting attainable, albeit audacious, new courses of actions, capable of gradually transforming society. The results attained, the maturity acquired during the long journey and the connectivity carefully constructed and maintained are valuable assets of the Movement to creatively deal with the present and upcoming challenges and opportunities.

References

Albuquerque, L.C. de (2004). 'Agradecimento'. XIV Seminário Nacional de Parques Tecnológicos e Incubadoras de Empresas. ANPROTEC, Porto de Galinhas, 11 November.

ANPROTEC (1987). Estatuto Social. Unpublished.

ANPROTEC (2007). Fiates, J. E. *et al*. Aventura do Possível: 20 anos Anprotec. Brasília: DF, 2007. Available at: www.anprotec.org.br. Accessed on 18 January 2016.

ANPROTEC (2008). Fiates, J. E. *et al*. Portfolio de Parques Tecnológicos no Brasil. Available at: www.anprotec.org.br/ArquivosDin/portfolio_versao_resumida_pdf_53.pdf. Accessed on 18 January 2016.

ANPROTEC (2014). Garcia, F. P. *et al*. 30+10: o Empreendedorismo Inovador em Movimento. Available at: www.anprotec.org.br/Relata/Anprotec_30+10_site.pdf. Accessed on 22 April 2016.

ANPROTEC (2015). Plonski, G. A. The Brazilian Innovation Framework. Study carried out for the European Commission. Unpublished. Accessed on 18 January 2016.

CDT/UnB (2014). Kimura, H. (coord.). Estudo de Projetos de Alta Complexidade: indicadores de parques tecnológicos. Study for the Ministry of Science, Technology and Innovation. Brasilia, Brazil. Available at: www.mct.gov.br/upd_blob/0228/228606.pdf. Accessed on 18 January 2016.

FUNDAÇÃO CERTI (2015). Coral E. and Carioni, L. (coords.). Estudo de Impactos do PNI: Programa Nacional de Apoio a Parques Tecnológicos e Incubadoras de Empresas. Study prepared for the Ministry of Science, Technology and Innovation. Brasilia, Brazil. Available at: http://ppi.certi.org.br/1-EstudodeImpactosdoPNI.pdf. Accessed on 18 January 2016.

Garcia, F. P. *et al.* (2015). Reference Center for Business Incubation: A proposal for a new model of operation. Available at: www.anprotec.org.br/Relata/artigoCernNBIA.pdf. Accessed on 18 January 2016.

Global Entrepreneurship Monitor: Reynolds, P. D. *et al.* (2000). file:///C:/Users/Ary/Downloads/ 1343295186GEM_2000_Global_Report%20(1).pdf. Accessed on 18 January 2016.

Ministry of Science and Technology (2009). Portaria 139, de 10.03.2009, que institui o Programa Nacional de Apoio a Parques Tecnológicos e Incubadoras de Empresas. Available at: http://projetos.unioeste.br/campi/nit/arquivos/Portaria%20MCT%20PNI%20%20n%5 B1%5D.pdf. Accessed on 18 January 2016.

Ryzhonkov, V. (2013). Entrepreneurship, Business Incubation, Business Models & Strategy Blog. Available at https://worldbusinessincubation.wordpress.com/business-incubation-models/. Accessed on 22 April 2016.

Zouain, D. M. and Plonski, G. A. (2015). Science and Technology Parks: laboratories of innovation for urban development — an approach from Brazil. *Triple Helix*, 2: 7.

Chapter 6

Assessing the Value Added by Incubators for Innovative Small and Medium Enterprises in Russia

Dina Williams and David Tsiteladze

Introduction

The role of innovation is universally recognized as a key source of competitiveness and economic development. Both in developed and emerging economies, governments devise policies, programs and instruments to support the development of new technology-based firms. Incubation mechanisms (IMs), such as science and technology parks, high-tech business incubators and innovation centers, are considered to be one of the instruments in fostering these firms. Despite initial inconclusive evidence on the effectiveness of incubation mechanisms, they remain an attractive proposition for the policy makers.

Recent years have witnessed a surge in research on business incubators and science/technology parks in developed and especially in emerging economies (Almeida, 2005; Bakouros *et al.*, 2002; Bruneel *et al.*, 2012; Chandra, 2007; Koçak and Can, 2014; Vaidyanathan, 2007; Williams *et al.*, 2013). In this respect, Russia is not an exception. A recent government white paper entitled, *Strategy of Innovative Development of Russian Federation for 2020*, emphasizes innovation as a key driver for the country's economic recovery and long-term future prosperity. The document

highlights the key issues in innovation development such as low innovation activities of state-controlled companies, low level of competition and
as a result lack of demand for innovation products and solutions as well as
low level of interaction between industry and research and low level of
commercialization of research outcomes. Although most of the policies
are focused on increasing level of innovation activities of established large
enterprises, the document recognizes the importance of new technology-
based entrepreneurship and the development of network of technology
parks[1] and high-tech business incubators alongside fiscal measures in
improving financial climate for venture financing is seen as a flagship
policy.

In Russia, high-tech business incubators and technoparks first emerged
in early 1990s; most of them were set up by universities and public research
organizations (PROs) under the Government's program 'Technology Parks
and Innovations', which aimed to promote technology transfer and commercialization of research outcomes from the universities and PRO.
Russian analysts (Эксперт РА, 2004) note that majority of university-
based technoparks are in fact another university department serving interests of its founding university and providing sheltered environment for
(not always commercially viable) university spin-off companies and very
little engagement with external stakeholders.

Universities and PRO were able to negate to an extent a negative
impact in state funding of higher education and research and to retain
skilled and enterprising members of staff allowing them to set up own
spin-off companies by setting up incubation facilities (Williams, 2011). By
the mid-1990s, the number of university-based technoparks increased;
alongside university-based technoparks, there is a process of establishing
regional technoparks set up by regional administration often in collaboration with regional research centers and industrial enterprises and focused
on the promotion of new technologies at established industrial enterprises
(Chistyakova, 2010).

---

[1] In the Russian context, Technology Parks could be considered as an equivalent to Science
Parks, e.g. areas designed to encourage the formation and growth of technology-based
companies to facilitate linkages with research centers and industrial enterprises.

According to different sources, in 2000, there were around 80 tech-noparks; however, only 30 of them were able to be qualified as high-tech technoparks in the accreditation process which took place in 2000 among which only 11 were recognized as having world-class standards. According to a survey commissioned by the Russian Venture Corporation (2013), at present, there are around 80–90 technoparks at different stages of develop-ment, and around 100 business incubators. Majority of IMs belong to regional or municipal administration (52% of technoparks and 67% of business incubators); some of them are in ownership of higher education institutions (26% of technoparks and 28% of business incubators). According to the official terminology, the differences between business incubators and technoparks lie in the target audience (newly established firms for business incubators and established companies for technoparks) and the scope of facilities and activities — technoparks are expected to be large scale integrated research and industrial complexes.

In 2006, the Government approved a Federal Program on "Creation of High-Tech Technoparks in Russian Federation". The program was aimed on acceleration of creation and development of new industries through establishing eight technoparks in seven regions of Russia offering services to both Russian and international high-tech companies. According to the data from Ministry of Communication and Mass Media[2] by 2014 over 19 billion RUB (around £325 million) was invested in the development of new regional technoparks. It was planned that by 2011 the total revenue would exceed p100 billion (~£1. 7 billion). However, by the end of 2011, only four out of planned eight technoparks were built accommodating 440 firms with a total turnover of around p33 billion (£55 million) (TAdviser, 2014). Although the results are far from expected, the government consid-ers them satisfactory and continues its plans in further development of new regional technoparks.

While official statistics reports encourage data in terms of employ-ment and turnover, many in the business community question the effec-tiveness of technoparks as an instrument of creation of new companies and new industries. Vice-president of Russia's association of privatized

---

[2] Ministry of Communication and Mass Media is responsible for implementation of the Federal Programme on "Creation of High-Tech Technoparks in Russian Federation".

and private enterprises notes that the emphasis should be focused on improving the effectiveness of existing incubation facilities; what attracts companies to technoparks and business incubators is services tailored to the needs of high-tech companies such as management training, access to markets and production facilities, etc.

Despite over 20 years in the development of incubation mechanisms in Russia, there is still a significant gap in understanding the role such mechanisms in the development of technology-based companies. More specifically, this research seeks to provide a better understanding of the nature of the tenants of the incubation facilities in Russia; to ascertain the needs of these firms and how they vary depending on the stage of company development as well as to assess the level of satisfaction with incubation support.

The next section of the chapter will discuss theoretical approaches based on most recent trends and empirical evidence on the development of incubation mechanisms in developed and emerging economies. The following section provides an outline of the methodology of the fieldwork. Then the empirical results are presented that reflect characteristics of the surveyed firms and analyze the motivation for IM location, level of satisfaction with incubation support and impact of IM on innovative performance of the surveyed firms. A discussion of the results underlining their policy implications concludes the chapter.

Theory

The main argument for the development of incubation mechanisms is negation of market failure in providing access to key resources that are crucial for long-term viability of the new technology-based firms. These firms face a 'liability of newness' which hinders their access to the resources they need to survive (Freeman *et al.*, 1983; Oakey, 1995). Therefore, a resource-based view of firms (Garnsey, 1998; Penrose, 1995) would be the most adequate framework to understand the contribution of the IMs in providing or easing an access to various physical (e.g. plants, equipment), financial (e.g. bank deposits), human (e.g. experiences, specialized knowledge), technological as well as a firm's reputation or intellectual property rights (Barney, 1991; Fahy, 2000). From this point of view, a more specific framework proposed by Mian (1996b) is particularly useful to assess the incubation mechanism value-added contribution to the tenant firm.

From their origins in the 1970s, technology business incubators, and science and technology parks were seen as mechanisms for linking talent, technology, capital, know-how to leverage entrepreneurial talent, accelerate the development of technology-based firms and speed up the commercialization of technology (Mian, 1997). Academic body of knowledge on incubation mechanisms grew substantially since early 1980s, yet empirical evidence did not produce conclusive results on the effectiveness on incubation mechanisms.

Early debates on the role of incubation mechanisms addressed the effect of science parks and incubator location on economic performance of their tenants (Lindelof and Lofsten, 2002; Lofsten and Lindelof, 2002, 2003, 2005; Mian, 1996a, 1997; Westhead and Storey, 1995) as well as accessibility to various tangible resources such as affordable and flexible office spaces, technology links, research collaborations, human resources (Mian, 1996b; Quintas *et al.*, 1992; Siegel *et al.*, 2003; Vedovello, 1997).

Initial studies focused on physical infrastructure and accompanied services such as physical space, laboratory and workshop facilities, staffing, management and external networks (Hisrich and Smilor, 1988; Mian, 1997). Although valuable for the tenant firms tangible factors such as physical infrastructure are less important to technology-based firms than the way in which such factors are configured to support business development (Patton *et al.*, 2009). Oakey and Mukhtar (1999) suggested that the problem with science parks and incubators lies in putting too much effort into creating the physical infrastructure and neglecting the real needs of high-tech firms such as capital, human resources and a local network.

Initial premise of creation of IMs was to link academic knowledge and business. However, studies suggest that tenant companies rarely develop formal links with universities and/or incubators and science parks (Oakey and Mukhtar, 1999; Schwartz and Hornych, 2010; Vedovello, 1997); incubator or science park location alone does not contribute to a firm's economic performance (Lindelof and Lofsten, 2002; Lofsten and Lindelof, 2003; Oakey and Mukhtar, 1999; Westhead and Storey, 1995). Furthermore, Quintas *et al.* (1992) noted that technology-based firms located in science parks did not perform well in comparison to other companies. Nonetheless, the geographical proximity of an incubator and science park location facilitates informal links though human interaction between firms and universities (Vedovello, 1997) and increases a likelihood of establishing links with local universities (Colombo and Delmastro, 2002; Lofsten and Lindelof, 2002). According to Colombo and Delmastro (2002), on-incubator firms perform better in terms of new technology adoption and participation in international collaborative R&D programs, especially with universities.

More recently, the emphasis in the debate on science parks and incubations shifted from location *per se* to clustering and networking effects of such location and the degree to which incubator firms integrate with one another and the external business community (Bøllingtoft and Ulhøi, 2005; Colombo *et al.*, 2006; Hansen *et al.*, 2000; Patton *et al.*, 2009; Sá and Lee, 2012). Hansen *et al.* (2000) suggest that facilitating inter-firm interaction, building links with external partners and providing access to existing networks incubators directly and indirectly facilitate tenants' technological and business development. Networks embed social capital that reduces the time and costs involved in accessing valuable information, partnerships and markets (Hansen *et al.*, 2000). Moreover, inter-firm interaction might contribute to knowledge sharing and synergy among tenant firms (Chan and Lau, 2005; Colombo *et al.*, 2006) while insufficient networking limits the ability of firms to fully benefit from proximity and collaboration with other tenants and research centers (Bakouros *et al.*, 2002; Sá and Lee, 2012) Schwartz and Hornych (2010) examined the role of specialization in fostering inter-firm collaboration and found out that incubator internal inter-firm networks are dominated by informal relationships between the tenant companies. In their study, Sa and Lee (2012) revealed that relatively low cost activities such as referral services, events, seminars and workshops are especially helpful for tenants in acquiring new contacts and developing collaborative projects.

Although the existing literature is inconclusive on the value of incubation mechanisms such as science parks and high-tech incubators as an engine for the development of technology-based firms, arguments from both supporters and critics indicate that the significance of incubation programs depends on the extent to which such programs are tailored to the specific challenges of the different stages of a firm's lifecycle (McAdam and

McAdam, 2008). In order to assess the value-added contribution of technoparks in Russia, we developed a framework (Table 1) comprising a number of factors based on the literature.

Table 1.   Assessment of Value-Added Contributions

Value-added contributions	Indicators
Technopark/Incubator facilities	
Physical Infrastructure	Fully equipped offices
	Research laboratories
	Workshop/small scale production facilities
	Convenient location
Services	Market research
	Support in market entry and promotion of new products/services
	Technical advice
	Business consulting
	Administrative support and bookkeeping
	Access to Governmental Funding programs
Cost reduction factors	Rental and other subsidies related to cost reduction
	Tax break/holidays[3]
Technopark/incubator specific factors	Transparency
	Brand/Reputation
Networking and clustering factors	
Access to resources and knowledge base	Access the leading experts/knowledge base
	Access to potential clients/suppliers
	Access to new business contacts
	Potential collaboration with regional research centers (universities and PRO)
	Potential collaboration and alliance formation with other tenant companies
	Opportunity for knowledge sharing/dissemination and inter-organization learning
	Access to VC
	Access to skilled workforce

---

[3] Some Technoparks in Russia are set up as a special economic zone with zero taxation for the tenant firms.

Methods

The main objective of this study is to provide an understanding of the impact of IMs on the development of innovative small firms in Russia (Table 2). Due to the scope of the project, the study focused on Nizhny Novgord region, which is regarded as one of the most innovative regions in Russia; it has an anchor research university in its heart, a number of large industrial enterprises and relatively developed support infrastructure for technology-based companies.

Based on a thorough review of existing research and matrices, a comprehensive questionnaire was developed. The questionnaire addressed the nature of the firm, age and stage of the development (from idea stage to maturity). To ascertain measures of growth, the questionnaire asked about changes in turnover and number of employees over last three years. Particular focus was given to the measures of innovation performance such as development and introduction of new products and processes. A set of questions was also asked to understand which factors impede innovation processes. Based on framework outlined in the previous section the questionnaire attempted to undertake a gap analysis in satisfaction of IM support. The respondents were asked a mixture of multiple response questions and Likert scale question to assess the level of importance of factors. To force respondents to provide more definitive answers a 4-point Likert scale was used with an additional option "Don't know/Refuse to answer/Not applicable".

At the initial stage of the data collection, we identified incubation organizations in the Region. Based on the regional government website, eight regional organizations were identified as high-tech/innovation business IMs. As stated by official data there was one modern technopark in operation, however, the field study uncovered that it was still unoperational and under construction. After initial screening of IMs, six technology business incubators were included in the list of IMs. Collecting quantitative data in Russia is a challenging process due to a number of factors.

First, business research based on primary data (such as survey and questionnaires) is relatively new and individuals and businesses do not like to answer mail survey, or in-person questionnaires (Hisrich and Grachev, 1995). Note that problems also arise from such factors as topic sensitivity,

Table 2.   Characteristics of Firms in Nizhny Novgorod Region of Russia

	Tenant firms	Non-tenant firms	Total
	Age		
Less than 1 year	13	9	22
1–3 years	13	7	20
4–6 years		2	2
7–10 years	1		1
Over 10 years	1	5	6
Total	28	23	51
	Stage of development		
Idea stage	0	1	1
Seed stage	7	2	9
Early development	16	8	24
Growth	4	7	11
Maturity	1	5	6
Total	28	23	51
	Number of Employees		
1–5 employees	23	12	35
6–25 employees	2	2	4
26–50 employees	1	0	1
51–100 employees	0	2	2
101–250 employees	1	2	3
over 250 employees	0	3	3
Total	27	21	48
	Activities		
Manufacturing	15	10	25
Service	12	12	24
Other	1	1	2

Source: Survey Data

tradition of silence and mistrust. To facilitate the data collection, we sought support from the executives of technology business incubators in the Region. Out of six organizations, only three incubators agreed to provide access to their tenant firms where the staff distributed and collected the questionnaire. No incubator allowed direct access to their tenants. The field work revealed inconsistency between official and real number of tenant firms. Overall, the survey data were obtained from 28 on-incubator firms.

Alongside on-incubator firms, we also distributed the questionnaire among wider population of SMEs to compare the nature of the firms and level of inter-firms cooperation. In total, 94 questionnaires were returned, only 51 of them were fully completed; 28 of them were from technopark/ business incubator tenants.

The questionnaire was followed by further interviews with managers of IMs and selected on-incubator firms to provide insight into issues highlighted by the questionnaire. Managers of 5 business incubators and 10 incubator tenants firms agreed to interviews. Managers of the incubators were asked to elaborate on incubator's specialization, selection criteria and services provided to the tenant firms. They were also asked to comment on the nature of cooperation between tenant firms with internal and external organizations. Follow-up interviews with on-incubator firms focused mainly on exploring in more detail reasoning for incubator location, use of its services as well as motivations and hindrances of collaboration with other organizations.

Results

Growth and innovation performance

Table 3 presents a summary of the sample including companies' size in terms of employment, age and stage of the development; it indicates that the majority of the surveyed firms are young, less than six years of age, microenterprises at early stages of the development. Taking into account that the role of IM is to support the very early development of innovative companies, it was expected to find more companies in pre-seed stage than among those companies that are located outside of technoparks/incubators. Data indicate approximately equal split between manufacturing and service sector with slightly larger proportion (60%) of manufacturing firms found in IM. The biggest firm cluster is found in IT (7 companies — 3 tenant and 4 non-tenant firms). Manufacturing includes a wide spectrum of activities from knife making to manufacturing LED lights; services

Table 3. Type and Sources of Innovation

| Type of innovation | Have the firm introduced innovation | | Who developed these innovations | | | | | | | |
| | | | Firm on its own | | Firm with other organizations | | Firm adopted existing solutions | | Other organizations | |
	on-incubator	off-incubator	on-incubator	off-incubator	on-incubator	off-incubator	on-incubator	off-incubator	on-incubator	off-incubator
New Products	20	14	14	7	0	5	3	1	3	1
New Services	7	10	6	8	0	2	1	0	0	0
New process	3	4	3	2	0	1	0	1	0	1
New Business Models	4	7	2	3	0	2	2	1	0	1
	34	35	25	20	0	10	6	2	3	3

include contract research, financial services, software development for education, on-line interior design and many others.

Based on the framework proposed in the theoretical part of the chapter, the survey data allow us to ascertain the contribution of IM on firms' growth, innovation performance as well as how on-incubator firms interact with IMs and other firms to gain access to relevant resources.

The value of IMs from a policy point of view is that they accelerate the growth of tenant firms and as a result they create more jobs for local economies. Results of our survey provide evidence to support such arguments in favor of regional incubators. While most on-incubator firms are very small with a majority with 1–5 employees (see Table 3), 54% of them reported increase in number of employees; this is in comparison to 35% of off-incubator firms. Turnover is another indicator of growth. However, companies in Russia find it to be a sensitive issue. Therefore, we asked surveyed firms to comment on changes in a company's turnover and growth expectations for the next five years. Survey data shows that more off-incubator firms reported increase in turnover over last three years (65% compare to 53% on-incubator firms). Nearly 60% of off-incubator firms also expected significant increase in turnover during this period. At the same time, more (68%) on-incubator firms have expectation of significant (over 25%) growth in the next year. Although the results are limited, they suggest that IMs are able to support their tenants and enable them to grow in terms of employment and inspire them for future growth.

Another premise of IM is to stimulate development and diffusion of innovation in the regional economy. We included education of company founders and number of R&D personnel as proxy measures of innovation potential which can enable companies to develop their own new products, services and technological processes. According to the survey results, founders of on-incubator firms are better educated — 96% of respondents indicated they had an university degree. At the same time, off-incubator firms reported slightly larger number of R&D personnel with research degrees. According to the survey data, introduction of a new product is a dominant type of innovation activity and larger proportion of on-incubator firms reported engagement in new products (see Table 3). At the same time, off-incubator firms are slightly more active in the introduction of new services and new business models. Follow-up interviews with companies indicated that in some instances the claim of level of newness is somewhat exaggerated and made without expensive market research. Interviews also point out that companies not always understand the true nature of their innovations, for example product versus business model innovation.

While the pattern of innovation is similar between on- and off-incubator firms, there are some differences in sources of these innovations. On-incubator firms are less likely to develop innovation solutions with other organizations; most of them developed new products, services, process and business models themselves, adopted existing solutions or introduced a product developed by other businesses or organizations, whereas off-incubator firms are more likely to work collaboratively with other businesses and organizations. Follow-up interviews with companies revealed effectual approach (Sarasvathy, 2008) to the innovation activities. Almost in all cases the idea came from previous knowledge and experience of the founding team, from discussion with friends, existing and potential customers. With regards to the level of innovation (new to the company versus new to the market), vast majority of firms reported that innovations were new to the company and there was no significant difference in this respect between on- and off-incubator firms — 24 tenant companies and 19 non-tenant companies reported that innovation solutions were new to the company.

Incubator value-added contributions

From a resource-based perspective, the contribution of IM is to correct market failure and provide and/or ease access to resources to the on-incubator firms without substantial costs (McAdam and McAdam, 2008; Rothaermel and Thursby, 2005). As the previous section outlined, we broadly defined value-added contribution in terms of IM facilities and networking/clustering factors.

Modern IM facilities are not limited to offering office spaces and associated telecom services but also a range of services to enable business development. Interviews with the managers of business incubators revealed that most of them could be considered as economic development incubators with the purpose to support the development of small business in their immediate location. Only one incubator of regional importance was specifically set up to support technology-based firms. Activities of business incubators are defined by the Region's government and include rental of fully-equipped office spaces with access to common use conference/meeting facilities, administrative and legal support (bookkeeping, secretarial services and advice on some legal matters). All surveyed business incubators serve as a gateway to regional and federal governments' support programs for SMEs including technology-based firms. In addition to basic services included in the rental fee, business incubators offer consulting services. According to the regional legislation, the fee for all services provided by the business incubators is set by the regional government. Fees for the basic services (offices rentals, administrative and legal support) are set in the following way: 40% for the first year, 60% for the second year and 100% for third year. After three years, companies are expected to leave the incubators. Characteristics of the incubators are presented in Table 4.

When the surveyed companies were asked to name the main reasons for on-incubator location, access to the regional and federal governments' support programs came on top of the list. 74% of on-incubator tenants and 72% of of-incubator firms named lack of financial resources as the main hindrance; nearly half of the companies also indicated the lack of available external finance. This fact is reflected in high importance given to access to governmental funding and grants for innovative SMEs associated with on-incubator location. In the interviews, managers of the incubators pointed that almost all their tenant firms were in receipt of some sort of governmental financial support. At the same time, when we asked firms if they had any financial support the response was "no". However, interviews with on-incubator firms revealed that by financial support they understood these to be bank loans and not government grants. The data indicated a tendency of state funding dependency. While VC investment requires a high level of accountability, state funding is viewed as "free money". This might explain why access to VC investment is low in terms of importance for technopark/incubator location. Similarly, in-depth follow-up interviews confirm this observation. Almost all interviewed companies mentioned that on-incubator location allowed them to get up-to-date information on available support; incubators also help

Table 4. Characteristics of IMs in Nizhiny Novgorod Region of Russia

Name	Year of founding	Ownership	Specialization	Services	Number of tenants
Innovation Business Incubator "CLEVER"	2007	Regional Government	No industry specialization, all Innovation-based firms	Office spaces Administrative & legal support PR & Marketing Information about and support in application process for Government's programs, Training Business planning	32
Business Incubator "Vyksa"	2013	Municipal Government	No industry specialization, all SMEs	Office spaces Administrative & legal support Information about and support in application process for Government's programs, Mentoring Training Business planning Networking events	14
Business Incubator "Bor"	2013	Municipal Government	No industry specialization, priority to manufacturing companies	Office spaces Administrative & legal support Information about and support in application process for Government's programs, Training Business planning	13

(Continued)

Table 4. (*Continued*)

Name	Year of founding	Ownership	Specialization	Services	Number of tenants
Business Incubator "Dzerzhinsk"	2011	Municipal Government	No industry specialization, Technology-based companies	Office spaces Administrative & legal support Mentoring Information about and support in application process for Government's programs, Training Business planning	15
Business Incubator "Pavlovo"	2013	Municipal Government	No industry specialization, all SMEs	Office spaces Technical and business consulting through external experts Information about and support in application process for Government's programs,	13

their tenants to fill in application documents and help with reporting if a company is successful in its application. Incubator managers also stressed that one of the objectives of all incubators is to help SMEs to get access to regional and federal support programs. To an extent, incubators also play a role of agents of funding bodies — successful companies have to submit all their reports on governmental grants through incubator administration. On-incubator firms find such process useful as they know who is their point of contact and incubator managers ensure that all reports are submitted on time. It is worthwhile mentioning that the need for government's support is expressed predominantly by firms at pre- and seed stage of the development.

Another main reason for on-incubator location is related to market development and product promotion, especially for companies ready to launch a product/service or expand their market. Respondents named lack of experience in marketing and sale as one of the main issues related to the business growth; in fact, it was regarded as the second most important problem for the on-incubators firms. The survey data indicate that on-incubator firms seek assistance with access to potential customers, business contacts, with launch and promotion of their products and services. Interestingly, on-incubator firms are mainly interested in regional and, with some exceptions, national markets. Exploration of foreign markets is not an important issue. One of the interviewed companies tried to penetrate the European market but was not successful due to the language barrier and lack of knowledge about international markets. Priority for the business incubators is to promote their tenants regionally by organizing trade fairs, competitions, local advertising campaigns. Generally, the level of satisfaction with services provided in this area is fairly low (see Table 5) as some of the firms expected incubator managers to get directly involved with a company's projects. Yet other companies have more pragmatic attitude towards solving their marketing issues; they indicated that incubators offer free PR and advertisement at the municipal level which contributes to wider awareness of business community about firms located in IM.

McAdam and McAdam (2008) state that young firms might lack credibility; in this respect, reputation and image of the incubation organization can make a significant difference in building relations and negotiating deals with external organizations Affiliation with high-profiled IMs allow

Table 5. Gap Analysis of the Importance and Satisfaction with Technopark/Incubator Location Factors (Scale from 1 to 5, 1 being 'disagree')

	Importance	Satisfaction	Gap
Governmental grants	3.46	3.08	−0.38
Convenient location	3.44	3.54	0.10
Transparency	3.43	3.12	−0.31
Access to potential customers	3.42	2.59	−0.83
Launch of new products/services	3.40	2.64	−0.76
Brand/Image	3.40	3.19	−0.21
Access to new business contacts	3.32	2.50	−0.82
Potential for joint innovation project with other companies	3.24	1.62	−1.62
Information on new technologies	3.04	2.92	−0.12
IP advice	2.95	2.10	−0.85
Potential for joint research project with PRO and universities	2.81	1.28	−1.53
Access to leading experts	2.67	2.42	−0.25
Subsidized administrative support and bookkeeping	2.38	2.88	0.50
Assistance in market promotion	2.12	1.79	−0.33
Tax break	1.88	1.31	−0.57
Access to skilled workforce	1.65	1.48	−0.17
Access to VC	1.58	1.09	−0.49
International market research of	1.39	1.19	−0.20
Access to research labs and equipment	1.38	1.39	0.01

companies to overcome "liability of newness"; the survey data support this argument — incubator brand image is one of main reasons for on-incubator location. Interviews with entrepreneurs revealed that even for successful companies, building awareness about their business outside the region is very costly and they tap into incubation PR campaigns to promote their businesses. Associated with incubator brand image is the issue of transparency. In the country where corruption and opaque business relations are endemic (Ledeneva, 1998), transparency is regarded highly important by the on-incubator firms.

Collaboration and clustering effect

Over 20–30 years of existence in the developed nations, IMs evolved from *merely property* projects to what Bøllingtoft and Ulhøi (2005) and Hansen *et al.* (2000) called "networked incubators" emphasizing the role of incubators in developing internal and external networks, which enabled tenant firms to access new knowledge, technical expertize, network of VC investors as well as to generate collective knowledge and learning between tenant firms.

While inter-firm collaboration is recognized as a source for growth and competitiveness among entrepreneurial firms in most Western countries (Lechner and Dowling, 2003), the results of the survey revealed that on-incubator firms tend not to collaborate with external partners on joint project (Table 6). Only two tenant companies reported collaboration with local universities; both companies are university spin-out firms with founders still working at the university. Nearly 70% of on-incubator firms reported that they met each other during incubator networking events but only 17% of them indicated that they shared information and discussed issues with fellow on-incubator firms both formally and informally.

Similarly, follow-up interviews supported survey data — respondents commented that they meet other firms at networking events but such acquaintances do not lead to further collaborative relations. Interviews allowed to shed some light on the reasons for weak inter-firms collaboration among on-incubator firms. In some instances, respondents said that they would like to collaborate with other on-incubator firms but hardly have any time for any other activities other than developing their own business.

Other explanations were related to specialization of incubators. On the one hand, on-incubator firms explained weak links with other firms by the lack of companies with similar industry specialization. On the other hand, incubator managers observed that their tenants are reluctant to share information and sometimes even attend the same event in fear of

Table 6. Collaboration with External Organization on Joint Projects

| | Do not collaborate | | | Collaborate | | | | |
| | | | | Regional and national | | International | | |
	On-incubator firms	Off-incubator firm	Total	On-incubator firms	Off-incubator firm	On-incubator firms	Off-incubator firm	Total
Suppliers	24	10	34	0	11		2	13
Clients and customers	17	4	21	6	18	1	4	29
Other companies	21	7	28	2	14		1	17
External experts	20	10	30	3	12		2	17
Universities	22	15	37	2	7		0	9
PROs	23	17	40	0	3		0	3
Large Industrial Enterprises	20	9	29	2	14		0	16

competition. These observations confer with Schwartz and Hornych (2010) who found weak internal inter-firm collaboration. They also observed that IMs have limited ability to foster formal collaboration between on-incubator firms. Nevertheless, although joint projects with external organizations are not particularly prominent among on-incubator firms, most of them (68%) reported business relations (client or supplier) with fellow on-incubator firms.

At the heart of any internal and external inter-firm collaboration are trust-building activities. Although the Russian economy and business environment have undergone significant change, personal informal networks still dominate inter-organizational relations (Ledeneva, 1998; Welter and Smallbone, 2006). At the same time, Jansson *et al.* (2007) observed that Soviet style informal networks gradually transform to the West European model of "firms in networks". It is vitally important therefore for the managers of technoparks/incubators to create opportunities where their tenant firms can meet and interact informally to foster trust-building relations. Activities such as mutual referral might facilitate this process, Sa and Lee (2012).

Despite absence of formal collaboration between on-incubator firms, the survey data indicated that one of the attractions for on-incubator location were collaborative opportunities (Figure 1). Gap analysis of the level of satisfaction with collaborative opportunities revealed that the greatest gap existed in opportunities for research collaboration as well as for internal inter-firm collaboration. The sample data indicate that there is very little synergy between companies located in technoparks/incubators. For most technoparks/incubators, the selection process is based on criteria related to the innovation project presented to an incubation organization. These might include quality of the business plan, type and level of innovation, market attractiveness, etc. However, to promote entrepreneurial growth incubator managers need to be more sensitive in selection process ensuring complementarity and interaction among tenant firms.

Even though empirical evidence linking on-incubator firms and research organizations is inconclusive, incubation organizations are viewed as vehicles to facilitate exchange of knowledge and talents between SMEs and universities and other PROs by initializing joint project, sharing knowledge and technical expertize as well as by providing SMEs with

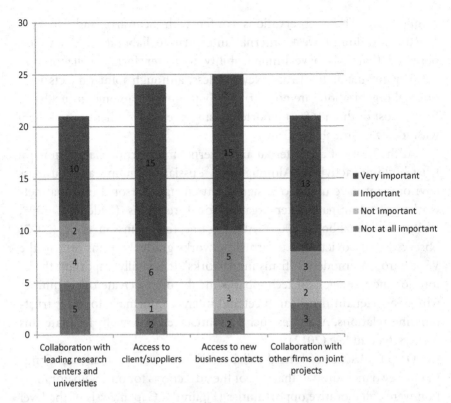

Figure 1.   Importance of Collaborative Opportunities for on-Incubator Firms

access to qualified workforce (university graduates, for example). As stated above, tenant firms are looking for collaborative opportunities with research organizations, yet they found that incubators did not provide such opportunities. Although access to leading experts and skilled workforce are not top priorities for the tenant firms, there is slight dissatisfaction with what incubation organizations can offer (see Table 5).

According to incubator managers, all incubators have links with local universities and PROs but interaction with such organizations depends on initiative from on-incubator firms. They also pointed out that very young firms too often focus on their own projects that they do not see the benefits of collaboration with PROs. Follow-up interviews with on-incubator firms pointed to the fact that on-incubator firms tried to keep all development "in-house". Moreover, with a number of Higher Education Institutions in the region, supply of skilled workforce is not considered an issue. Although incubators offer recruitment services, interviewed companies prefer to rely on their own contacts for hiring new personnel.

Conclusion

Over the last 20–25 years, more than 100 technology parks and high-tech business incubators were created in Russia. The results of this study suggest that incubators in Nizhny Novgorod Region of Russia hardly could be called facilitators of high-tech businesses; they mainly fulfil the function of a need for support to small firms in their respective municipalities. They set up to overcome market failure providing subsidized office spaces, free administrative and legal support as well as consulting services in obtaining financial support from governmental sources. The findings suggest relatively limited value-added contribution to the development of the on-incubator firms — incubators are perceived more as convenient office spaces and a gateway to governmental funding. The results indicate a tendency of state funding dependency by on-incubator firms.

Although on-incubator firms demonstrate higher growth rate in employment and higher growth aspiration than their off-incubator counterparts, it is important to point out that majority of them remain very small micro-enterprises limiting their market offer to the regional market.

Successful IM is an environment that fosters business development and synergy between residents, technopark management team, regional government and universities and PROs. The findings suggest that on-incubator firms are seeking support in launching new products/services as well as access to new market; however, they dissatisfy with what host incubators have to offer in this respect. At the same time, incubators are important for newly formed firms to overcome "liability of newness" by sharing their brand image and reputation. Analysis of collaborative opportunities yield rather paradoxical outcomes — potential collaboration with other companies and PRO including universities were stated as of high value/importance to the companies; yet on-incubator firms are less likely to collaborate on joint projects with other external organizations. This could be due to the selection process which focuses mainly on the market indicator but neglects potential synergy among tenant firms. Level of collaborative activities among all SMEs is very low. Lack of trust, reluctance to share information, role of informal personal relations and lack of inter-firm trust are some of the explanations for that.

The results of the study are limited to one region of Russia and require further investigation. Yet they provide implications for the incubation organizations. Incubation organizations need to focus on developing high-value services to facilitate access to markets, customers and suppliers. These might include a network of business mentors and coaches as well as formal links with universities to assist on-incubator firms in acquiring business and management skills. It has been proven that formal or informal networking is a key resource for business growth. Hence, incubation organizations need to pay greater attention to building complementarity and synergy among tenant firms fostering interaction between companies going beyond the so-called networking event and implement mechanisms which might encourage internal inter-firm collaboration.

Acknowledgment

The authors would like to express their gratitude to the High School of Economics in Moscow for the financial support in undertaking this research.

References

Almeida, M. (2005). The evolution of the incubator movement in Brazil. *International Journal of Technology and Globalisation*, 1(2): 258–277.

Bakouros, Y. L., Mardas, D. C., and Varsakelis, N. C. (2002). Science park, a high tech fantasy? An analysis of the science parks of Greece. *Technovation*, 22(2): 123–128.

Barney, J. B. (1991) Firm resources and sustained competitive advantage, *Journal of Management*, 17(1): 99–120.

Bøllingtoft, A. and Ulhøi, J. P. (2005). The networked business incubator — leveraging entrepreneurial agency? *Journal of Business Venturing*, Special Issue on Science Parks and Incubators, 20(2): 265–290.

Bruneel, J., Ratinho, T., Clarysse, B., and Groen, A. (2012). The evolution of business incubators: Comparing demand and supply of business incubation services across different incubator generations. *Technovation*, 32(2): 110–121.

Chandra, A. (2007). *Approaches to Business Incubation: A Comparative Study of the United States, China and Brazil* (SSRN Scholarly Paper No. ID 1077149), Social Science Research Network, Rochester, NY. Available at: http://papers. ssrn.com/abstract=1077149 [Accessed 24 March 2015].

Chan, K. F. and Lau, T. (2005). Assessing technology incubator programs in the science park: The good, the bad and the ugly. *Technovation*, 25(10): 1215–1228.

Chistyakova, O. (2010). Role of Technoparks in the development of innovation infrastructure of the regions, *Proceedings of the Irkutsk State Academy of Economics*, 3: 103–106

Colombo, M. G. and Delmastro, M. (2002). How effective are technology incubators?: Evidence from Italy. *Research Policy*, 31(7): 1103–1122.

Colombo, M. G., Grilli, L., and Piva, E. (2006). In search of complementary assets: The determinants of alliance formation of high-tech start-ups, *Research Policy*, Special issue commemorating the 20th Anniversary of David Teece's article, "Profiting from Innovation", *Research Policy*, 35(8): 1166–1199.

Ernst and Young (2013). Issues and Solutions: Business Incubators and Technoparks, Russian Venture Corporation, Moscow, p. 28.

Expert, R. A. (2004). Technoparks as a tool to intensify the development of production, Moscow, p. 38

Fahy, J. (2000). The resource-based view of the firm: Some stumbling-blocks on the road to understanding sustainable competitive advantage. *Journal of European Industrial Training*, 24(2/3/4): 94–104.

Freeman, J., Carroll, G. R., and Hannan, M. T. (1983). The liability of newness: Age dependence in organizational death rates. *American Sociological Review*, 48(5): 692–710.

Garnsey, E. (1998). A theory of the early growth of the firm. *Industrial and Corporate Change*, 7(3): 523–556.

Hansen, M. T., Chesbrough, H. W., Nohria, N., and Sull, D. N. (2000). Networked incubators. Hothouses of the new economy. *Harvard Business Review*, 78(5): 74–84, 199.

Hisrich, R. D. and Smilor, R. W. (1988). The university and business incubation: Technology transfer through entrepreneurial development. *The Journal of Technology Transfer*, 13(1): 14–19.

Jansson, H., Johanson, M., and Ramström, J. (2007). Institutions and business networks: A comparative analysis of the Chinese, Russian, and West European markets. *Industrial Marketing Management*, Opening the network — Bridging the IMP tradition and other research perspectives 2006 IMP Conference

Special Issue, 22nd Industrial Marketing and Purchasing Group Conference, 36(7): 955–967.

Koçak, Ö. and Can, Ö. (2014). Determinants of inter-firm networks among tenants of science technology parks. *Industrial and Corporate Change*, 23(2): 467–492.

Lechner, C. and Dowling, M. (2003). Firm networks: External relationships as sources for the growth and competitiveness of entrepreneurial firms. *Entrepreneurship & Regional Development*, 15(1): 1–26.

Ledeneva, A. V. (1998). *Russia's Economy of Favours: Blat, Networking and Informal Exchange*, Cambridge University Press. Available at: http://www.cambridge.org/us/academic/subjects/sociology/political-sociology/russias-economy-favours-blat-networking-and-informal-exchange [accessed 23 September 2014].

Lindelof, P. and Lofsten, H. (2002). Growth, management and financing of new technology-based firms — assessing value-added contributions of firms located on and off Science Parks. *Omega*, 30(3): 143–154.

Lofsten, H. and Lindelof, P. (2002). Science Parks and the growth of new technology-based firms — academic-industry links, innovation and markets. *Research Policy*, 31(6): 859–876.

Lofsten, H. and Lindelof, P. (2003). Determinants for an entrepreneurial milieu: Science Parks and business policy in growing firms. *Technovation*, 23(1): 51–64.

Lofsten, H. and Lindelof, P. (2005). R&D networks and product innovation patterns — academic and non-academic new technology-based firms on Science Parks. *Technovation*, 25(9): 1025–1037.

McAdam, M. and McAdam, R. (2008). High tech start-ups in University Science Park incubators: The relationship between the start-up's lifecycle progression and use of the incubator's resources. *Technovation*, 28(5): 277–290.

Mian, S. A. (1996a). The university business incubator: A strategy for developing new research/technology-based firms. *The Journal of High Technology Management Research*, 7(2): 191–208.

Mian, S. A. (1996b). Assessing value-added contributions of university technology business incubators to tenant firms. *Research Policy*, 25(3): 325–335.

Mian, S. A. (1997). Assessing and managing the university technology business incubator: An integrative framework. *Journal of Business Venturing*, 12: 251–285.

Oakey, R. P. (1995). *High Technology New Firms*. Paul Chapman, London.

Oakey, R. P. and Mukhtar, S.-M. (1999). United Kingdom high-technology small firms in theory and practice: A review of recent trends. *International Small Business Journal*, 17(2): 48–64.

Patton, D., Warren, L., and Bream, D. (2009). Elements that underpin high-tech business incubation processes. *The Journal of Technology Transfer*, 34(6): 621–636.

Penrose, E. T. (1995). *The Theory of the Growth of the Firm.* Oxford University Press Inc, New York.

Quintas, P., Wield, D., and Massey, D. (1992). Academic-industry links and innovation: Questioning the science park model. *Technovation*, 12(3): 161–175.

Robert D. Hisrich, Mikhail V. Grachev, (1995) "The Russian entrepreneur: Characteristics and prescriptions for success", *Journal of Managerial Psychology*, 10(2): 3–9

Rothaermel, F. T. and Thursby, M. (2005). University-incubator firm knowledge flows: Assessing their impact on incubator firm performance. *Research Policy*, 34(3): 305–320.

Sá, C. and Lee, H. (2012). Science, business, and innovation: Understanding networks in technology-based incubators. *R&D Management*, 42(3): 243–253.

Sarasvathy, S. D. (2008). *Effectuation: Elements of Entrepreneurial Expertise.* Edward Elgar Publishing Ltd, Cheltenham.

Schwartz, M. and Hornych, C. (2010). Cooperation patterns of incubator firms and the impact of incubator specialization: Empirical evidence from Germany. *Technovation*, 30(9–10): 485–495.

Scillitoe, J. L. and Chakrabarti, A. K. (2010). The role of incubator interactions in assisting new ventures. *Technovation*, 30(3): 155–167.

Siegel, D. S., Westhead, P., and Wright, M. (2003). Science parks and the performance of new technology-based firms: A review of recent U. K. evidence and an agenda for future research. *Small Business Economics*, 20(2): 177–184.

Tadviser. (2014). Technoparks in Russia, Available at: http://tadviser.ru/a/53883 [Accessed 11 September 2014].

Vaidyanathan, G. (2007). Technology parks in a developing country: The case of India. *The Journal of Technology Transfer*, 33(3): 285–299.

Vedovello, C. (1997). Science parks and university–industry interaction: Geographical proximity between the agents as a driving force. *Technovation*, 17(9): 491–502.

Welter, F. and Smallbone, D. (2006). Exploring the role of trust in entrepreneurial activity. *Entrepreneurship Theory and Practice*, 30(4): 465–475.

Westhead, P. and Storey, D. J. (1995). Links between higher education institutions and high technology firms. *Omega*, 23(4): 345–360.

Williams, D. (2011). Russia's innovation system: Reflection on the past, present and future. *International Journal of Transitions and Innovation Systems*, 1(4): 394–412.

Williams, N., Vorley, T., and Ketikidis, P. H. (2013). Economic resilience and entrepreneurship: A case study of the Thessaloniki City region. *Local Economy*, 28(4): 399–415.

Chapter 7

How Business Incubators Create a Conducive Environment for the Development of Innovative Tunisian Startups

Selma Mhamed Hichri, Zouhaïer M'chirgui and Wadid Lamine

Introduction

In the last two decades, the political establishment of business incubator as an instrument dedicated to the support, coaching and supporting young businesses has spread throughout the world. Several studies then focused in analyzing their impacts (OECD, 1999, 2015; Schwartz, 2013), including the development and growth of young companies. If the work has generally made a better understanding of their role in supporting and assisting young companies, they nevertheless remain divided on their effectiveness (Tamasy, 2007; Hackett and Delts, 2008; Schwartz, 2013). In addition, the responses are applied to experiences from developed countries (Mian et al., 2012), and the question still remains unanswered for developing countries. Indeed, studies are rare and sometimes almost non-existent.

Furthermore, the literature has emphasized the importance of the link between incubators and universities and research centers to facilitate access to knowledge, and hence to improve the performance of incubated companies (Rothaermel and Thursby, 2005). However, this literature remains rather fragmented (Siegel 2006; Rothaermel *et al.*, 2007) and focused on the European and American context (Pena, 2004; Rothaermel and Thursby, 2005; Cooper and Park, 2008; Scillitoe and Chakrabarti, 2010).

Thus, we wonder about the role of political and incubation facilities in developing countries, including both the effect of the support and the impact of knowledge sources on the growth of young firms. To fill this gap, we propose in this chapter to examine these issues by looking at the case of Tunisia. The purpose is to understand the way in which these structures are involved to promote the development and growth of young firms. Such an approach will not only assess the efficiency of the entrepreneurial instrument but also to suggest advice and recommendations to the government. The chapter will be structured as follows: first, we develop hypotheses about the determinants of the growth of young firms. Then, we describe the methodology used to test these hypotheses. Afterward, we present and discuss the results of the estimates. Finally, we conclude.

The determinants of growth in young firms

Three sets of factors likely to influence the success of a young firm are often highlighted in the literature. These are factors that are associated with the entrepreneur, the firm and the environment. They help produce predictive models for firm growth.

The impact of entrepreneur characteristics on the growth of young firms

The characteristics of the entrepreneur and firm growth are strongly linked (Barringer *et al.*, 2005) and for at least three reasons. Firstly, the founder influences their firm by bestowing it with their personality and by conveying their own values to it (Mullins, 1996). Davidsson (1989) characterized the entrepreneur's individual attributes as the overriding determinant of firm growth. Next, investors and stakeholders gauge the firm's potential and its growth by assessing its founder's attributes (Barringer *et al.*, 2005). Finally, the decision to create their firm requires variables linked to the entrepreneur's own characteristics.

There are three important factors primarily associated with entrepreneur characteristics that are likely to influence their firm's growth: human capital, past experience and the motivation of the entrepreneur.

The entrepreneur's human capital, which is often assessed by their level of education, is generally higher than that of the population as a whole (Gasse and D'armours, 2000), especially for high-value technical firms. These companies are mostly knowledge-based and gain their competitive advantage from the skills and the level of training of their founders. The latter can influence how efficiently the accomplishment of tasks is perceived which, itself, can influence the entrepreneur's vision. The level of education serves as a *proxy* for entrepreneurial skills, especially in intensive knowledge sectors such as ICT, or biotechnology (Sapienza and Grimm, 1997). A high level of education nurtures and feeds entrepreneurial abilities and therefore fosters the growth of young firms.

Hypothesis 1.a: *The growth of young firms is positively correlated with the entrepreneur's level of education.*

The level of academic education is, however, a necessary element but not sufficient on its own (Cooper and Park, 2008). The entrepreneur's previous experience is an important determinant in the success of their business (Wiklund and Shepherd, 2001) and is considered one of the most reliable factors in forecasting potential entrepreneurial performance. Managerial and entrepreneurial knowledge acquired from previous work experience largely explains success in business. This is all the more probable if the previous experience corresponds to the business activities of the firms created (Cooper *et al.*, 1994) where the entrepreneur can broaden their knowledge base on the different aspects of management (MacMillan and Day, 1987). Benefiting from previous professional experience constitutes a means of acquiring knowledge in the sector in which the promoter wants to start their business. This knowledge is less a source of business ideas than a way of minimizing risk and of building a distinct advantage (Barringer *et al.*, 2005). Business techniques are at the heart of company life. This is why Cooper and Park (2008) emphasize business experience which helps understand the reality and workings of the market. In this context, Thornhill and Amit (2003) argue that the handicap of entrepreneurs' inexperience matters in firm growth. As the firm evolves, the entrepreneur broadens and develops their knowledge and general leadership aptitudes. In other words, adopting better management methods and more promising strategies significantly influences the growth of firms (Cooper *et al.*, 1994). Consequently, entrepreneurs with previous experience are better placed to succeed in the entrepreneurial process and avoid making certain costly errors (Cooper *et al.*, 1989).

Hypothesis 1.b: *The growth of young firms is positively correlated with the entrepreneur's previous professional experience.*

Finally, the psychological factor is of no small significance in business success. The entrepreneur who succeeds is generally one with a strong desire for personal achievement. Having positive reasons, we might expect that these entrepreneurs will have greater motivation and ambition and be strongly committed to success (Pena, 2002). These motivations are further accentuated if the entrepreneur has a role model in their entourage who provides support in 'taking the plunge' and can affect the perceived desirability in entrepreneurial behavior.

Hypothesis 1.c: *The growth of young firms is positively correlated with the presence of an entrepreneurial role model in the entrepreneur's entourage.*

The impact of firm characteristics on the growth of young firms

The firm's own attributes such as its age, capital, strategic positioning, etc. constitute another group of factors likely to influence its growth.

The effect of size has been widely discussed in literature. Gibrat's research (1932) is of vital importance in this context. His model explains the dynamics of firm size and industry structure. It give rise to the famous law Gibrat or the law of proportionate effect (Law of Proportionate Effect) stating that the growth rate of a firm is independent of its original size. However, if some previous empirical studies have validated this law (Simon and Bonini, 1958; Chesher, 1979), more recent studies, incorporating populations of small sized enterprises, have rejected it (Harris and Trainor, 2005; Mata and Portugal, 2002). They lead to the conclusion that small businesses show a growth rate higher than large.

In a recent study, Fort *et al.* (2013) argue that the negative relationship between firm size and employment growth is due in fact to inadequate data. The authors reach the conclusion that the annual net employment growth average rates increase (rather than decrease) by size of business, especially for companies with fewer than 20 employees. Similarly, Fotopoulos and Giotopoulos (2010), studying a sample of Greek firms, find that Gibrat's Law is rejected for small firms and startups, while older firms appear to follow a random pattern of growth.

In addition to the size of the firm, age is also considered as another important factor in business growth. The age of the firm is usually associated with the accumulation of experience and learning. Geroski (1995) mentioned that one of the most interesting topics in business dynamics is the ability to learn. It is essential to business growth and is strongly correlated with the age of the firm or experience. Depending on the model of the selection of firms (Jovanovic, 1982), the youngest companies take time to become aware of their relative efficiency. The process of selection removes the less efficient. It is more selective in the early years of the existence of companies. Indeed, when creating, entrepreneurs are generally in a situation of incomplete information. Over time, they get to know their skills by observing their performance in a difficult environment. Those who exceed their expected gain and demonstrate a proven managerial ability are expanding their production volumes and their market share. While those who overestimated their abilities will close. Therefore, young efficient firms (not ruled out by the process of selection) are reaching the maturity with a fairly stable level of employment. The first years of the company's existence are decisive. They constitute a trial period in which the company evaluates its own performance and updates its expectations (Mata and Portugal, 2002).

As such, the age of the startup company can be considered as an indicator of the learning period. The longer it gets, the more she learns. Similarly, the amount of the initial investment (Cooper *et al.*, 1994; Wiklund, 1999) can also be an indicator of the initial size of the company. A larger amount of money as an initial investment devoted to the venture gives the entrepreneur more flexibility and protection against the unexpected. Indeed, the chances of survival rise sharply with the amount of resources allocated to start the firm. De Meza and Webb

(1987) demonstrated that firms which startup without any recourse to external financing show that they are founded on risky ventures leading to a high probability of failure.

Hypothesis 2.a: *The growth of young firms is positively correlated with their age.*

Hypothesis 2.b: *The growth of young firms is positively linked to the amount of financial resources invested when establishing the business.*

Other authors have shown that strategic position is not without significance in the survival and growth of young firms. The extent of the market (local, national and international), the number and type of customers (small businesses, public institutions, large companies) are all major determinants in business success. Nevertheless, although certain studies have underlined the risk of failure for firms adopting early international development strategies,[1] others have highlighted the importance of international development in the survival of the business. But, despite the risk of adopting a strategy for international expansion early on, finding a foreign market gives the entrepreneur greater commitment and responsibility. Indeed, internationalization constitutes an excellent school of management which tends to accelerate the learning process and assimilation of best practice. It might therefore be expected that foreign customers have a strong propensity for growth.

Hypothesis 2.c: *The growth of young firms is positively linked to engagement in international business activities.*

Furthermore, the type of customers the business caters for also constitutes another important vector for the growth of young firms. In general, newly established firms cater for a clientele made up of very small companies and individuals. The more they grow, the more the size of their customers grows. Consequently, firms that have succeeded in serving some big customers have a greater propensity to grow than others.

---

[1] A theoretical framework specifically for international new ventures was initiated by Oviatt and McDougall (1994, 2002a, 2000b, 2002, 2005), Zahra and George (2002), Knight and Cavusgil (1996, 2004) to name just a few.

Hypothesis 2.d: *The growth of young firms is positively linked to types of customers.*

The role of the incubator in the growth of young firms

The term, incubator, covers structures accommodating recently established businesses, i.e. firms already with a volume of business. According to the European Commission (1990), a business incubator is, "*a place where newly created firms are concentrated in a limited space. Its aim is to improve the chance of growth and rate of survival of these firms by providing them with a modular building with common facilities (telefax, computing facilities, etc.) as well as with managerial support and back-up services. The main emphasis is on local development and job creation*".

Incubators supply logistical support, assistance and connections to a network of technical and commercial partners. They provide a favorable environment in which firms can develop interactions and commercial and non-commercial links with centers of creativity and knowledge for mutual benefit. According to Mian (1996), the value-added contribution of incubators corresponds to the way in which the services are solicited to supply the newly created firms.

The value-added in the business incubation and support sector corresponds to the way in which training and apprenticeship programs contribute to the long-term future of the graduate companies and improve their survival rates. Business incubators regularly organize training courses for project promoters and newly established firms to ensure continuous learning on themes linked to the startup process, management and the development of firms (UNIDO, 2005) because they generally feel the need for assistance in management, accounting, finance and marketing (Rice and Matthews, 1995). Marketing assistance is particularly important in the sense that it helps entrepreneurs to better showcase their products to sell them (Rice and Matthews, 1995). According to the UNIDO definition (2005), assistance from the incubator and its network of consultants and experts will help provide firms in the process of creation and development with content relating to the marketing strategy, market research, the commercial strategy, promotional policy, the marketing plan and databases (UNIDO, 2005). Litvak and Maule (1980) showed that the most problematic commercial element is marketing. The adoption of an inefficient marketing strategy reduces the chances of success.

Similarly, the quality of management plays a significant role in the performance of young firms. It also matters in the bankruptcy of young firms (Thornhill and Amit, 2003). Several studies have highlighted that management skill deficiencies in certain aspects restrict firms' chances of survival (Gaskill *et al.*, 1993). Consequently, training and support programs are meant to improve the entrepreneur's skills so that they can manage their firm and comprehend its market. We would therefore expect these training and support programs to have a positive effect on firm growth.

Hypothesis 3.a: *The growth of young firms is positively linked to the frequency of recourse to experts and to training support offered by the business incubator.*

The incubator manager and staff constitute a primary source of social capital and access to new knowledge through the offer of support and advice services (Rice, 2002; Scillitoe and Chakrabarti, 2010). The determination and commitment of the incubator director and their team remains one of the most significant determinants of its success (OECD, 1999, p. 53). The incubator managers provide direct support by interacting on a one-to-one basis with tenant entrepreneurs. They pass on their knowledge to them and offer assistance (Rice, 2002). The frequency with which a service is used shows its usefulness and importance for young firms (Mian, 1996) and strengthens the ties between the two parties. From this angle, the intensity in how frequently the services are used involves the creation of strong links (Granovetter, 1973) conducive to the learning process and knowledge transfer, both for the firms and the incubator. The frequent interactions enable the latter to better understand young firms' needs (Hacketts and Dilts, 2004) and to better serve them. A dyadic co-production process consequently arises (Ahmed and Ingle, 2011). So, the frequent interactions form the basis for the creation of values as much for the entrepreneurs as for the incubator managers (Rice, 2002).

Hypothesis 3.b: *The growth of young firms is positively linked to the frequency of recourse to business incubator managers.*

The easy access to a network of contacts that the business incubator could offer graduate firms constitutes another important indicator of its performance (Scillitoe and Chakrabarti, 2005). This network enables graduate firms to build up contacts with relevant partners in technical, economic and institutional spheres which would not have been possible if the firm was out with the incubator. Firms with the opportunity to access sources of knowledge will have significant potential to learn from and exploit these sources and to grow. Being part of intra-company and intra-institutional networks helps entrepreneurs to find new openings, new solutions and to consequently boost the chance of survival of their firm.

In this situation, the incubator constitutes an excellent networking tool (Bøllingtoft, 2012) as it enables entrepreneurs to establish both formal and informal contacts with the different parties involved in the creation and the development of firms and to benefit from seminars and meetings organized by the incubator (McAdam and McAdam, 2008; Scillitoe and Chakrabarti, 2010). The incubator can therefore consolidate the link between the market and the entrepreneur (Smilor, 1987).

Hypothesis 3.c: *The growth of firms is positively linked to the frequency of contacts established with assistance from the business incubator.*

Universities and research centers constitute an important source of knowledge particularly in developed countries (Siegel, 2006; Fini *et al.*, 2011). Firms can access these sources by developing formal and informal links with the latter (Mian *et al.*, 2012). This allows academics to test their ideas and give entrepreneurs the chance to acquire the latest scientific knowledge.

Incubator services extend to consolidating the link with universities (Mian, 1996). Moreover, the interest in incubators is based on their potential to transfer academic results to industry. They are not simply a learning lab for entrepreneurial skills, but should be a point of convergence between academic research and industry. On the other hand, firms need technical assistance[2] enabling them to consolidate their technological and

---

[2] Technical assistance *"is designed to encourage innovation in firms in the process of starting up and technological support of SME's/SMI's. It therefore addresses the needs of innovative project promoters (IPP) and entrepreneurs wanting an idea in terms of a technological solution, a product, or a high value-added service"* (UNIDO, 2005).

scientific gains (Scillitoe and Chakrabarti, 2010). Technical assistance consists of advising and informing the entrepreneur in terms of technological monitoring, R&D, innovation, technological transfer and foresight (UNIDO, 2005). The incubator must therefore facilitate the use of university-related services (Mian, 1996). These services are related to the use of consultants and employees/interns from the university, to the university's prestigious image (Smilor, 1987), to the use of library information and databases (Smilor, 1987; Allen and Levine, 1986), to the use of laboratories (Doutriaux, 1987) IT units (Hisrich and Smilor, 1988), to access to research and development units (Allen and Levine, 1986; Smilor *et al.*, 1988; Doutriaux, 1987), to the technological transfer program (Allen and Levine, 1986; Smilor, 1987; Hisrich and Smilor, 1988; Abetti and Stuart, 1985) and to the employee training (Allen and Levine, 1986; Hisrich and Smilor, 1988). The amount of use of these types of services will prove the ability of incubators to be a bridge between academic research and industry. Consequently, locating a business incubator in the vicinity of a university establishment is important because geographical coincidence can play a facilitating role in interactions (Vedovello, 1997), the learning process and the reduction of the probability of new venture failure (Rothaermel and Thursby, 2005).

Hypothesis 3.d: *The growth of firms is positively linked to the frequency of contacts with researchers from the neighboring university.*

Hypothesis 3.e: *The growth of firms is positively linked to the frequency of employing students/interns from the neighboring university.*

Methods

First, we justify the choice of framework for analysis. Next, we present the data and the sample and finally, we describe the variables.

The case for Tunisian incubators

The Tunisian case study is significant since the majority of research on the subject focuses on the study of entrepreneurship and its 'instruments' in developed countries. This study concerns a country in transition where ventures are rather repetitive in character. Innovation is rare, incremental and the *high tech* sector is rudimentary.[3] Moreover, the *Système National d'Innovation* (National Innovation System) is weak, the firms established are fragile, the supply of key inputs for innovative activities (technical, commercial, marketing, management, etc.) suffers from serious problems and there is market failure. Given these conditions, we might expect that the spatial concentration of firms in a confined space close to a university might compensate for some of these shortcomings.

Clearly, the incubator is not a universal remedy to tackle these gaps, but it can be one instrument among others used to nurture the development of young firms and represents an alternative solution to the weaknesses in the market. The introduction of incubators has consequently become an effective resource supporting new innovative companies in Tunisia as well as for industry–university dialogue.

In accordance with public authorities' desire to encourage the creation of new firms in Tunisia, the Ministry of Industry, Energy and SME's together with the Ministry of Higher Education, Scientific Research and Technology signed a framework agreement on October 19, 1999 stipulating the introduction of business incubators in collaboration with both academia and industry. This national program to create and promote business incubators was launched by the Agency for the Promotion of Industry and Innovation (APII) and the higher education institutions concerned, particularly the Higher Institutes for Technological Studies (ISET). Its purpose is to strengthen the support process for new promoters and to develop a synergy between academia and enterprise. The academic institutions acceding to this agreement provide the APII with appropriate premises and laboratories together with the scientific and technological knowledge required. The APII is responsible for incubator management, operation and logistics.

The incubator works closely with several regional and national structures, political bodies (Governorate, delegation), financial organizations

---

[3] Exports of high-tech products are weak in comparison to all exports (4% compared to 34% and 31% for Ireland and Holland).

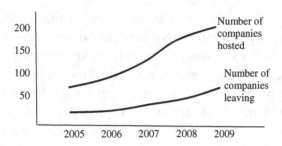

Figure 1.   Number of Firms Housed and Leaving
Source: APII.

(SICAR's,[4] the BFPME,[5] etc.), associative bodies (association of chartered accountants, chambers of commerce, etc.) and certain Ministries (such as the Ministry of Education and Training, etc.).

Figure 1 shows the evolution in the number of firms housed in these incubators as well as the number of firms leaving them.

Sample and data

The sample was drawn from a database provided by the APII of firms housed in incubators as of May 31, 2010, see Appendix A (Table A.1). We only targeted firms operating in the information and communication technology sector. This database provided information on the firm's business activities, its age and size as well as the amount initially invested. In addition, it provided the names and contact details of entrepreneurs and incubator-housed firms in the country's different Governorates. This facilitated direct contact with the entrepreneurs.

The total number of firms currently housed in the various business incubators throughout the country comes to 205.[6] We identified 106 firms

---

[4] Société d'Investissement à Capital Risque (Risk Capital Investment Companies).

[5] Banque de Financement des Petites et Moyennes Entreprises (Bank for Financing Small and Medium Enterprise).

[6] This figure corresponds to operational firms and those registered for future entry to the incubators. According to CSCE managers (Centre du Soutien à la Création d'Entreprises), the number of incubated firms comes to 186.

operating in the ICT sector. As part of our research, we targeted the region of Grand Tunis as it is a pioneering region in terms of incubation. The Grand Tunis region alone represents 26% of incubated firms and 25% of all the incubators in the country. Efforts in terms of startup and incubation are considerable compared to other Tunisian regions.

There are seven incubators based in Grand Tunis: Centre d'Innovation et de Développement at INSAT, Radès Technologie Plus, Carthage Innovation at the EPT, Manouba Tech, Manartech at ENIT (incubator non-operational), Innotech at the Borj Cedria Technology Park and the communications business incubator at the El Ghazala Technology Park. We did target other incubators based in regions known for their entrepreneurial drive and energy, namely, Sousse and Sfax. So as to give a fuller picture of business incubators, we also conducted interviews with tenant entrepreneurs in regions that were less entrepreneurial and furthest from the capital, namely, Gafsa, Tozeur and Tataouine.

We conducted 51 interviews with all the entrepreneurs based in the incubators referred to above (see annex). We excluded eight questionnaires where the firm (in the process of setting-up) and the entrepreneur were not able to give meaningful answers to our questions. In all, our sample included 43 firms established in the incubators and which were still in activity up until the time of our visit.

The survey

To gather the necessary information to test the validity of our hypotheses, we drafted a questionnaire to describe the characteristics of the entrepreneur (age, motivation, educational attainment, past experience, etc.), the firm created (age, organizational positioning, turnover, etc.) and the incubator's role in the development of the young tenant firms. This choice is primarily justified by the lack of comprehensive official databases which simultaneously take into account a set of elements that are essential and indispensable for the completion of this work. Among these elements, we stress the need to have information available on the reasons for setting up the firm, the frequency of interaction with the incubator team, the nature of relationships with other tenant firms sharing the same facility and the nature of the relationship with the university and research units.

Consequently, the framework around which the questionnaire was structured includes questions seeking to explore the characteristics of the entrepreneurs, the characteristics of the firm and the added-value of the business incubator.

Measures

The dependent variable that we consider is the variation in employment between the number of persons employed at startup and number of persons employed at the time of our survey. Firm growth is a complex phenomenon (Caschandler and Hanks, 1993; Davidsson and Wiklund, 2000) in which several variables are implicated. Delmar (1997) stresses that there is no consensus in literature on factors affecting growth. The variation of firm growth indicators over time, the process of growth itself as well as the variation in characteristics of these firms and the environment in which they evolve (Delmar *et al.*, 2003) makes studying growth difficult. Furthermore, the literature shows that there are two major trends dominating work on growth. The first trend considers growth as an independent variable and focuses more on explaining its consequences. The second trend considers it as a dependent variable and concentrates on analyzing its determinants (Cooper *et al.*, 1994). As part of our research, we approach growth according to the latter trend which, from a theoretical point of view, seems to provide meaningful elements.

According to Nègre (1987), the growth of firms corresponds to their increase in size over time. This results from increased demand for the firm's products or services. The effect of this will be increased sales and will enable the firm to acquire new factors of production (capital investment, or the creation of new jobs) to meet the additional demand.

Some studies use sales turnover to measure growth (Donckels, 1990) and tend to recognize it as the preferred indicator (Ardichvili *et al.*, 1998) and the most appropriate measure of firm growth (Davidsson and Wiklund, 2000). However, this indicator presents certain shortcomings concerning the reticence of firms to provide such data. In addition, sales turnover is sensitive to inflation and currency exchange rates (Delmar *et al.*, 2003).

Economists often use employment growth (Child, 1973; Delmar, 1997) although this measure presents numerous drawbacks (Garnsey and

Heffermann, 2005). Indeed, it is possible for firms to grow without additional hiring (Delmar, 1997), productivity improvements or the use of sub-contracting to increase production without the recruitment of additional staff. However, employment growth is highly important as it enables economic growth to be measured (Kirchoff, 1991) as well as the contribution of firms to the common good (Dunkelberg and Cooper, 1982). Furthermore, it seems to be the most appropriate measure, especially for established technological firms and newly established ones where staffing levels often grow before sales increase (Delmar *et al.*, 2003). The use of employment growth therefore appears to be the natural choice to help understand the growth of newly-created young firms.

In order to test our hypotheses, we assembled the following explanatory variables (Table 1):

The variable, *nive educ*, measures the entrepreneur's level of education. If this is up to Bac + 4 (*Baccalaureate + 4 years higher education*), the variable is coded "1", if it is Bac+4 or more, it is coded "0".

The variable, exp *p*, measures the entrepreneur's professional experience. If they possess professional experience, the variable is coded "1", if not, it is "0".

The variable, *ent fam*, indicates the presence (or not) of entrepreneurs in the entrepreneur's family or the social entourage. If they are present, the variable is coded "1" and "0" if not. These variables enable testing of hypotheses 1.a–1.c respectively.

The variable, *age*, measures the age of the firm. The variable *march* indicates the type of market the firm is in: domestic as opposed to international. If the customers are mainly located in the local market, the variable is coded "1" and if they are mainly located in the foreign market, the variable subsequently takes the value of "0".

The variable, *montdepar*, measures the amount originally invested. This takes the *neperian logarithm* of the amount of capital initially invested.

The variable, *typeclient*, indicates the firm's type of customers: small as opposed to big. If the customers are mainly small and medium enterprises, the variable is coded "1", or otherwise, "0". These variables enable testing of hypotheses 2.a–2.d, respectively.

Table 1. Summary of the Variables in this Study

	Variables	Definition and measure	Hypothesis	Predicted outcome	Reference
Dependent variables	$Y_{i,t}$	The variation between numbers of persons employed at startup and the numbers of persons employed at the time of our survey.			
Explanatory variables concerning entrepreneur characteristics	nive educ	Level of education of the entrepreneur	H.1.a	Positive	Cooper *et al.* (1994)
	exp p	Professional experience	H.1.b	Positive	Cooper *et al.* (1994); Brüderl *et al.* (1992); Cooper and Park (2008); Pena (2004); Wiklund and Shepherd (2001);
	ent fam	Presence of entrepreneurs in the family	H.1.c	Positive	Pena (2002);
Explanatory variables concerning firm characteristics	Age	Age of firm	H.2.a	Negative	Evans (1987); Papadaki and Chami (2002)
	montdepar	Amount initially invested	H.2.b	Positive	Cooper *et al.* (1994); Wiklund (1999)
	march	Type of market: serving foreign customers	H.2.c	Positive / Negative	Sapienza *et al.* (2004).
	typeclient	Type de customers: serving 'big' customers	H.2.d	Positive	Verhoef *et al.* (2009).

Explanatory variables concerning the added value of the incubator	Training and assistance: frequency of use of experts.	form	H.3.a	Positive	Gaskill et al. (1993); Fayolle et al. (2010); Pena (2004)
	Relationship with incubator managers and operators	rpep	H.3.b	Positive	Rice (2002); Scillitoe and Chakrabarti (2010); Hackett and Dilts (2004a)
	Network integration	res	H.3.c	Positive	Smilor (1987); Hackett and Dilts (2004); Rice and Matthews (1995); Scillitoe and Chakrabarti (2005; 2010).
	Frequency of contacts with university staff and research laboratories.	ulab	H.3.d	Positive	Allen and Levine (1986); Smilor et al. (1988); Doutriaux (1987); Mian (1996); Colombo and Delmastro (2002)
	Frequency of hiring students/interns from the neighboring university.	usal	H.3.e	Positive	Allen and Levine (1986); Smilor et al. (1988)

Recourse to experts and training programs offered by the business incubators (Hypothesis 3.a) is acknowledged by the variable *form* (training and assistance): Entrepreneurs must be willing to request assistance from the incubator (Rice and Matthews, 1995). The incubator's level of expertize must be considered in relation to its ability to offer technical and managerial assistance (Scillitoe and Chakrabarti, 2010) through a network of experts and coaches. However, the use of experts varies widely (Hannon, 2005). It is for this reason that we questioned our interviewees on the frequency with which they used experts and attended training courses. They had to give an answer on a scale of 1 to 5 showing that they had hardly or frequently requested services offered by experts.

Recourse to incubator managers (Hypothesis 3.b) is addressed through the variable, *rpep*, (relationship with the incubator operators): To understand the nature of the relationship with incubator managers, we tabled a question measuring the frequency of interactions with the personnel. The entrepreneur was encouraged to give an estimate ranging from 1 (never used) to 5 (once a day). The term, incubator manager, refers to those persons meant to be listening to the needs of the entrepreneurs. These persons can in turn refer to the Director as well as the operators having a key role in the incubator. This measure of the frequency of interactions is adapted to that used by Scillitoe and Chakrabarti (2010). Furthermore, Cuzin and Fayolle (2006) identified five key notions characterizing the entrepreneur/incubator link upon which support is based: the interpersonal relationship, duration, frequency of meetings, learning and access to material and non-material resources. The frequency of interactions or meetings therefore appears to be a suitable measure.

The frequency of contacts established with the help of the business incubator (Hypothesis 3.c) is tested by forming the variable, *res*, (network integration). This variable measures the degree of integration in networks through initiatives and events organized by these incubators. These events constitute an opportunity to form new relationships with investors, new promoters as well as academics and other key players involved in the startup and development of firms. The frequency of attendance at these events gives an idea of the significance of new contacts established by the entrepreneur. It also gives an indication of their ability to assemble a network of external links through the incubator. It is measured by asking the following question: "*What is the significance of contacts made through activities and events organised by the incubator?*" Our interviewee is encouraged to estimate the significance of the number of contacts made through the incubator: 1 (*barely significant*) to 5 (*very significant*). This measure of networking is adapted to that used by Buche and Scillitoe (2007) and Scillitoe and Chakrabarti (2010).

Finally, in order to form variables acknowledging the nature of the link with academic services, we questioned firms on the frequency of hiring student interns or graduate employees (Allen and Levine, 1986; Smilor *et al.*, 1988). Qualified employees are a critical resource enabling young firms to grow (Barringer *et al.*, 2005). Consequently, growth is strongly dependent on the ability of firms to attract qualified employees (Harrison and Taylor, 1997). The variable is entitled *usal* and enables Hypothesis 3.d to be tested.

Similarly, we questioned them on the frequency of informal contacts with university staff and research laboratories (Westhead and Storey, 1995; Vedovello, 1997). The entrepreneurs had to specify the degree of involvement (or use) of these services by selecting one of the options: "*no involvement*", "*occasional involvement*" and "*frequent involvement*". This measure is adapted to that used by Mian (1996). The variable is entitled *ulab* and allows Hypothesis 3.e to be tested.

Results

We used the Generalized Least Squares (GLS) to assess the effect of explanatory variables on firm growth. The results of the regression analysis are presented in Table 2. Some descriptive statistical elements are presented in Appendix B.

A review of the literature shows that there is no genuine consensus on growth determinants. Of the 12 explanatory variables tested, we found that eight variables significantly affect firm growth.

Table 2.   The Determinants of Business Growth

Emplcre	Coef.	Std. err.	t	P>|t|	[95% Conf. interval]	
Nivform	−2.53	1.46	−1.74	0.10*	−5.51	0.44
Profante	0.56	0.22	2.52	0.03**	0.12	0.99
Entrfami	1.78	1.89	0.94	0.35	−2.08	5.63
Age	0.75	0.28	2.67	0.02**	0.20	1.30
Lmontdepa	2.47	1.31	1.88	0.07*	−0.21	5.16
Typmarch	2.23	1.21	1.83	0.08*	−0.25	4.71
Typclien	0.06	0.02	2.93	0.01**	0.019	0.10
Rexpfr	−0.10	1.17	−0.09	0.93	−2.48	2.28
Rpepfr	−0.70	1.00	−0.71	0.47	−2.74	1.33
Rressa	2.34	1.28	1.82	0.08*	0.28	4.96
Ulabfr	2.16	2.14	1.01	0.32	−2.20	6.53
Usalfr	0.42	0.18	2.40	0.03**	0.08	0.77
Constant	−34.21	13.92	−2.46	0.02**	−62.63	−5.78

$N = 43$.
$F(12, 30) = 2.22$.
Prob $> F = 0.0382$.
R-squared $= 0.6811$.
Root MSE $= 5.5416$.

Variables related to the characteristics of the entrepreneur and the firm

The high level of education

The results of estimates show that a high level of education does not promote firm growth. An average level (Bac + 4 at the most) goes hand in hand with firm growth. This result shows that spending many years studying does not go in tandem with firm growth. This outcome is not consistent with work highlighting the importance of higher education on firm growth. Nevertheless, it concurs with the remarks of Cooper *et al.* (1994) emphasizing that 10 of the 17 studies that they consulted find a negative link between entrepreneurs' level of education and firm performance. Similarly, moving directly from the status of young doctor to company manager is far from easy.

Professional experience

In accordance with the results of Cooper *et al.* (1994), and those of Brüderl *et al.* (1992), previous professional experience is positively correlated to firm growth. Knowledge and skills acquired from a previous work experience largely explain business success as it helps understand how the market works (Cooper and Park, 2008). These results are entirely consistent with those of previous studies (Cooper *et al.*, 1994; Brüderl and Preisendörfer, 2000).

Opening up to international markets

As for the firm characteristics, estimates show that there is a positive relationship between firm age and growth. This result is consistent with the argument advanced by the literature, which considers this variable as an indicator of entrepreneurial learning process. It is a continuous and incremental process. That is to say what is learned during a period comes to add to what was learned in a previous period (Minniti and Bygrave, 2001). Thus, the knowledge gained during this process has an immediate self-reinforcing role in the learning process to regenerate over time. Companies that have managed to refine their strategies are those that have passed through this learning process and experiment successfully. They persisted and managed to increase their chances of survival over time (Birley and Westhead, 1990).

Similarly, the initial size of the company (Hypothesis 2b) is positively associated with business growth. This result shows that the micro-enterprise growth rate is not independent of their original size as postulated Gibrat's Law. This result is consistent with those found by Fort *et al.* (2013), for example. The initial size is thus an especially important determinant for the survival of young companies.

In contrast to 2.c and 2.d hypotheses, successful companies are those that target the local market and serving a clientele of small businesses and individuals. This result shows the vulnerability of these companies on foreign markets. Indeed, entrepreneurs who unearth a foreign customer claim that these customers are "hard" and "very demanding". In other words, the company must be able to quickly develop a culture dedicated to the international that can respond effectively to the requirements of international markets (Oviatt and McDougall, 1995). In this sense, early internationalization may be antithetical to entrepreneurial logic characterizing the starting phases.

The role of the incubator in the growth of young firms

All the entrepreneurs who participated in this study have asserted that their enterprises are widely nourished in an incubator. For this purpose, we examined the effect of services offered by the business support program on business growth. Estimates show that incubators play a very modest role in business growth. Indeed, apart from hiring students/trainees from the nearby university and the networking, the remaining variables do not contribute to the growth of companies. This is, in part, in agreement with that found by Pena (2004), Scillitoe and Chakrabarti (2010) and Fayolle *et al.* (2010), in which the incubators do not play for the development of the capital entrepreneurs.

Zghal and Mezghani (2009) have asked officials of Tunisian incubators to define their missions. The responses show that very important missions — including those related to networks (seeking new partnerships — networking, facilitating access to information, information monitoring) — are rarely mentioned (1–2 responses of 25 results). Despite this lack of awareness and experience, it seems that incubators were able to provide a network of business relationships to their tenants. This shows that companies operating in incubators are not simply juxtaposed in a designated area. There is some momentum revealing the existence of a dense social fabric in nurseries.

In fact, Fayolle *et al.* (2010) have already mentioned that the proposed training is not in harmony with the needs of the enterprises. During our interviews we observed the existence of a latent demand (Westhead and Storey, 1995) and a real need for assistance. However, according to one of the experts, the benefits are provided for "punctual missions "and "the demand is at random". This situation pushes experts to further conceive a new intervention plan and offer their services in a more proactive way.

Regarding the links with the university, our results show that only hiring employees from the nearby university contributes to the growth of emerging companies. This shows the lack of real relationships between universities and companies from incubators. This is explained in part by the weakness of scientific research in Tunisian universities and the lack of a real relationship between academia and the business. In an analysis of the Tunisian entrepreneurial context, the OECD report (2012) reported that partnerships with Tunisian universities are often limited to recruitment and hiring arrangements. These partnerships are very limited and remain "the major flaw of the Tunisian system of innovation" (Tili, 2009). For example, ISET Rades is located in an industrial area that concentrates 20% of Tunisian industry. This geographical coincidence has not received any partnership relationship with this institution of higher education (OECD, 2012). Furthermore, the Tunisian experience in the promotion of scientific knowledge from public research institutions, technological innovations in the technology parks and business incubators is still at the embryonic stage.

This result is not consistent with past work applied to the Western context (Rothaermal and Thursby, 2007). For example, in the case of Italy, Colombo and Delmastro (2002) showed that companies based in incubators grow better than their counterparts off-incubators. Indeed, they proceed better in terms of adoption of advanced technologies, ability to participate in international R&D programs and establishment of collaboration agreements, particularly with universities.

Inevitably, the support systems for entrepreneurs fit and evolve in the economic development process (Brooks, 1986). They cannot be separated from a comprehensive public policy on innovation and entrepreneurship. They depend heavily on the degree of integration of the country in the economy of knowledge and development of the national innovation system. In developed countries, the overall policies are clear and the national innovation systems are at an advanced stage (Gu, 1999). To varying degrees, these countries have managed to gather the necessary framework conditions for the development of entrepreneurial activities. The assessment of business incubators in these countries shows some effectiveness. If we use the survival rate as an indicator, Albert *et al.* (2002) emphasize the effectiveness of such structures. In fact, 85–90% of companies from incubators are still operating five years after their release. Moreover, they show a growth rate stronger than companies that were not accompanied. Aerts *et al.* (2007) highlight the effectiveness of European business incubators in promoting innovation and entrepreneurship (although they draw attention to the fact that among the 107 analyzed structures, a minority investment in tenants and provides real support).

Unquestionably, the incubation and coaching sector is suffering from the bad economy (Aert *et al.*, 2007) and put constraints on business dynamics.

Tunisia is characterized by "a system [of innovation] obviously too heavy" "immature" and "poor linkages" (Narula, 2004). Researchers, like all institutional entrepreneurs, face many pitfalls opposing their production efforts, coordination and innovation. Institutional structures are complete but they are not operational due to the lack of a clear policy on technological development, too centralized governance and disability interactional. Given all these reasons, we believe that our results are consistent with a national innovation system located in a rather primitive stage (Gu, 1999).

For incubators to become the premises of powerful entrepreneurial levers, it would be interesting to explore the way of against-cyclical: in a recession, stimulating creativity, innovation, entrepreneurship and providing better support for entrepreneurs is crucial, indeed urgent. This can be achieved in two stages: first, the government must define a clear policy on technological development. Second, we must support the business aid programs to the enterprises that had to further obey an actual adherence to entrepreneurship and entrepreneurial culture as legitimate search logic (creation of companies and jobs).

Conclusion

Today, incubators are spread around the world and have become a real industry (Albert *et al.*, 2002). In this chapter, we proposed a study on the usefulness and effectiveness of incubators as intermediary structures in the development of neophytes companies in the case of developing countries, while emphasizing their potential to mobilize university resources. This work is an extension of previous research on business incubation (Mian, 1996; Rice, 2002; Pena, 2004) and focuses on the business itself, as the unit of analysis, rather than the incubator.

It appears from our results that the success of hosted companies is essentially connected to the human capital of the entrepreneur. Specifically, an average higher level of education and previous work experience are important ingredients in endurance companies. We also draw attention to the positive effect of the initial size, organizational learning, the extent of the market and the type of clients on corporate survival. Indeed, it seems that companies that survive are those that have gone through a long process of learning and experimentation. The longer they survive, the more they learn (Pena, 2004).

It also appears from the results that the majority of variables related to the assistance of the incubator are not significant. This shows that startup businesses trying to succeed by themselves. To survive, they rely on their own organizational skills and resources. The human capital of the entrepreneur then seems a key variable for success. Therefore, governments and incubator operators' need to further strengthen human capital and organizational resources startup companies.

We therefore think that the quality of flows (essentially ISET flows) must lend itself to numerous improvements. In our opinion, we think that the incubator concept must evolve. New instruments, new methods and new approaches must be designed to make support and assistance more efficient and more operational. Similarly, it is interesting to deliberate on other methods to guarantee a flow of entrepreneurs that is both quantitatively and qualitatively more significant. In particular, we emphasize the necessity of breaking with a 'wait-and-see' approach to reach out to other academic establishments to ensure a higher level of flow. In other words, incubators must define new qualitative objectives and equip themselves with new instruments to better ensure the survival and growth of young firms.

References

Abetti, P. and Stuart, R. (1985). Entrepreneurship and technology transfer: key factors in the innovation process, In Sexton, D.L. and Smilor, R.W. (Eds.), The Art and Science of Entrepreneurship (Ballinger Publishers, Cambridge, MA).

Aerts, K., Matthyssens, P. and Vandenbempt, K. (2007). Critical role and screening practices of European business incubators. Technovation, 27: 254–267.

Ahmed, A. and Ingle, S. (2011). Relationships matter: Case study of university campus incubator. International Journal of Entrepreneurial Behavior and Research, 17(6): 626–644.

Albert, P., Bernasconi, M. and Gaynor, L. (2002). Incubators: the emergence of new industry, Research report, CERAM Sophia-Antipolis.

Allen, D. and Levine, V. (1986). Nurturing Advanced Technology Enterprises: Emerging Issues in State and Local Economic Development Policy. Prager, New York.

Ardichvili, A., Cardozo, R. N. and Gasparishvili, A. (1998). Leadership styles and management practices of Russian entrepreneurs: implications for transferability of Westerns HRD interventions. *Human Resource Development Quarterly*, 9(2): 145–155.

Barringer, R., Jones, F. and Neubaum, F. (2005). A quantitative content analysis of the characteristics of rapid-growth firms and their founders. *Journal of Business Venturing*, 20: 663–687.

Birley, S. and Westhead, P. (1990). Growth and performance contrasts between types of small firms. *Strategic Management Journal*, 11(7): 535–557.

Bollingtoft, A. (2012). The bottom-up business incubator: Leverage to networking and cooperation practices in a self-generated, entrepreneurial-enabled environment. *Technovation*, 32(5): 304–315.

Brooks, O. J. (1986). Economic development through entrepreneurship: Incubators and the incubation process. *Economic Development Review*, 4(2): 24–29.

Brüderl, J. and Preisendörfer, P. (2000). Fast-growing businesses: Empirical evidence from a German study. *International Journal of Sociology*, 30(3): 45–70.

Buche, M. W. and Scillitoe, J. L. (2007). The impact of female founders on facilitated human networking within technology incubators. *Mid-American Journal of Business*, 22(1): 59–68

Brüderl, J., Preisendörfer, P. and Ziegler, R. (1992). Survival Chances of Newly Founded Business Organizations. *American Sociological Review*, 57: 227–242.

Caschandler, G. N. and Hanks, S. H. (1993). Measuring performance of emerging businesses. *Journal of Business Venturing*, 8: 32–40.

Chesher, A. (1979). Testing the law of proportionate effect. *Journal of Industrial Economics*, 27(4): 403–411.

Colombo, M. G. and Delmastro, M. (2002). How effective are technology incubators? Evidence from Italy. *Research Policy*, 31: 1103–1122.

Cooper, A. C., Gimeno-Gascon, F. J. and Woo, C. Y. (1994). Initial human and financial capital as predictors of new venture performance. *Journal of Business Venturing*, 9(5): 371–395.

Cooper, A. C., Woo, C. Y. and Dunkelberg, W. C. (1989). Entrepreneurship and the initial size of firms. *Journal of Business Venturing*, 4: 317–332.

Cooper, S. Y. and Park, J. S. (2008). The impact of 'incubator' organizations on opportunity recognition and technology innovation in new, entrepreneurial high-technology ventures. *International Small Business Journal*, 26(1): 27–56.

Cuzin, R. and Fayolle, A. (2006). *What is the support for new venture creation?* l'Expansion Management Review, 92–97.

Davidsson, P. and Wiklund, J. (2000). Conceptual and empirical challenges in the study of firm growth'. In Sexton, D. and Landström, H. (Eds.), *The Blackwell Handbook of Entrepreneurship*. Oxford, MA: Blackwell Business.

Davidsson, P. (1989). Entrepreneurship-and after? A study of growth willingness in small Firms. *Journal of Business Venturing*, 4: 211–226.

Delmar, F. (1997). Measuring growth: Methodological considerations and empirical results. In Donckels, R. and Miettinen, A. (Eds.), *Entrepreneurship and SME Research: On its Way to the Next Millennium*. Aldershot, UK: Ashgate, pp. 199–216.

Delmar, F., Davidson, P. and Gartner, W. (2003). Arriving at the high-growth firm. *Journal of Business Venturing*, 18: 189–216.

De Meza, D. and Webb, D. C. (1987). Too much investment: a problem of asymmetric information. *The Quarterly Journal of Economics*. 102(2): 281–292.

Donckels, R. (Ed.) (1990). *Les leviers de croissance de la P.M.E.* King Baudouin Foundation, Roularta Books, Brussels.

Doutriaux, J. (1987). Growth patterns of academic entrepreneurial firms, *Journal of Business Venturing* 2: 285–297.

European Union (1990). Official journal OJ, C186-51/52, 27 July 1990.

Evans, D. S. (1987). The relationship between firm growth, size and age: estimates for 100 Manufacturing industries. *Journal of Industrial Economics*, 35: 567–581.

Fayolle, A., Basso, O. and Bouchard, V. (2010). Three levels of culture and firms' entrepreneurial orientation: A research agenda. *Entrepreneurship and Regional Development*, 22: 7–8.

Fini, R., Grimaldi, R., Simone, S. S. and Sobrero, M. (2011). Complements or substitutes? The role of universities and local context in supporting the creation of academic spin-offs. *Research Policy*, 40: 1113–1127.

Fort, T. C., Haltiwanger, J., Jarmin R. S. and Miranda, J. (2013). How firms respond to business cycles: the role of firm age and firm size. *IMF Economic Review*, 61: 520–559.

Fotopoulos, G. and Giotopoulos, I. (2010). Gibrat's law and persistence of growth in greek manufacturing. *Small Business Economics*, 35(2): 191–202.

Garnsey, E. and Heffernan, P. (2005). Growth setbacks in new firms. *Futures*, 37(7): 675–697.

Gasse, Y. and D'Amours, A. (2000). Profession: Entrepreneur: Avez-vous le profil de l'emploi? Montréal : Les Éditions Transcontinental inc. Et la Fondation de l'Entrepreneurship.

Gaskill L. R., Van Auken H. E. and Manning R. A. (1993). A factor analytic study of the perceived causes of small business failure. *Journal of Small Business Management*, 31(4): 18–30.

Geroski, P. (1995). What do we know about entry? *International Journal of Industrial Organization*, 13: 421–440.

Gibrat, R. (1932). The law of proportional effect. Feedbacks from the Academy of Science for 1932, presented by E. Jouguet March 7, pp. 843–845.

Granovetter, M. (1973). The strength of weak ties. *American Journal of Sociology*, 78(6): 213–233.

Gu, S. (1999). Concepts and methods of NIS approach in the context of less developed economies. DRUID conference, Aalborg school, Denmark.

Hackett, S. M. and Dilts, D. M. (2004). A systematic review of business incubation literature. *Journal of Technology Transfer*, 29: 55–82.

Hackett, S. M. and Dilts, D. M. (2008). Inside the black box of business incubation: Study B-scale assessment, model refinement, and incubation outcomes. *Journal of Technology Transfer*, 33: 439–471.

Hannon, P. D. (2005). incubation policy and practice: building practitioner and professional capability. *Journal of Small Business and Enterprise Development*, 12(1): 57–78.

Harris, R. and Trainor, M. (2005). Plant level analysis using the ARD: Another look at the Gibrat's law. *Scottish Journal of Political Economy*, 52(3): 492–518.

Harrison, S. and Taylor, A. D. (1997). Empirical evidence for metapopulation dynamics. In I. A. Hanski and M. E. Gilpin (eds.), *Metapopulation Biology: Ecology, Genetics, And Evolution*. Academic Press, San Diego, California, USA, pp. 27–42.

Hisrich, R. and Smilor, R. (1988). The university and business incubation: technology transfer through entrepreneurial development, *Technology Transfer* (fall), 14–19.

Jovanovic, B. (1982). Selection and evolution of the industry. *Econometrica*, 50(3): 649–670.

Kirchoff, B. A. (1991). Entrepreneur's contribution to economics. *Entrepreneurship Theory and Practice*, 16(2): 93–112.

Litvak, I. A. and Maule, C. J. (1980). Bill C-58 and the Regulation of Periodicals in Canada, *International Journal* 36: 70–90.

MacMillan, I. C. and Day, D. L. (1987). Corporate ventures into industrial markets: Dynamics of aggressive entry. *Journal of Business Venturing*, 2(1): 29–39.

Mata, J. and Portugal, P. (2002). The survival of new domestic and foreign-owned firms. *Strategic Management Journal,* 23(4): 323–343.

Mayer-Haug, K., Read, S., Brinckmann, J., Dew, N. and Grichnik, D. (2013). Entrepreneurial talent and venture performance: A meta-analytic investigation of SMEs, *Research Policy,* Elsevier, 42(6): 1251–1273.

Mcadam, M. and Mcadam, R. (2008). High tech start-ups in University Science Park incubators: The relationship between the start-ups's lifecycle progression and the use of the incubator's resources. *Technovation,* 28: 277–290.

Mian, S. (1996). The university business incubator: A strategy for developing new research/technology- Based firms. *The Journal of High Technology Management Research,* 7(2): 191–208.

Mian, S., Fayolle, A. and Lamine, W. (2012). Building sustainable regional platforms for incubating science and technology businesses: Evidence from US and French science and technology parks. *International Journal of Entrepreneurship and Innovation,* 13(4): 271–297.

Minniti, M. and Bygrave, W. (2001). A dynamic model of entrepreneurial learning. *Entrepreneurship Theory and Practice,* 25: 5–16.

Mullins, L. J. (1996). *Management and Organizational Behavior.* Prentice Hall, London.

Narula, R. (2004). Understanding absorptive capacities in an innovation systems context: Consequences for Economic and Employment Growth. DRUID Working Paper N°04-02, Aalborg School, Danemark.

Nègre, C. (1987). La croissance de l'Entreprise, Cahiers Français, n° 234: 21–25.

OECD (1999). The Incubators Worldwide, Case studies. OECD.

OECD (2012). Entrepreneuriat, PME et développement local, promouvoir l'entrepreneuriat dans les universités tunisiennes. Available at: http://www.oecd.org/fr/cfe/leed/Tunisia%20Entrepreneurship%20Skills%20Report_FINAL_FR.pdf.

OECD (2015). Policy brief: Financing SMEs and entrepreneurs. Available at: http://ifuturo.org/documentacion/Financing%20SMES%202015.pdf.

Oviatt, B. and Mcdougall, P. (1995). Global start-ups: Entrepreneurs on a worldwide stage'. *Academy of Management Executive,* 9(2): 30–44.

Papadaki, E. and Chami, B. (2002). Growth Determinants of Micro-Businesses in Canada, Ottawa: Industry Canada, Small Business Policy Branch (July). Available at: http://www.ic.gc.ca/eic/site/sbrp-rppe.nsf/eng/h_rd01522.html (Accessed on: September 28, 2010).

Pena, I. (2002), Intellectual capital and business start-up success. *Journal of Intellectual Capital*, 3(2):180–198.

Pena, I. (2004). Business incubation centers and new firm growth in the Basque country. *Small Business Economics*, 22: 223–236.

Rice, M. P. and Mattews, J. B. (1995). *Growing New Ventures, Creating New Jobs: Principles and Practices of Successful Business Incubation*. Quorum Books, Westport, CT.

Rice, M. P. (2002). Co-production of business assistance in business incubators. An exploratory study. *Journal of Business Venturing*, 17: 163–187.

Rothaermel, F. and Thursby, M. (2005). Incubator firm failure or graduation? The role of university linkages. *Research Policy*, 34: 1076–1090.

Rothaermel, F., Agung, S. and Zhang, L. (2007). University entrepreneurship: A taxonomy of the literature. *Industrial and Corporate Change*, 16(4): 691–791.

Rothaermel, F. T. and Thursby, M. (2007). The nanotech versus the biotech revolution: Sources of productivity in incumbent firm research, *Research Policy*, 36: 832–849.

Sapienza, H. J. and Grimm, C. M. (1997). Founder characteristics, start-up process, and strategy/structure variables as predictors of shortline railroad performance. *Entrepreneurship Theory and Practice*, 22(1): 5–24.

Sapienza, H. J., Parhankangas, A. and Autio, E. (2004). Knowledge relatedness and post-spinoff growth, *Journal of Business Venturing*, 19(6): 809–29.

Scillitoe, J. L. and Chakrabarti, A. K. (2005). The sources of social capital within technology incubators: The roles of historical ties and organizational facilitation. *International Journal of Learning and Intellectual Capital*, 2(4): 327–345.

Scillitoe, J. L. and Chakrabarti, A. K. (2010). The role of incubator interactions in assisting new ventures. *Technovation*, 30: 155–167.

Siegel, D. S. (Ed.) (2006). *Technology Entrepreneurship: Institutions and Agents Involved in University Technology Transfer*, Vol. 1. Edgar Elgar, London.

Simon, H. A. and Bonini, C. P. (1958). The size distribution of business firms. *American Economic Review*, 58(4): 607–617.

Smilor, R. W. (1987). Commercializing technology through new business incubators. *Research Management*, 30: 36–41.

Schwartz, M. (2013). A control group study of incubators' impact to promote firm survival. *Journal of Technology Transfer*, 38(3): 302–331.

Schwartz, M. and Hornych, C. (2010). Cooperation patterns of incubators firms and the impact of incubator specialization: Empirical evidence from Germany. *Technovation*, 30: 485–495.

Tamasy, C. (2007). Rethinking technology-oriented business incubators: developing a robust policy instrument for entrepreneurship, innovation, and regional development?. *Growth and Change*, 38(3): 460–473.

Thornhill, S. and Amit, R. (2003). learning about failure: bankruptcy, firm age and the resource-based view. *Organization Science*, 15(5): 497–509.

Tlili, A. (2009). Genèse, caractéristiques et évolution du Système National d'Innovation en Tunisie, Économie et Société, Série «Dynamique technologique et organisation», 11(6): 1031–1048.

UNIDO (2005). Capability building for catching-up. Development. United Nations Industrial Development Organization.

Vedovello, C. (1997). Science parks and university–industry interaction: geographical proximity between the agents as a driving force. *Technovation*, 17(9): 491–502.

Verhoef, P., Lemon, K. N., Parasuraman, A., Roggeveen, A., Tsiros, M. and Schlesinger, L. A. (2009). Customer experience creation: Determinants, dynamics and management strategies. *Journal of Retailing*, 85: 31–41.

Westhead, P. and Storey, D. (1995). Links between higher education institutions and high technology firms. *Omega, International Management Science*, 23(4): 345–360.

Wiklund, J. and Shepherd, D. A. (2001). Intentions and growth: The moderating role of resources and opportunities. *Academy of management Proceedings*, ENT: F1, 2001.

Wiklund, J. (1999). The sustainability of the entrepreneurial orientation performance relationship. *Entrepreneurship Theory and Practice*, 24(1): 37–48.

Zghal, R. and Mezghani, L. (2009). Le développement de l'entrepreneuriat. Rapport intermédiaire de mission, Période du 11 mars au 18 avril 2009, PMI n°686.

Appendix A

Table A.1.   Sample Composition

Surveyed incubators	Site	Hosted companies	Number of ICT companies	Number of companies interviewed
Innovation and Development Centre of the INSAT	Higher Institute of Applied Science and Technology (INSAT)	10	7	7
Rades Technology More	ISET	19	12	11
Carthage Innovation	Polytechnic School of Tunis	6	5	4
Business Incubator Communications	El Ghazala Technopole	10	10	10
Innotech technopole of Borj Cedria	Technopole of Borj Cedria	4	2	2
Soft Tech Sousse incubator	Technopole of Sousse	13	12	4
Sfax Innovation	National School of Engineers of Sfax	12	9	6
Gafsa Technology of the Future	ISET Gafsa	6	4	3
Tozeur incubator dare undertaking Djerid	ISET Tozeur	4	4	3
Tataouine Technological Innovation	Head Regional Direction of Industry Promotion Agency	1	1	1
TOTAL		80	66	51

Appendix B

Descriptive statistics

Table B.1.   Percentage of Entrepreneurs who took a Training Course Prior to Starting their Firms

Training prior to startup	%
No	18.9
Yes	81.1
Total	100.0

Table B.2.   Percentage of Entrepreneurs Linked to with Firms in the Incubator (Internal Network)

Internal network	%
No	8.2
Yes	91.8
Total	100.0

Table B.3.   Reasons for Establishing Firms

Reason for startup	Valid %	Cumulative %
Need for achievement	35.1	35.1
Commercial exploitation of research	8.1	43.2
The taste for enterprise	51.4	94.6
Following job loss	5.4	100.0
Total	100.0	

Table B.4.   Presence of an Entrepreneurial Role Model in the Family

Family business	%
No	56.7
Yes	43.3
Total	100.0

Table B.5.   Family Opinion on the Decision to Start a Business

Family opinion	%
Agree	73.5
Disagree	26.5
Total	100.0

Table B.6.   Type of Market

Type of market	%
Local	61.1
Foreign	38.9
Total	100.0

Table B.7.   Number of Products on the Market

Number of products	%	Cumulative %
A single product	22.6	22.6
2 products	9.7	32.3
3–5 products	25.8	58.1
More than 5 products	41.9	100.0
Total	100.0	

Chapter 8

A Resource-Based View of Business Incubation in South Africa with a Focus on the Selection Process

Goosain Solomon and Per Lind

Introduction

Business incubation (BI) has proved to be an effective multi-faceted small business economic development mechanism. Documented successes include: effective high value-added job creators (Abetti, 2004); job creators at a cost lower than a person on welfare (Albert *et al.*, 2002; Abetti, 2004) and return on investment of five dollars for every dollar of public funding from a taxation perspective (Abetti, 2004; Lalkaka and Shaffer, 1999).

Business incubators have also been shown to be a counter measure to unemployment (Albert *et al.*, 2002; Abetti, 2004). Colombo and Delmastro (2002) have found that incubated firms outperform similar non-incubated firms; they also access public funding more easily, and they are more growth-orientated than their non-incubated counterparts. Business incubators generate synergy and a nurturing ecosystem that provides and unlocks resources to overcome potential market failure of the incubatees (Bøllingtoft and Ulhøi, 2005). Therefore, depending on the specific objectives, business incubators may be used as an added mechanism for small business development by various actors such as government, universities and industry, albeit for different objectives. Even though the type of

213

projects incubated vary according to the different contexts and objectives of the incubators (Etzkowitz *et al.*, 2005), there is opportunity for synergistic collaboration by the various stakeholders in the BI domain.

A significant body of research on BI has been developed since the mid-1980s with limited research on the incubation process. Solomon and Hough (2008) in their study of 317 peer reviewed journal articles found that less than 1% of the articles reviewed addressed the BI process. Other areas of focus included incubation configuration, entrepreneurship, knowledge, economic development and impact studies. Better understanding of the incubation process is required (Hackett and Dilts, 2004b) and Hackett and Dilts (2004a) propose building and testing of new predictive process theories.

In South Africa, BI is under-researched and based on a pilot study during the initial exploration of this study the key issue raised was finding the right caliber of incubatee. Among the issues raised was that incubatees lacked initiative, displayed a culture of entitlement and expected things to be done on their behalf. These issues suggest a lack of co-creation and entrepreneurial orientation from the incubatees which strongly suggests that the incubatee selection process (SP) was not effective. It cannot be expected that incubatees should have excellent management skills; that is one of the reasons why they need to be incubated. Based on the strategy and characteristics of the incubator, the relevant qualifications, experience and incubatee characteristics should be determined during the SP. More importantly, incubatees should at least demonstrate an appropriate attitude towards being proactive and cooperative in terms of acquiring and developing the deficient resources in the form of knowledge and skills required. Ineffective incubatee selection will obviously have a negative impact on the efficacy of BI and ultimately on the projects selected for incubation. It is therefore important to better understand the SP which forms the focus of this study.

In the South African small business context, subsequent to the political transformation in South Africa of 1994, the then newly elected democratic government developed a National Strategy for the Development and Promotion of Small Business in order to create an enabling environment for Small, Micro and Medium Enterprise (SMME) growth (Department of Trade and Industry, 1995). The small business sector was identified as a priority for job creation, as well as a means of transferring equity to disenfranchised communities by facilitating participation of previously disadvantaged communities into the formal economy, as a means to address economic imbalances. Institutional support was developed to facilitate SMME growth, but the institutional support suffered from a number of weaknesses which included uneven distribution of services, limited outreach to SMMEs, cumbersome administration, and discontinuity of programs as well as the need for development of trust (Berry *et al.*, 2002). Large numbers of emerging and established small enterprises were unaware of support institutions (Orford *et al.*, 2004).

The small business sector has been under the auspices of the Small Enterprise Development Agency (SEDA), an agency of the Department of Trade and Industry that has always been subjected to changes and transformations over the last two decades. There was an increase in the number of small business support agencies and programs. However, these initiatives suffered from weaknesses and limitations such as lack of cooperation and therefore duplication, lack of depth of understanding and professionalism amongst support staff (Department of Trade and Industry, 2004). During 2014, a ministry for small business was established which underlines the relative importance of small business development in South Africa.

With the successes reported from BI elsewhere in the world BI was introduced as another mechanism for small business development in South Africa. The BI foundation was laid in the year 2000 when the Department of Trade and Industry and the Department of Science and Technology in conjunction with the European Union established the GODISA trust to create a BI framework (Ramluckan and Thomas, 2011). Therefore, BI as a mechanism for small business development is relatively young in South Africa. In view of the novelty of BI, it can be expected that there would be a lack of experience in the application of BI processes in South Africa compared with countries where BI is at an advanced stage. During 2006, SEDA established the Seda Technology Programme (STP) which oversees the BI in South Africa. The focus of STP was to enhance entrepreneurship, promote and improve quality, performance, productivity and competitiveness in small enterprises and reduce the failure rate of small businesses (SEDA, 2015).

The purpose of this chapter is first to improve understanding of the SP by conceptualizing it from a resource-based view (RBV), and second to make a data-driven contribution towards a more effective and efficient SP and thereby to the BI process itself. The BI process generally consists of four sub-processes; *Selection,* the focus of this chapter, refers to activities that result in incubatees being contracted to incubation; *Business* support refers to activities addressing resource deficiencies, which should preferably be co-produced episodically or continually, either incubatee- or incubator-initiated (Rice, 2002); *Mediation* refers to facilitating networks between incubatees and external parties (Bergek and Norrman, 2008) to build social capital and *Graduation* refers to the exit of the incubatee from the incubation program.

By definition, the BI process concerns growing and/or developing a fledgling enterprise from its present state to a preferred state where the enterprise is self-sustainable and able to compete in a dynamic environment by providing required resources and business support services. Barney (1991) states that a firm's ability to compete is underpinned by appropriate resources astutely configured. Barney further adds that competitive advantage is attainable with heterogeneous resources that are valuable, rare, inimitable and non-substitutable (VRIN). From a RBV perspective, a primary function of business incubators is to increase the resource base of the incubatees. RBV of the firm is a concept rooted in Penrose's (1980) definition of a firm as a bundle of resources. RBV suggests an internal evaluation of the firm's potential based on its resources in order to engage opportunities in the external environment.

It is argued that, consistent with RBV logic, BI primarily concerns the acquisition and development of resources to grow the resource base of fledgling enterprises towards improved competitiveness. In addition, the selection of incubatees is the process that determines the fit between the resource capabilities of incubator management and the resource deficiencies of potential incubatees. It stands to reason that the incubator management should have access to a higher level of the resources found to be deficient in the resource base of the potential incubatee. From an incubatee perspective, a negative resource gradient is meant that the resource level of the incubator is higher than the resource base of the incubatee. A negative resource gradient is necessary for a positive incubation outcome. Positive incubation outcome implies that a fledgling firm during incubation has undergone business growth from a present unpreferred state to a preferred state which is more competitive based on its developed base of resources.

Business growth is a complex issue (Delmar *et al.*, 2003) and to assess growth of small business it is important to understand what is meant by the "growth" referred to (Lind, 2012). In this study, firm growth is interpreted as a net positive increase in the effective resource base of a firm. It is useful to employ theoretical or conceptual models in order to understand and develop perspective and insight of growth of an enterprise. The resource-based, motivation, strategic and resource configuration theories are such models (Gupta *et al.*, 2013). Theories or models of the firm are but representations of reality, while no single theory can explain everything about a firm (Grant, 1991) their usefulness may be enhanced with integration of the advances made due to extended research of the theory. The three aspects: the SP, a resource-based assessment model and incubator-specific characteristics form the conceptual framework of this study and are presented as follows. This is followed by the methodology, the findings, a discussion on the findings, conclusions and recommendations.

The Selection Process (SP)

The SP is a critical aspect of the incubation process. Hackett and Diltz (2004) postulate that business incubation performance (BIP) is dependent on the SP, monitoring and business assistance intensity (M&BAI), and resource munificence (RM) together with contextual factors such as the political context. Selection refers to the process determining the ventures accepted for incubation (Bergek and Norrman, 2008) based on incubator-specific criteria (Lumpkin and Ireland, 1988). Selection is an important aspect of the BI process (Lumpkin and Ireland, 1988; Merrifield, 1987; Kuratko and LaFollette, 1987) as it determines the degree of success of incubation. An effective SP highlights the critical areas of need of the incubatees that must be strengthened in order for the firms to be successful. Mian (1996) found that tenants from well selected technology-based firms, reported positively to value-added incubatees by universities. Thus, selection is the process of matching incubatees with the incubator, based on determining the appropriate resource gradient between them.

The criteria for selection seem to be primarily focused on the incuba-tee. Lumpkin and Ireland (1988) argue that critical success factors (CSFs) are necessary to ensure success and conversely those factors that would reduce project failure be used for selection. In general, an effective SP is such a factor. More specifically, Lumpkin and Ireland, (1988) consider the market, incubatee team characteristics, financials and incubator character-istics as CSFs for the SP. Aerts *et al.* (2007) suggest that selection strategies that are well-balanced and consider a wide range and diversified sets of criteria will impact positively on project failure. As incubators evolve through the different stages of its lifecycle learning and experience accu-mulates therefore the selection strategies should be adapted accordingly (Allen and McCluskey, 1990). In addition, from the literature, the dimen-sions found to be most influential on the selection component of BI are incubator type and characteristics (Smilor 1987; Allen and McCluskey, 1990; Bøllingtoft and Ullhøi, 2005) stage in the lifecycle of the incubator (Allen and McCluskey, 1990), incubator objectives (Hannon, 2004), and CSFs of the incubator and the incubatee (Lumpkin and Ireland, 1988), illustrated in Figure 1.

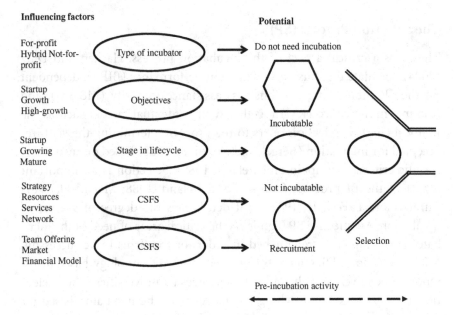

Figure 1.   Conceptual Map of the Selection Process

Figure 1 shows the primary influencing factors to the SP to be the type and characteristics of the incubator, the objectives of the incubator, the stage in the lifecycle of the incubator and CSFs for the incubator and the potential incubatee. The figure also shows that three categories of applicants for incubation are possible: (1) those that cannot be helped through incubation because of too large a resource gradient due to below threshold resource levels; (2) hold promise but need incubation because of resource gaps as identified in an effective screening process, an appropriate resource gradient and (3) those that do not need incubation because the resource gradient is insufficient or even positive (Hackett and Dilts, 2004b).

From the SP in Figure 1, a resource assessment framework is required to assess the incubatee as well as to determine the resource capability of the incubator based on the incubator type and characteristics. It would be difficult to assess growth and development as well as the resource gap without set criteria against which incubatees are benchmarked, (Smilor and Gill, 1986). To this end, a resource-based capability matrix for strategic assessment of incubatees and incubators is discussed, followed by a discussion concerning the incubator type and characteristics.

Resource-based assessment model

The model developed is rooted in theories emanating from the resource-based view of defining a firm. There are different levels at which firms operate in an industry, based on their strategic intent. When the advances in RBV research from the literature are integrated, a useful matrix evolves and is proposed in Figure 2 as the RBV Competitive Capability Matrix. From the RBV perspective, fledgling new firms entering the market operate at the threshold level of resources shown as A in Figure 2, and it can be assumed that these enterprises initially function in survival mode. How the firm manages its resources provides it with potential competitive advantage to deliver preferred customer value and thereby gain traction in the market (Wernerfelt, 1984; Barney, 1991; Peteraf, 1993).

If a firm manages such that it owns resources with attributes that are VRIN the firm can generate value which other firms are not able to use (Barney, 1991) and will have a competitive advantage for a period of time. Firms that have acquired a resource base that has the VRIN attributes are

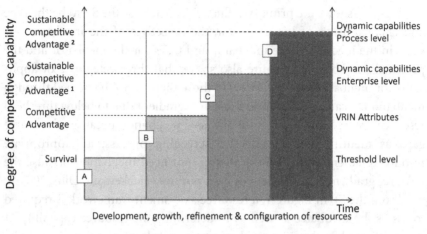

Figure 2.   RBV Competitive Capability Matrix

[1] At this level of sustainable competitive advantage, the level of analysis for competitive advantage is the organization.

[2] At this level of sustainable competitive advantage, the level of analysis is much deeper than the organization it is at the process, routine and configuration level.

Source: Adapted from Barney (1991), Eisenhardt and Martin (1991) and Ray *et al.* (2004).

able to attain a competitive advantage and thereby acquire rents on their resources that other firms that lack resources with VRIN attributes are not able to. These firms are at the VRIN attribute level of resources shown as B in Figure 2. Over time the competitive advantage will be eroded primarily due to innovative responses by competitors in the industry. Therefore, competitive advantage is not enough, and needs to be sustainable.

Sustainable competitive advantage (SCA) is driven by more than owning resources with VRIN attributes. SCA requires a dynamic response to the dynamism in the environment. The agility to respond to sudden market changes is an important competitive advantage to small firms (Lind, 2012). Eisenhardt and Martin (2000) propose that firms should acquire dynamic capability to respond to rapidly changing markets. They define dynamic capability as "the organizational and strategic routines by which firms achieve new resource configurations" (Eisenhardt and Martin, 2000, p. 1107), which is more than owning resources with VRIN attributes. It implies processes and routines of the firm that continually reconfigure resources with VRIN attributes in response to market evolution, maintaining and sustaining the firm's competitive advantage. This level of activity is shown as C in Figure 2, where dynamic capabilities yield SCA on aggregate at enterprise level.

Firm level performance can be assumed to be an aggregation of all business process level performance, whereas net positive performance at firm level does not imply net positive performance for every activity at business process and routine level. Some of the technological processes or routines employed might not be as effective and/or efficient, and then the management has to focus on the specific technologies, processes or routines to improve their level of competitiveness. Attainment of this level of competitive capability indicated on the Degree of competitive capability axis, as SCA^2 in Figure 2, according to Ray *et al.* (2004) is to focus at the level of routines and business process and maximize the opportunity for competitive advantage to be generated from routines and business processes. It might require focusing on core competencies and outsourcing non-core competencies to suppliers who specialize in that in order to improve competitiveness.

Competence in developing sustainable competitiveness refers to the ability to assess resources and capabilities in relation to competition, and to leverage advantage by configuring resources and capabilities to exploit opportunities (Grant, 1991). In the context of this discussion, resource configuration and routines must be approached from a small business perspective and targeted at the position the business finds itself in the supply or value chain with a limited degree of complexity, and limited strategic analytical skills (Rangone, 1999).

The RBV Competitive Capability Matrix as a framework may be useful in assessing and positioning the potential incubatee, and also to assess the progress made with the incubation process over time. The idea of the incubation program is to assist incubatees with growing their resource baseline at the point of entry into the incubation program to as far up the competitive capability axis as possible. The further the incubatee moves from the threshold level of competitive advantage, the more sustainable the business should be. These shifts are not easy to attain; the reality of failure of small businesses bear testimony, as Headd and Kirchhof (2009) found the survival rate of single establishment firms over a 10-year period (1992–2002) in the USA at just over 40%. In South Africa, 1.96 million closed corporations (a proxy for a small business) registered during the period 2000–2012 and 1.56 million deregistered and/or liquidated, (Solomon *et al.*, 2013).

Thus, BI is a complex process that requires specific and complementary suites of resources to develop and grow the incubated enterprises from their entry reference point to enterprises with the dynamic capabilities to sustainably compete in their chosen industry after their incubation period over time. As mentioned earlier, the resource development capability of the incubator has to be greater than the resource base level of the incubatees. Inability of incubator management to respond positively to any resource deficiency of incubatees will impact negatively on trust, and ultimately on the incubatee–incubator relationship. This requires alignment of incubators with the stage of development and nature of projects accepted. Based on the understanding of the objectives of the incubation process, there follows a conceptual development discussion about specificity of incubator characteristics.

Incubator characteristics

Incubator characteristics are important for the SP because it determines the type of incubatees to be selected and is influenced by four factors briefly discussed as follows. These factors are classification, objectives, position in the lifecycle of the incubator and CSFs.

Classification of incubators

Smilor (1987) classified business incubators into two main categories either for-profit or not-for-profit. Since the study concerns public business incubators the focus will be on the latter of the categories. Public incubators are intended for public good and therefore also funded with public money.

Classification of incubators determines the objectives of the incubator, the style, role and function of the management as well as the level and degree of sophistication with regard to networking activities. It also influences the SP. Public incubators selection criteria are influenced by funder's objectives, (Lumpkin and Ireland, 1988) which may be economic, social and/or political by nature. In the case of South Africa, small enterprise creation and job creation are key performance indica-tors (KPIs), especially for the designated groups. Designated groups are defined as previously disadvantaged, women, youth (18–35 years of age) and the disabled. These are the groups who were disenfranchised in the pre-1994 era.

Objectives

The primary objective concerns providing business support and conse-quently as highlighted earlier, contribute to employment generation, stimulate economies and rejuvenate industrial zones. Business incubator objectives can be divided into strategic objectives and stakeholder objec-tives. These objectives are briefly explored as follows.

Hannon (2004) proposes three strategic objectives for incubators: germination, incubation and acceleration. Germination refers to bringing new ventures into existence not necessarily with growth ambition, while incubation refers to supporting new and existing ventures to grow and acceleration concerns accelerating the growth of ventures with high-growth potential. Each of these objectives has different risk profiles and specific resource implications and they also require specific skill sets and different management approaches (Hannon, 2004).

Stakeholders, especially if they are primary sponsors of incubators or projects, have potential to influence objectives, (Lee and Osteryoung, 2004). They link the KPIs of business incubators they support to their agendas (Lumpkin and Ireland, 1988). If the government's concern is about starting businesses and job creation, the number of enterprises started and jobs created should reflect as KPIs. These influences may be counterproductive to the BI process, because misalignment between pri-mary and secondary objectives creates tension for incubator manage-ment. The management may then not necessarily act in the best interest of the BI. Starting enterprises and creating jobs may then become more important than improving productivity and competitiveness of incuba-tees compromising on effective selection of appropriate incubatees. Effective and efficient incubation requires alignment between the BI process and the strategic objectives of the incubator (Lumpkin and Ireland, 1988).

Position in incubator lifecycle

Factors influencing selection based on incubator lifecycle position are determined as business incubators evolve through different stages of their lifecycle and selection strategies have to be adapted accordingly (Allen and McCluskey, 1990). The business incubator lifecycle spans three distinct stages, each with its own identifiable characteristics. Allen and McCluskey (1990) refer to these stages as startup, business development and maturity. The "startup" is characterized by managing the real estate issues and attracting tenants. This is also when the incubator must become known in its region in order to gain traction in the market. The "business development" stage is when the incubator breaks even the focus then shifts more to business development stage and the management's primary activity will be to nurture the businesses. When the incubator reaches this stage, it has developed legitimacy in the market. The "maturity" stage is characterized by a demand for space in the incubator outstripping supplies, and the issues around increasing throughput, entrance and exit policies receive high priority (Allen and McCluskey, 1990). Peters *et al.* (2004) found that incubators learn the needs of tenants as they grow.

Owing to learning and experience developed over time, the age of the incubator is a significant differentiator in quality business service in the business incubator industry (Allen and McCluskey, 1990). In addition, incubation management plays a significant role in the performance of BI (Albert *et al.*, 2002) and by implication, incubator management must be able to adapt to the management roles required throughout the lifecycle of a business incubator and adapt their selection policies accordingly in order to underpin incubatee and incubator success. It can be understood that relative competence of the incubator management in small business development is a CSF for incubation.

Critical Success Factors (CSFs)

A CSF approach is a comprehensive approach to identify factors critical to the success of the firm. It is defined as internal or external factors sufficiently significant that they require special attention (Dickinson *et al.*, 1984). CSFs can be both positive factors that need to be reinforced and negative factors to be eliminated.

A distinction is made between the factors deemed necessary and sufficient for the success of a small business and the factors deemed necessary and sufficient for the success of the business incubator. It is reasonable to assume that the probability of a successful BI process will be enhanced if the requirements for success of incubatees as well as the requirements for success of the business incubator are met. Furthermore, understanding the difference and relationship between the success factors for a business incubator and the success factors for a small business will assist in profiling clients for selection, enhancing understanding of the capabilities of the business incubator, managing resources and finally focusing the effort in supporting and/or developing the businesses admitted to the incubation program.

Critical success factors for business incubators

Business incubators are also businesses and there will be some commonality between success factors for a small business and success factors for an incubator. Lee and Osteryoung (2004) developed a broad framework of success factors for business incubators which include the goals, resources (physical and human), services and the network program. In the South African context, Buys and Mbewana (2007) found access to expertize and facilities of science and technology, funding, quality of entrepreneurs and management, stakeholders, government policies, sustainability and networking to be important factors for success of incubators.

CSFs for incubatees

In their study, Lumpkin and Ireland (1988) found 85% of the cases CSFs were considered for screening incubatees, and suggests that CSFs be used by business incubators in selecting viable projects. From the literature, CSFs proposed for selection of incubatees are:

1. Attractive markets which are characterized by groups of homogeneous customers where premium and sustainable revenues are realizable and verifiable (Timmons and Spinelli, 2007);

2. Unique value propositions (Dickinson *et al.*, 1984), with preference over what is available in the market (Katz and Green, 2014);

3. A viable financial model (Lumpkin and Ireland, 1988), where innovation drives the optimization between value, price and cost, (Hoopes *et al.*, 2003). This should preferably be from an added value perspective especially in developing countries which will require closer engagement in dialogue with customers (Lind, 2012) and

4. Competent management, (Buys and Mbewana, 2007). Competent management requires incubatees to show potential for business management and entrepreneurial management competencies. Business management competencies refer to business functional competencies such as marketing, finance, operations and human resource. Entrepreneurial management requires problem solving, communication, as well as decision-making skills (Timmons and Spinelli, 2007). Cognizance must be taken that entrepreneurial orientation is an antecedent for entrepreneurial activity (Frese and De Kruif, 2000).

Methods

The research was conducted on public business incubators in South Africa. All the business incubators studied are supported in various degrees by public funding provided by SEDA. SEDA has a technology program, (STP), responsible for managing BI. To better understand the SP, the dialogue between the incubator management and the incubatees was empirically explored since they represent the most appropriate sources of data.

Initially, an attempt was made to survey the population of incubatees using a self-administered questionnaire. A very low response rate (in most cases, no responses) and responses of low quality were experienced. Reasons for the low response rate and quality of responses were investigated and some of the causes identified were logistics, low literacy levels, and cultural issues. In the case of the cultural issues, high power distance, which refers to the perception of inequality among people (Hofstede, 1993) and paternalism were identified as influences to the low quality of responses. Incubatees felt they needed approval from the incubator managers for their responses and thought that they had to show-case incubator management in a good light, by simply ticking the high scoring boxes on the Likert scales in the questionnaires. Therefore, an alternative strategy was employed. Face-to-face semi-structured interviews with a smaller sample of incubatees proved successful.

Two incubators had been in operation for less than one year and were removed from the original list of 26 incubators and incubation centers. Two incubators had more than one center and were purposefully selected for inclusion. Four of the incubator manager interviews were disrupted by operational issues and one of the incubators did not yet have any incubatees owing to lengthy processes of starting and registering businesses specific to the particular industry.

Around 31 interviews were held with various members of incubator management and administrative staff nationally, 18 of which were held with incubator managers or members of the management that had a strategic influence on the incubation process; these interviews were deemed useful for this study. The data was captured on questionnaires. The data was both qualitative and quantitative in nature. A quota sample of three incubatees from each of the incubators was requested from the incubator management for selection. The criteria given to the incubator management for the three incubatees were that they must constitute an above-average an average, and a below-average performing incubatee that had preferably been incubated for at least a year. Average was explained as being specific to the incubator and not a national average. The data was collected using semi-structured interviews from 18 public business incubator managers or management team members with strategic influence, and 42 incubatees. The data collected from the incubatees was primarily of a qualitative nature, using semi-structured interviews which were audio-recorded and transcribed. From the incubator management, the data was both quantitative and qualitative and was captured on a questionnaire. Field notes were taken during the interviews, and observations were noted. The qualitative data was analyzed using a content analysis technique manually and with the assistance of the Atlas.ti7 program. Quantitative analysis is limited to descriptive statistics, means and modes.

Findings

In general, most of the incubator managers had a fairly good idea of the quality of incubatees they would prefer to work with. The contexts in which incubators operated were not in all cases supportive of their expectations and in some cases compromised effective SPs. The nature and context of local conditions are diverse, and the degree of diversity varies from incubator to incubator. Local contexts are influenced by many factors ranging from distance to public transport to nature of power relations of local communities. In addition, the concepts of productivity and competitiveness did not appear to be foremost on the agenda of most of the incubators, which raises questions about the focus of public incubation. Following are the findings from the perspectives of the incubator management and the incubatees respectively.

Incubator management perspective

The following findings are based on the data collected from the interviews held with the incubator managers pertaining to the SP. Qualitative as well as quantitative data was collected, where possible, some basic statistic calculations were performed, primarily ranking and means. Incubator management represents the supply side of BI and the issues of concern were the expectations of incubator management, key problems experienced and occupation and funding issues. The findings concerning these issues are dealt with as follows.

Incubator management expectations

Responses from incubator managers to the request: "Please rank in order of priority which criterion has the highest influence on selection of incubatees" responses were indicated on a 5-point Likert scale presented in Table 1, 1 representing the highest influence and 5 representing the lowest.

Table 1. Responses to Selection Criteria

Criteria	Mean
The quality of the potential incubatee or team	2.2
The availability and stage of development of a unique product and/or service	2.8
The availability of a market (growing)	2.9
The ability of the potential incubatee to compete in the industry	3.2
The profitability potential of the opportunity	3.8

Note: $n = 17$.

Table 2.   Ranking of Qualities for Assessment of Incubatee based on the Mean

Qualities	Mean
Entrepreneurial orientation (innovative, risk taking, pro-activeness)	1.6
Entrepreneurial management (problem solving, negotiating, ext-relations)	2.9
Leadership competence (ability to influence behavior of others)	3.4
Technical competence	3.5
Business management competence	3.6

Note: n = 17.

The incubator managers were also asked to "Please rank from 1–5 in order of importance the qualities listed below with respect to the assessment of the quality of incubatee". The ranking, based on the responses from the incubator managers is presented in Table 2, where 1 represents the highest priority and 5 represents the lowest priority.

Incubator managers' experiences of key problems

The idea was to understand the most frequently occurring type of problems hampering the incubation process and that the incubator management had to deal with. To this end, the incubator managers were asked: "What would you describe as the three most frequent problems faced by the incubator in the incubation process, in order of priority?"

The data for this category was qualitative. To try and understand the source of the problems, the items listed were classified and sorted into the categories as shown in Table 3.

The vast majority of the issues raised by the incubator management could be linked to weaknesses of the incubatees in one of the three categories listed in Table 4. For example, in terms of attitude, "Lack of focus" or "Abuse of machinery & equipment" were mentioned, for knowledge "lack understanding of the business process" or "confusion of concepts" were mentioned. In terms of skills, "Lack of business skills" would be an example of the issues raised. The most frequent problems raised were linked to incubatee competence, presented in Table 4.

Table 4 shows that according to the incubator managers the primary source of all frequent problems was the competence of the incubatees

Table 3. Representation of the Categories of Problems Raised

Incubatee competence issues	1
Incubation process issues	2
Stakeholder issues	3
Business Market issues	4
Industry context issues	5
Resource issues	6
Infrastructure issues	7
Social context issues	8

Table 4. Representing Three Most Frequent Problems in Order of Priority

Most frequent problems raised	Rank
Incubatee competency issues, attitude	1
Incubatee competency issues, knowledge	2
Incubatee competency issues, skill	3

selected. This finding supports the initial pilot study which also suggested weakness in the SP.

It was also important to understand the nature of the most significant problems. The incubator managers were asked: "What would you describe as the three most significant problems identified during the incubation process?" The significance of the problem was explained to the incubator managers as relating to the problems that had the most significant hampering effect on the incubation process, as opposed to daily operating issues, presented in Table 5.

Similar to the frequent problems, the data for this category was qualitative. The items were also listed and grouped into various categories to understand the source of the problems raised. Table 5 shows that according to the incubator managers, the most significant problems related to resources of which funding was mentioned the most. This was followed by problems related to incubation process issues and incubatees for example issues raised as significant problems included: "Targets, KPIs were linked

Table 5. Representing Three most Significant Problems
in Order of Priority

Most significant problems raised	Rank
Resource issues (primarily funding)	1
Incubator process & incubatee quality issues	2
Business and market access issues	3

to funding", "Graduation and post incubation" and "Lack of understanding of technical training to staff of incubatee". The third category of problems was found to be business and market access related, the issues raised included, "Access to markets" and "Counterfeit products entering our markets".

Occupation and funding

Average occupancy figures were difficult to finalize because figures were not up to date, and occupancy rates fluctuated over short periods of time during any year as incubatees left and new ones were taken up. The available statistics showed that incubator occupancy ranged between 50% and 85%. Only in the case of agri-incubators, occupancy was 100% because incubatees had their own land, a requirement for agri-incubation. One agri-incubator rented land to the incubatees. They had a turn-over problem, the incubatees could not leave the incubator at graduation, because acquisition of land is expensive and the time period was too short for the incubatees to build up enough capital to purchase land. So, the incubator was in a difficult situation with respect to turnover of incubatees. They also had a significant number of off-incubator or virtual clients to make up the required KPIs.

As for funding, incubator managers spend a significant amount of their time on fund raising. On the question of time spent for raising funds, incubator managers' responses ranged from 30% to 80% of their time on raising funds for their incubator. This is worrying, since they should be engaged in managing the incubation process, of which funding is not a part, especially for public incubators. One incubator manager stated that in spite of meeting and exceeding the KPIs for the previous year, the funding for the incubator was subsequently reduced. The reason(s) for the reduction in funding was not known at the time.

Incubatees' perspective

From the incubatees' side, only qualitative data was collected. The incubatees represent the demand side of the BI process, and of primary concern were the positive incubation experiences, selection issues of incubatees and negative incubation experiences. Incubatees were asked to relate their positive incubation, selection and negative incubation experiences. Some of the responses are tabulated in Table 6 followed by a brief analysis of the responses.

Table 6.   Responses from Incubatees for Positive Incubation Experiences, Selection and Negative Incubation Experiences, Respectively

Reference	Incubatee responses reflecting positive experiences
A1	"Technical support, financial support and the fact that opportunities, we've got more access to, if I can say access, to opportunities and more exposure".
A2	"Now people get more information about business, skill development, approaches how to source finance, how to market your business, how to do business the right way".
A3	"They take you in detail and some of the things that I thought no, this I can't do, you know its compliance".
A4	"Improving manufacturing skills".
A5	"Facilitating the manner in which we will get access to finance so that we can have the machinery".
A6	"I think the resources. When I say resources, I mean having an office space. I know most people would actually look down at this fact but having a decent office space actually adds to the credibility of the business itself".
A7	"They actually bring to your attention the things that you tend to overlook on a daily basis and you think they are not important ... time management. The first coaching programme that the Incubator put me on, really it changed the way I managed my time, the way I do things".
A8	"The facilities are good, you know, the network's stable, the print facilities, the rent, secure environment, we haven't had any hassles".

(Continued)

Table 6.   (*Continued*)

Reference	Incubatee responses reflecting the SP.
B1	"They identified my requirements, business skills, learn more about manufacturing, increase my knowledge in marketing, get more information about funding".
B2	"They say they will take a well performing company, a middle one and a struggling one. I'm not sure where do I feature, but I can evaluate myself".
B3	"They did have space but they would rather give that space to a different set of skills ... but upon me showing them the samples of my work, they changed their mind".
B4	"I don't think they find anything. Nobody told me... You see the mentor he will always ask you about what your turnover will be".
B5	"... this is now my understanding, in order for the incubator to be up and running and also receiving the funds they receive, therefore they need the incubatees that they can show ... ".

Reference	Incubatee responses reflecting negative experiences
C1	"I try to make the point that meetings are limited. Because sometimes you will find that it's meetings and meetings and you can't cope with your business activities properly".
C2	"It is the time. Time, time, time ... access to the centre, to the work ...".
C3	"...when they bring in the incubatees, I think that they must be categorised...".
C4	"...the biggest disadvantage is working with resources that are not... working properly. That's not operational. Resources that's not operational".
C5	"I would say the technology is not up to date. I think they still working – with paraffin not really, but if you can put it that way and it's still outdated. But, we struggle with the old *technology* and we getting some bad *outputs*. We have improved a lot now because we have worked on ...".
C6	"Ja, you see. Everyone who comes here, okay, let me see your business plan. Okay, this is what you have? You can put that aside, let's work on a new business plan. You see, so...".
C7	"I have only one machine ... that I think is a big problem. So I can't maybe, if we have a lot of *work*, I can't hire other person ...".
C8	"There's no marketing, always I was asking them about marketing, they say, no, you must market yourself". This incubatee was further questioned: "So how are they adding value?" the response of the incubatee was: "No. I can't say they have".
C9	"No ... We needed the office space." – in response to the question "Did you really need the incubator?"

Positive incubation issues

It is not unusual to find that the incubatees in general derived some benefit from being incubated. The results from the interviews with the incubatees show that the incubatees derived benefit from the incubators in terms of access to information, business support and physical resources. Analysis of the selected responses of incubatees A1–A8 from Table 6 indicates that incubators serve as network nodes, provide physical resources and facilitate acquisition of basic business skills. The incubator management encourages compliance with statutory regulations, and encourages a shift to professionalization of the business. These activities can be reasonably expected as entry-level activity of an incubator that is keen to germinate new business ventures. The response of the participants in general indicated a positive disposition to being incubated.

Selection of incubatees

Many factors may influence the SP for incubatees. In South Africa, recruitment for selection of incubatees is primarily target driven. There are three factors that influence the target of incubators. To begin, preference is given to designated groups and unemployed. In South Africa, designated groups are defined as previously disadvantaged, women, youth (18–35 years of age inclusive) and the disabled. These are the groups who were discriminated against in the pre-1994 era. However, employed people who intend to start their own business are not excluded.

Another factor is funder preference; for example, a funder would make R1 million (ZAR) available for training a certain number of unemployed female youth to develop a business plan, with the hope of starting their own businesses. They would engage an incubator to manage the project if it is industry-specific, alternatively, incubators would tender for the project. The successful incubator would then go about recruiting the preferred cohorts to fulfil the funders' specifications.

A third factor was a combination of the strategy of the incubator management and the context of the incubator environment and how the incubator management responded to the external environment. Tribal customs are also prevalent in certain areas in South Africa. The sociocultural attributes of tribes influence power relations in these communities and unless the tribal chiefs are consulted, it is difficult to obtain support from the general community. The incubator managers in such cases had to include the tribal chiefs or elders as stakeholders in their networks in order to gain support from the communities. At times, these relations take much time and energy, especially if the incubation concept is not understood by the chieftains.

Following is the general SP that most incubators use as a guide:

1. Recruitment, a process where the incubator seeks incubatees to fill the spaces available at the incubator. In the case where there are many spaces to fill, incubators would go on to recruitment drives such as open days and advertising of the incubator and services available.
   a. Application by incubatees, potential incubatees are required to fill in application forms, a business plan or business concept, identity documentation and documents specific to each incubator.
2. A pre-incubation period might be available, where the business plan is developed usually based on a template that is incubator specific and also a development plan for the incubatee based on the assessment and 'level of knowledge' of the incubatee.
3. Incubatees are assessed in terms of their technical, entrepreneurial and business management competencies.
4. Most of the aforementioned steps are done by the management of the incubator or center and the potential incubatees are recommended to the board of directors for final selection decisions.

There are exceptional cases where certain preconditions are required for consideration in incubation programs, for example, agriculture requires potential incubatees to have access to land, water and power at least and in some instances physical ability (ability to physically work the land).

The responses from the incubatees indicate that the selection policies were not uniform across the public business incubators. Not all incubatees were sure that they understood why they were selected for incubation. There are indications of different strategies being employed in managing the spaces available, seeking turnover potential, mixing skill agendas and accommodating different levels of incubatees which could imply startups, existing businesses and potential fast-growers, and in one case no weakness being identified and by implication the SP was not implemented.

Negative incubation issues

Incubatees did not have only positive issues to report. The following are some responses to the question concerning negative aspects of being incubated.

From the incubatee comments in Table 6, it is evident that the expectations of incubator management and incubatees are not aligned. There is a disparity between incubator management and some incubatees concerning the time factor and meetings. Incubatees whose businesses have found traction in the market place a high premium on their time. Incubatees with near positive resource gradients found the bureaucratic approach a significant hampering factor. In some cases, incubatees are treated as a homogenous group where new recruits had to be brought up to the level of the existing incubatees in terms of training. This impacted negatively on the progress of incubation causing tension between incubator management and incubatees.

Discussion

As highlighted earlier, small business supporting institutions and development policies in South Africa is politically driven in order to address socio-economic issues. Therefore, the objectives for small business development and in turn incubation are primarily determined by macroeconomic policies and the number of small businesses and jobs created are key indicators in this regard. Also, small business institutional support has transformed significantly since 1994 with integration of various mechanisms from the then business hive concepts to the present day BI concept into the small business development, (Masutha and Rogerson, 2014). BI should not be seen as a substitute for small business development support mechanism.

As highlighted earlier, BI is specialized and a focused support. Therefore, incubation should be appreciated as complimentary to the existing institutional support mechanisms within SEDA such as support programs for startups, skills development of existing businesses and business growth programs, as well as Donor agencies including USAID, DFID and GTZ that support SMME development in South Africa. BI has the potential to attract and ring-fence required resources from specialized resource pools for specific objectives to more effectively and efficiently deliver to these objectives which should inform selection strategy.

Effective selection strategy is executable when the demand for incubation is higher than the supply. Occupation levels less than 100% due to low levels of demand for BI services. This is of concern for a country where unemployment levels hover around 25%, (Statistics South Africa, 2015). Part of the explanation is that awareness of the incubation concept as an option for support to new and fledgling businesses is not well diffused into the community, (Berry *et al.*, 2002). Another reason for the lack of interest as highlighted earlier is the lack of trust in the state support agencies who do not deliver according to promise due to lack of integration of support structures, competence and professionalism of the staff, (Department of Trade and Industry, 2004). Consequently, people are reluctant to commit to contractual relations with other state support agencies such as the incubation programs.

Incubator management perspective

From Tables 1 and 2, it can be seen that there is a relatively good alignment between incubator managers' perception of criteria for selection and qualities of assessment of incubatees when compared to the CSFs framework for selecting incubatees. However, ranking competitiveness and business management low raises a concern about the depth of insight and experience of the incubator staff. This is not surprising in that productivity and competitiveness were not of concern to incubator managers, and it partially supports the Department of Trade and Industry's (2004) report concerning the quality of staff.

The most frequent problems reported by incubator managers are quality of incubatees as shown in Table 4. This finding indicates that the incubator management is not able to exercise their preference in choice of candidates for incubation and there are factors beyond their control that influence the SP adversely. The most significant problems illustrated in Table 5 suggest that a key influencing factor is limited resources, and deeper analysis pointed to limitations on funding and more importantly, long-term funding. It can be seen from Table 3 that incubator management also raised issue with stakeholders and incubation processes. During discussions held with incubator managers, it was noted that goals of stakeholders and goals of incubation processes are not necessarily aligned. This makes it very difficult for incubator managers to deliver to the objectives of the incubation process and to the stakeholder objectives.

Owing to low levels of demand for incubation services, two options are exercised by incubator management. Option one is that inappropriate candidates will now be accepted for incubation in order to fill the spaces and meet requirements of funders. The second option is that management of incubators engages in recruitment activities, such as open days to attract clients. Some have extended their focus to pre-incubation phase where they develop business plans in order to develop their own supply or pipeline of potential incubatees placing strain on scarce resources. It is thus not surprising that some incubatees have negative experiences from incubators who are forced to spread their resources beyond their explicit mandate in order to achieve short-term objectives.

Strategic objectives

As indicated earlier, according to Hannon (2004), incubators should limit their focus to germination or incubation or acceleration. When they extend their focus, they also spread their resources further and place strain on their expertize. This is evident in that the difference in competence and experience of incubatees seems problematic when they are dealt with as homogenous groups. Advanced incubatees are frustrated when their time is wasted to accommodate new and less experienced incubatees. This is expressed in the words of an advanced incubatee:

> "...when they bring in the incubatees, I think that they must be categorised..."

There were businesses incubated with positive resource gradient that did not need incubation. This behavior is indicative of incubators in survival mode, seeking 'anchor tenants' and success stories. These incubatees benefited from the subsidized rental and no other value was added to them. They were also the incubatees that expressed dissatisfaction with the time spent in meetings and bureaucratic reporting processes. The spaces and resources spent on them could have been better utilized for more needy incubatees.

Integration of small business support

Due to a lack of integration of support programs, 'double-dipping' is common since similar programs such as business plan development are offered by other agencies. Business incubators should ideally be at a second-tier level. More baseline (first-tier) small business developing agencies should be growing potential incubatees for incubators to select from, and business incubators should not attempt to grow their own. A strategy that is indicative of incubators trying to survive as organizations rather than focusing on providing effective business support.

Compliance, productivity and competitiveness

Based on the evidence from the incubatees, business support was focused on compliance with statutory regulations for example registration for taxation purposes and operational process issues. Very limited support of strategic and/or entrepreneurial nature was evident. The business support in general is more incubator- or program-driven and not incubatee-specific. Incubatee needs were not defined and catered for specifically. As highlighted earlier, STP is mandated to promote improved levels of quality, performance, productivity and, competitiveness in small businesses. It is of concern that deliberate intervention focused productivity and competitiveness of incubatees from incubator management was not evident.

Incubatee needs are context-specific; as entrepreneurs, they have to make decisions and forecast in dynamic environments with uncertainty (Storey and West Lead, 1994) and an assumed lack of experience. They need to be supported in what they specifically need to do and know on the job. Incubator support has to be contextual; while it might make economic sense to provide generic training in groups, incubatees' it is then necessary that the groups being trained be relative at the same level.

It has long been identified that lack or low quality of management skills hampers small business survival, growth and development and that small business services and support should be demand-driven, (Bolton, 1971). In the case of the incubatee who was deficient in the resource of marketing skills, the incubator management was not able to respond positively to the incubatee's need or demand. It was left for the incubatee to attain the required resource on his/her own.

Technology and equipment

The focus of incubators can also be extended to levels of technology employed by the incubator. If the incubator is focused on germination of new businesses then the employment of the latest technologies may not be necessary. However, when growing or accelerating existing ventures, it becomes critical that the most appropriate technology be employed in order for the incubatees to effectively compete in the market place. This is a major hampering factor for those incubatees who have the potential to compete which is evident in the following comment:

"…we struggle with the old *technology* and we getting some bad *outputs*".

Similarly, when some equipment of incubators are defective or of low capacity, the urgency for re-commissioning defective equipment and increasing capacity seems to be less than desired. The issue here seems to be the different approaches in response to needs between the bureaucratic approach of incubator management and the market approach of business. Incubator management has to manage their resources as effectively as possible and with limited and targeted funding their capability to respond to needs arising from dynamic contexts are inhibited.

Funding

Funding represented the primary lack of resources from the incubator managers' perspective, which impacted negatively on long-term planning; therefore incubators in general were forced to adopt a short-term view. Business incubators have a relatively short-term funding cycle which impacts negatively on effective strategic planning. Funding mechanisms are structured based on KPIs set for the incubator management. Therefore meeting KPIs is a key objective for the management of incubators to secure funding. Incubator managers spend a significant amount of their time to secure funding. SEDA requires quarterly reporting on progress and performance and consequently funding is linked to reporting the performance of the incubator on a quarterly basis. This being the case, the priority of incubator managers becomes securing the funding in order to determine the survival of the incubator.

Some of the incubators have alternative revenue streams and funding partners providing incubator management with some slack in resources and latitude in their operations. It was noted that these managers spend more time with their incubatees and in these instances the management are seemingly more creative and strategic.

There appears to be a lack of confidence and understanding of the value of the contribution by BI. As pointed out earlier, Abetti (2004) and Lalkaka and Shaffer (1999) have shown BI has potential to provide significant returns from a tax perspective, it is important to understand who the customers are, especially of publicly funded business incubators, and they ultimately are the taxpayers. The real question then would have to be whether the investment in public BI is worth the return for the investor. Have the resources been efficiently used to achieve the projected outcomes? Has an optimum degree of incubation intensity been achieved? Could the resources be invested elsewhere to achieve the same outcomes at reduced costs?

Conclusion

The objective of the study was to develop increased understanding of the SP of BI. The methodology employed enabled the contribution of the detailed voice of the incubatees and the incubator management which provided much needed insight to the SP and its impact on BI. It was, however, limited in that it does not provide quantification of variables for example growth, throughput rates, profitability, return on investment and costs per incubate.

Based on the findings, analysis and discussions, firstly it can be concluded that the SP is critical to the BI and that ineffective selection will impact negatively on the quality of incubation and that the SP be reviewed. Secondly, the SP is hampered by a number of factors including but not limited to macroeconomic agendas, lack of alignment of stakeholder and incubation objectives, limited marketing of small business institutional support, lack of integration of support agencies and inappropriate funding strategy. Thirdly, incubator management is constrained to short-term strategies and the core focus of the incubator as a highly specialized small business development mechanism is diluted.

Consequences of these hampering factors are that limited indicators are used to determine incubator performance. Instead of directly assessing the contribution to the incubatee in terms of resource transfer towards growth, productivity and competitiveness, indirect indicators such as jobs created are used as key indicators of incubator performance.

The SP should be reviewed, and consideration should be given to integrating strategic positioning of incubators. Strategic positioning will of course require that incubators review their market and sharpen their focus on whether their primary objectives are to play a supporting role in germinating new ventures, incubating new ventures, or accelerating ventures (Hannon, 2004). The SP should be redefined as a strategic component incorporated in the BI process, where it defines the resource gap of the incubate. It is at this point that effect and direction must be given if a business is to have support, mediation and facilitation components from the perspective of graduating an effective business able to compete in the business environment. A conceptual selection framework is proposed in Figure 3 below.

The process of selection should be incubator and context specific. Figure 3 shows the potential incubatee submits a formal application for

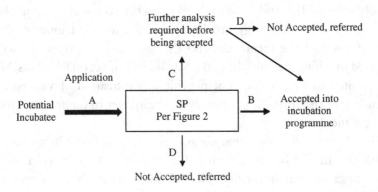

Figure 3.   Proposed Conceptual Selection Framework

admission to the incubation program (A). The selection program starts with a recruitment program when advertising for a specific profile of potential incubatees. The profile may be determined by any or a combination of:

- The type of incubator;
- Objectives of the incubator and
- The stage in the lifecycle of the incubator.

Should the incubator be in the mature stage of its lifecycle, preferred clients can be selected, and others may be referred to another incubator or alternative SMME development program.

When a good fit between resource gap of potential incubatee and incubator potential is found, incubatees are accepted into the incubation program, Figure 3, (B). This means that the CSFs for the business is sufficiently satisfied. When the fit is not good, the gap between resource requirements of incubatee and resource potential of incubator (includes ability to unlock potential of the team) must be defined, which can of course change with time, Figure 3, (C). Once the gap is defined, a plan for incubation of the business must be developed whereby the incubatee and incubator management agree on the role distribution for co-production of the envisaged firm for that specific incubatee, (Rice, 2002). Of course, when the potential incubatee is not incubatable, (Figure 3), path (D) is followed. It is evident that only actively new ventures and high-growth ventures be recruited at a later stage in the lifecycle of an incubator, after they acquired and developed the understanding and competence. It is argued here that the output of the SP is the input for planning management of resources the incubator and the distribution of roles in the co-production of the firm.

In summary, the findings indicate that incubation in South Africa has not reached levels of maturity along the incubator lifecycle. The incubators are trying to manage real estate and attract tenants (Allen and McCluskey, 1990). The incubator manager has to be tasked and tooled to effectively manage the incubator along its venture lifecycle over time. This could preferably be achieved by training and allowing the incubator managers to manage the quality and interaction of the variables affecting the

BI process. Better integration platforms must be developed between incubation and general small business development programs to facilitate diffusion of the incubation concept, as well as working towards a positive pipeline of incubatees. Incubatees should be referred to incubators for selection, not incubators going on recruitment drives for incubatees.

Finally, more focused research is required to better understand aspects of BI processes. Future research should also incorporate longitudinal methodology in order to track the incubation process over time, as well as doing comparative studies between incubated ventures and non-incubated ventures. Furthermore, research on quantification of incubation outputs, inclusive of business growth, throughput rates, profitability, return on investment, costs per incubatee, must be performed in order to develop benchmarks.

References

Abetti, P. (2004). Government supported incubators in the Helsinki Region, Finland: infrastructure, results, and best practices. *Journal of Technology Transfer,* 29: 19–40.

Albert, P., Bernasconi, M., and Gaynor, L. (2002). *Incubators: The Emergence of a New Industry — A Comparison of the Players and their Strategies: France–Germany–UK–USA,* Research Report CERAM Sophia Antipolis, December.

Aerts, K., Matthyssens, P., and Vandenbempt, K. (2007). Critical role and screening practices of European business incubators. *Technovation,* 27(5): 254–267.

Allen, D. N. and McCluskey, R. (1990). Structure, policy, services, and performance in the business incubator industry. *Entrepreneurship: Theory and Practice,* 15(2): 61–77.

Barney, J. (1991). Firm resources and sustained competitive advantage. *Journal of management,* 17(1): 99–120.

Bergek, A. and Norrman, C. (2008). Incubator best practice: A framework. *Technovation,* 28: 20–28.

Berry, A., von Blottnitz, M., Cassim, R., Kesper, A., Rajaratnam, B., and van Seventer, D.E. (2002). The economics of SMMES in South Africa. *Trade and Industrial Policy Strategies, Johannesburg, South Africa.*

Bolton, J. E. (1971). Small Firms: Report of the Committee of Inquiry on Small Firms. London: HMSO, Cmnd, 4811.

Bøllingtoft, A. and Ulhoi, J. P. (2005). The networked business incubator – Leveraging entrepreneurial agency? *Journal of Business Venturing*, 20: 265–290.

Buys, A. J. and Mbewena, P. N. (2007). Key success factors for business incubation in South Africa: The Godisa case study. *South African Journal of Science*, 103: 356–358.

Colombo, M. G. and Delmastro, M. (2002). How effective are technology incubators? *Research Policy*, 31: 1103–1122.

Delmar, F., Davidsson, P., and Gartner, W. B. (2003). Arriving at the high-growth firm. *Journal of Business Venturing*, 18(2): 189–216.

Department of Trade and Industry (2004). Review of ten years of small business support in South Africa. Pretoria: DTI.

Dickinson, R. A., Ferguson, C. R., and Sircar, S. (1984). Critical success factors and small business. *American Journal of Small Business*, 8(3): 49–57.

Elsenhardt, K. M., and Martin, J. A. (2000). Dynamic capabilities: What are they? *Strategic Management Journal*, 21(1): 1105–1121.

Etzkowitz, H., de Mello, J. M. C., and Almeida, M. (2005). Towards 'meta-innovation' in Brazil: The evolution of the incubator and the emergence of a triple helix. *Research Policy*, 34: 411–424.

Frese, M. and De Kruif, M. (2000). Psychological Success Factors of Entrepreneurship in Africa: A Selective Literature Review. In Frese, M. (Ed.), *Success and Failure of Microbusiness Owners in Africa: A Psychological Approach*. Quorum Books, London, pp. 1–30.

Grant, R.M. (1991). The resource-based theory of competitive advantage: Implications for strategy formulation. *California Management Review*, 33(3): 114–135.

Gupta, P. D., Guha, S., and Krishnaswami, S. S. (2013). Firm growth and its determinants. *Journal of Innovation and Entrepreneurship*, 2(1): 1–14.

Hackett, S. M. and Dilts, D. M. (2004). A systematic review of business incubation research. *Journal of Technology Transfer*, 29: 55–82.

Hackett, S. M. and Dilts, D. M. (2004b). A real options-driven theory of business incubation. *Journal of Technology Transfer*, 29: 41–542.

Hannon, P. (2004). A Qualitative sense-making qualification of business incubation environments. *Qualitative Market Research*, 7(4): 274–283.

Headd, B. and Kirchhoff, B. (2009). The growth, decline and survival of small businesses: An exploratory study of life cycles. *Journal of Small Business Management*, 47(4): 531–550.

Hofstede, G. (1993). Cultural constraints in management theories. *The Academy of Management Executive*, 7(1): 81–94.

Hoopes, D. G., Madsen, T. L., and Walker, G. (2003). Why is there a resource-based view? Toward a theory of competitive heterogeneity. *Strategic Management Journal*, 24: 889–902.

Katz, J. A. and Green, R. P. (2014). *Entrepreneurial Small Business*, 4th Edn. McGraw-Hill/Irwin, New York.

Kuratko, D. F. and LaFollette, W. R. (1987). Small business incubators for local economic development. *Economic Development Review*, 5(2): 49–55.

Lalkaka, R. and Shaffer, D. (1999). Nurturing entrepreneurs, creating enterprises: Technology business incubation in Brazil. In *International conference on effective business development services*, March 2–3. *Technolgy Business Incubation in Brazil* — 26 Committee of Donor Agencies for Small enterprise Development, International Conference on Effective Business Development Services, Rio de Janeiro, Brazil.

Lee, S. S. and Osteryoung, J. S. (2004). A comparison of critical success factors for effective operations of university business incubators in the United States and Korea. *Journal of Small Business Management*, 42(4): 418–426.

Lind, P. (2012). *Small Business Management in Cross-Cultural Environments*. Routledge: London.

Lumpkin, J. R. and Ireland, R. D. (1988). Screening practices of new business incubators: The Evaluation of critical success factors. *American Journal of Small Business*, 2(4): 59–81.

Masutha, M. and Rogerson, C. M. (2015). Business Incubation for Small Enterprise Development: South African Pathways. *Urban Forum*, 26(2): 223–241.

Merrifield, D. B. (1987). New business incubators. *Journal of Business Venturing*, 2: 277–284.

Mian, S. A. (1996). Assessing value-added contributions of university technology business incubators to tenant firms. *Research policy*, 25(3): 325–335.

Orford, J., Herrington, M., and Wood, E. (2004). *Global Entrepreneurship Monitor 2004: South African Report*. Centre for Entrepreneurship and Innovation, Graduate School of Business, UCT: Cape Town.

Penrose, E. T. (1980). *The Theory of the Growth of the Firm*. Oxford University Press.

Peteraf, M. A. (1993). The cornerstones of competitive advantage: A resource based view. *Strategic Management Journal*, 14(3): 179–191.

Peters, L., Rice, M., and Sundararajan, M. (2004). The role of incubators in the entrepreneurial process. *Journal of Technology Transfer,* 29(1): 83–91.

Ramluckan, S and Thomas, W. (2011). Raising Businesses. *Agenda,* 2: 18–21. Available at: http://thoughtprint.usb.ac.za/Leaders%20Lab%20PDFs/ Raising_Businesses.pdf [Accessed 2 September 2014].

Rangone, A. (1999). A resource-based approach to strategy analysis in small-medium sized enterprises. *Small Business Economics,* 12: 233–248.

Ray, G., Barney, J. B., and Muhanna, W. A. (2004). Capabilities, business processes, and competitive advantage: Choosing the dependent variable in empirical tests of the resource based view. *Strategic Management Journal,* 25(1): 23–37.

Rice, M. A. (2002). Co-production of business assistance in business incubators An exploratory study. *Journal of Business Venturing,* 17(2):163–187.

Smilor, R. W. (1987). Commercializing technology through new business incuba-tors. *Research Management,* 30(5): 36–41.

Smilor, R. W. and Gill Jr, M. D. (1986). *The New Business Incubator: Linking Talent, Technology, Capital, and Know-How.* Lexington books, Toronto.

Solomon, G., Frese, M., Friedrich, C., and Glaub, M. (2013). Can personal initia-tive training improve small business success? A longitudinal South African evaluation study. *The International Journal of Entrepreneurship and Innovation,* 14(4): 255–268.

Solomon, G. and Hough, J. (2008). Business incubators: A review of literature towards a research agenda. Paper delivered at the annual SAIMS Conference, Johannesburg, 14–16 September.

Storey, D. J. and Westhead, P. (1994). Management training and small firm perfor-mance: A critical review. Working Paper No. 18, Warwick Business School, Coventry.

Statistics South Africa. (2015). Available at: http://www.statssa.gov.za [Accessed March 27, 2015].

SEDA (2015). *Seda Technology Program.* [ONLINE] Available at: http://www.seda. org.za/MyBusiness/STP/Pages/AboutSTP.aspx. [Accessed December 21, 15].

Timmons, J. A. and Spinelli. S. (2007). *New Venture Creation: Entrepreneurship for the 21st Century.* McGraw-Hill/Irwin, New York.

Wernerfelt, B. (1984). A resource based view of the firm. *Strategic Management Journal,* 5(2): 171–180.

Chapter 9

Science Parks and Incubators: Observations, Synthesis and Future Research[1]

Phillip Phan, Donald S. Siegel and Mike Wright

Introduction

A by-product of the technological revolutions in manufacturing processes and telecommunications in the early-1980s is the perception among policy makers and scholars that innovation results in wealth creation at the regional and national levels. Developmental and growth economists assert that an increase in the rate of investment in R&D can allow advanced industrial countries to compete with emerging economies, which have significantly lower labor costs in manufacturing and service industries. Another common perception is that new-technology-based firms are likely to be a critical source of new job creation.

This focus on the need to increase the population of small, high-technology firms has contributed to a substantial increase in public and private spending on science parks and business incubators. We define

---

[1] Updated reprint from Phan, P. H., Siegel, D. S., and Wright, M. (2005). Science parks and incubators: Observations, synthesis and future research. *Journal of Bussiness Venturing*, 20(2): 165–182. Copyright March 2005, with permission from Elsevier Ltd., Kidlington, Oxford, OX5 1GB,UK (Lic: 3735991328628)

these institutions as property-based organizations with identifiable administrative centers focused on the mission of business acceleration through knowledge agglomeration and resource sharing.[2] Many universities have established science parks and incubators in order to foster the creation of startup firms based on university-owned (or licensed) technologies. Public universities (and some private universities) also view these institutions as a means of fostering regional economic development.

Science parks and incubators have become an international phenomenon. In 2003, the Association of University Research Parks (AURP) reports that there were 123 university-based science parks in the U.S. (Link and Link, 2003) and by 2012 that number had swelled to 174 (Battelle, 2013). The National Business Incubation Association (NBIA, 2015) reports that the number of business incubators in North America rose from 12 in 1980 to 1250 at the end of 2012, while U.K. Business Incubation estimates 250 business incubators in 2002, rising from 25 in 1997 (UKBI, 2003). The U.K. Science Park Association (UKSPA) reports that there were 32 science parks in 1989, 46 in 1999 (Siegel *et al.*, 2003b), and by 2015, more than 100 (UKSPA, 2015). According to the European Commission's Enterprise Directorate General, there were 850 business incubators in the European Union, as of 2001.[3]

In Asia, the first science park, Tsukuba Science City, was built in Japan in the early 1970s with other Asian countries following suit in the mid-1980s. Today, there are more than 200 science parks in Asia and still growing, with Japan topping the list at 111. China, which built the first one in the mid-1980s, now has about 100. India established 13 parks in late-1980s but with the exception of Bangalore, India's Silicon Valley, all have failed. Hong Kong and South Korea report two parks each while Macau, Malaysia, Singapore, Taiwan and Thailand have one each.

This increased level of activity has stimulated an important academic debate concerning whether such property-based initiatives enhance the performance of corporations, universities, and economic regions. More

---

[2] The U.S.-based NBIA (www.nbia.org) defines a business incubator less specifically as "an economic development tool designed to accelerate the growth and success of entrepreneurial companies through an array of business support resources and services".

[3] http://www.europa.eu.int/comm/enterprise/bi/[Accessed August 14, 2014].

practically, it has also led to an interest among policy makers and industry leaders in identifying best practices. This raises important questions relating to strategy formulation by organizations that manage science parks and incubators and also for tenants of these facilities.

While there is an increasing number of academic studies addressing such issues, the rapidly evolving nature of the prototypical incubator, and the fact that the organizations that have established these facilities, i.e. universities and governments, are non-profit entities have made research challenging. These challenges render standard economic explanation assumptions invalid or in need of substantial modification. It is also important to note that science parks and incubators are often the result of public–private partnerships, which means that multiple stakeholders (e.g. community groups, regional and state governments) have enormous influence over their missions and operational procedures. Thus, developing theories to characterize the precise nature of their business models and managerial practices beyond simple descriptions has not proceeded very far.

Theoretically, there has been a recurring problem of definitions in which science parks and incubators can encompass almost anything from distinct organizations to amorphous regions (Storey and Tether, 1998). As such, the relevant government agencies (e.g. the National Science Foundation) have not collected systematic data on these institutions (Siegel, 2003). Thus, there are no publicly available data for comparative analysis or benchmarking. This makes it difficult to conduct an econometric analysis of the antecedents and consequences of the performance of firms on such facilities and their impact on universities, regions and other firms in the local region.[4]

The purpose of this chapter is to discuss the theoretical and empirical gaps in the literature and highlight some of the best available international quantitative and qualitative evidence. We highlight some exemplar papers

---

[4] In contrast, the research on the patenting and licensing process for university based startups, for example, has been richer (Bray and Lee, 2000; Bercovitz *et al.*, 2001; Siegel *et al.*, 2003a). This is because data is widely collected by such industry associations as the Association of University Technology Managers (AUTM) in the U.S. and NUBS/UNICO/AURIL in the U.K. and by financial institutions with interests in embryonic industries such as the Securities Data Company, Recombinant Capital, Corporate Technology Directory and Venture Economics.

to illustrate three themes that we believe are prevalent in the literature: the role of networks in business incubation, entrepreneurial strategies by firms, universities and regions to exploit university created intellectual property and the impact of science parks and incubator on firms and universities. The extant research features a variety of theoretical approaches such as the theory of the firm, institutional theory, resource dependence theory, agency theory, social capital theory and organization learning; at multiple levels of analyzes — firm, industry, region, country; that employ a mix of quantitative and qualitative methods to build and test theoretical frameworks. Yet, there is still no consensus over the appropriate theoretical framework for studies in this domain. As such, questions on the appropriate dependent variables, levels of analyzes, measurement and, therefore, policy and managerial implications are still in play.

In the next section, we outline some problems with the extant literature on science parks and incubators. This is followed by a brief review of exemplar papers we identified as illustrating unexplored dimensions of this literature. In the conclusion, we provide a synthesis and outline a broader research agenda.

Reflections on the literature

Academic studies of science parks and incubators can be divided into studies that focus on the companies located on these facilities, those that attempt to provide an assessment of the science parks and incubators themselves, those that focus on the systemic level of the university, region or country and those that examine the individual entrepreneur or teams of entrepreneurs in these facilities. Thus, there are four streams of research in the literature. From a theoretical perspective, efforts to connect these four research streams have not been very fruitful. First, that is because there is currently no systematic framework to understand the connection between these multiple levels of analyses, as there is, for example, for the relationship between the headquarters of a multinational corporation and its subsidiary office in or the relationship between a venture capitalist and an investee firm.

In addition to their multilevel nature, science parks and incubators are also dynamic because the mission and operational procedures of an incubator change over time. We have yet to encounter such a dynamic model.

We also observe that what constitutes an appropriate measure of performance for a business incubator remains unclear even after three decades of research. Specifically, few studies have explicated the level of analysis of the construct — the performance of the incubator or the firms in the incubator. We know that simply locating in a business incubator does not guarantee success (Lumpkin and Ireland, 1988). In fact, apart from the location and administrative support advantages, the value of business incubators has been called into question (Mian, 1997; Hansen *et al.*, 2000). A serious problem with research in this area is that the typical dependent variable, the rate of firm survival (or failure), has little construct validity, since incubators are specifically designed to maintain and increase life span. In short, such studies are selecting on the dependent variable, which creates an endogeneity problem. One way to deal with this is to choose to compare survival rates among different incubators (e.g. for different types of incubators), an approach that few authors have undertaken.

In addition to the general theoretical problem of identifying valid dependent variables, there is the normative problem of demarking the transition between the efficient (acceleration) and inefficient (life support) organizational form of the same entity. Lendner and Dowling (2003) and others have used the metaphor of a greenhouse to illustrate the growth acceleration orientation of a business incubator. However, it is quite easy for incubation to turn into life support, a metaphor with negative implications — government bailouts, and the inefficient deployment of public resources. For example, Bollingtoft and Ulhoi (2005) report that 50% of the companies in the incubator they examined remained in the incubator after four years.

Attempts to construct theories of science parks have proven to be quite difficult, due to the lack of systematic data collection. An exception is a series of studies conducted by the Centre for Small and Medium Size Enterprises at the University of Warwick created a matched-pair sample of on-park and off-park U.K. firms that have been used successfully in a series of studies (see Westhead, 1997; Westhead and Storey, 1994). Even so, much of what constitutes theory, on closer examination, is usually an inventory of typologies, and causations and outcomes. Perhaps, no general theory is possible because the causes and consequences of science parks and incubators may be idiosyncratic to their geographic locations, political and social contexts and economic systems. However, to make such a conclusion at this time would probably represent a rush to judgment on very thin evidence, which is the why we believe this chapter is still relevant and timely, in spite of the original paper being published a decade ago.

In this chapter, we adopt the perspective that science parks and incubators are distinct organizations within the technological entrepreneurial value chain. This value chain comprises the set of organizations whose activities are linked by the successive transformation of resource and knowledge inputs to marketable outputs in the period leading to and shortly after the creation of a new firm. Science parks and incubators are the intermediate organizations that provide the social environment, technological and organizational resources and managerial expertize for the transformation of a technology-based business idea into an efficient economic organization. Therefore, to advance the research on science parks and incubators we first need to understand their role in the value chain of entrepreneurial wealth creation.

This is the approach taken by Markman *et al.* (2005) and Clarysse *et al.* (2005). Specifically, Markman *et al.* (2005) outline a model that links a university's knowledge assets (patents) to business creation in university-based incubators with university technology transfer offices (TTOs) acing as the intermediaries. The focus on universities is due to the fact that they are responsible for a large share of the technology oriented incubators in the U.S. Although there have been several field studies of university TTO licensing activities (e.g. Bercovitz *et al.*, 2001; Siegel *et al.*, 2003b; Mowery *et al.*, 2001; Nerkar and Shane, 2003), they have largely been based on data from a set of elite research universities (e.g. Stanford, UC Berkeley and MIT) or from a small sample of more representative institutions. These results may not be generalizable to the larger population of institutions that do not enjoy the same favorable environmental conditions. To build a theoretically saturated model of TTOs' entrepreneurial development strategies, the authors collected qualitative and quantitative data from virtually the entire population of university TTOs.

A surprising conclusion of the Markman *et al.* (2005) study is that the most "attractive" combinations of technology stage and licensing strategy for new venture creation, i.e. early stage technology, combined with licensing for equity, are *least* likely to be favored by the university and thus, not likely to be used. That is because universities and TTOs are typically focused on short-term cash maximization, and are extremely risk-averse with respect to financial and legal risks. Their findings are consistent with evidence presented in Siegel *et al.* (2003a and 2003b), who found that university TTOs appear to do a better job of serving the needs of large firms than small, entrepreneurial companies and taken together the studies suggest that universities need to change their technology transfer strategies if they are serious about promoting entrepreneurial development.

The work by Markman *et al.* (2005) highlights the importance of identifying the interests and incentives for those who manage the technology transfer process and their interactions with those who manage the science parks and incubators and entrepreneurs who work in these institutions. Theoretically, the relationship between TTO managers, the university administration and entrepreneurs can be modeled as a multi-level agency problem. In the case of university-based incubators, an internal market for the efficient allocation of resources does not exist. Thus, decisions on technology transfer and new venture creation may be driven by internal bargaining, which would bring to the fore the question of incentives versus university mission.

More generally, we believe that a good explanatory model of incubators cannot be achieved without direct reference to the individuals or teams[5] involved in the creation and management of ventures in them. There is a paucity of research on the human capital of the administrators and entrepreneurs, and the opportunity identification process that occurs in science parks and incubators. There are several interesting research questions: are there systematic differences in the demographics of entrepreneurs that locate on science parks and incubators compared with those

---

[5] For our purposes, defined broadly as the entrepreneur, TTO officer managing the transfer of intellectual property to startups, surrogate entrepreneurs, members of the research team, business development officers from the incubator or science park, venture capitalists, business angels and non-executive directors.

involved in the creation of ventures outside these locations? To what extent do science park and incubator managers take an active role in identifying opportunities? Existing studies of entrepreneurs indicate that individuals scan the environment according to schemas and heuristics that confine the scope of their search (Gaglio, 1997; Venkataraman, 1997). These schemas are found to be related to the level of education, demographic factors and work experience. Thus, scientists in science parks and incubators may be those who have recognized the need for more help in identifying the market for their inventions. This brings in a discussion of the entrepreneurial team.

There is increasing attention to the phenomenon of entrepreneurial teams. However, this research has yet to explore the different contexts in which they are found. Team members can contribute the requisite range of human capital necessary to develop a venture that may not be available in a single individual. However, team heterogeneity may lead to increased level of conflict and the administrative inefficiency that it causes (Ensley *et al.*, 2002). When viewed dynamically, entrepreneurial teams can be seen to evolve with the entry of new team members who bring the requisite human capital at a particular stage and the exit of others when their contributions cease to be relevant (Ucbasaran *et al.*, 2003). Thus, the extent to which science parks and incubators assist in team building as a venture matures should be seriously considered. Administrators of science parks and incubators may, for example, fulfill a team role in helping to identify a market for the innovation, providing intellectual property protection advice, offering business development skills, identifying surrogate entrepreneurs and venture capitalists (Franklin *et al.*, 2001).

Clarysse *et al.* (2005) follows the same inductive tradition, using qualitative analysis to document the "spinout" strategies of European research institutions. It employs a two-stage approach to developing and validating a set of seven "scientific regions of excellence" in France, Belgium, Germany, U.K. and the Netherlands. Their case studies of these regions revealed three generic strategies (low selective, supportive, incubator) for managing the spin-out process. The selective model is based on a "let a thousand flowers bloom" strategy that maximizes the investment options in highly uncertain technology startups. The supportive model is designed to maximize the survival odds of a startup by providing extensive pre-startup financial, technical and administrative support. The incubator model is based on the clear goal of creating financially attractive spin-outs. Each model is configured differently, in terms of its organizational, human, financial, technological, network and physical resources.

An interesting finding from the study, which would not have been apparent if the authors had employed a large sample, deductive approach, is the revelation that two "sub-optimal" categories existed: research institutions that are *resource deficient* and those that are *competence deficient*. Competence deficient organizations have sufficient resources, but insufficient capabilities whereas resource deficient ones may suffer from unrealistic expectations, as they tend to follow visibly successful startups in their immediate region.

Koh *et al.* (2005) elaborates on this line of research. They outline an analytical framework for predicting the factors influencing the growth and evolution of science parks, based on a deductive analysis of three exemplars: Silicon Valley, the Cambridge Science Park and the Hsinchu Science District. Their model considers three aspects of science parks that have been separately discussed in the literature but never together in a cohesive framework: growth mechanisms, sophistication of technological capabilities and the degree of integration in the value chains of national and global markets. This framework is then used to evaluate an emerging science park strategy in Singapore.

As a contribution to the extant literature, the use of exemplars to build a theoretical model is simultaneously controversial and unique. The approaches by Koh *et al.* (2005), and Clarysse *et al.* (2005) are quite instructive to researchers, especially those who try to induce a general model from a set of well-known case studies. Typically, the use of individual case studies has been linked to inductive approaches to theory building. However, when multiple case studies are considered, general lessons may be deduced by looking for commonalities among the case studies. An issue with such an approach is the problem of left censorship, in which only successful exemplars or models are picked for building the general model. This can lead to an under-specification of the model or worse, incorrect theoretical conclusions. Koh *et al.* (2005) avoided this in three ways. The exemplars they selected have been extensively studied in the literature and have themselves been the bases for entire streams of work on national innovation systems. Second, they were careful to anchor their conclusions on well-known theories, such as knowledge spillovers. Third, in testing the model by application to another case study, they were careful to limit their generalizations.

It turns out that the main growth mechanisms for the exemplar science parks are government-led infrastructure provisions that create opportunities for knowledge agglomeration and self-renewal through the continual creation of new businesses. Strong self-renewal capabilities result in new firm formation and a high level of sustained R&D. Silicon Valley evolved into a global hub for R&D because of its proximity to world class universities and the world's largest domestic consumer market. Hsinchu exploited Silicon Valley's R&D capabilities by exploiting the overseas Chinese network already established in the Valley. Cambridge acted as a magnet for technology startups keen to take advantage of its proximity to a world class university. In each of the exemplars the most important trait for creating and sustaining new technologies and products for the global market is the access to talent. In a sense, the authors' framework reinforces some of the work by Saxenian (1991) and others but by making the science park central to the innovation network and highlighting the three success factors, they suggest a higher level of control over the trajectory of entrepreneurial intensity than previously implied in the literature.

Koh *et al.* (2005) test the generalizability of their framework on Singapore's evolving science park strategy and conclude that it represents a macro-economic policy driven infrastructure-led growth strategy. According to the framework, they assess that whether these efforts would succeed would depend on how successfully the science park can acquire the other success factors such as greater private sector participation, formal linkages with Silicon Valley and other successful science parks and a continual supply of knowledge creating talent.

Both Clarysse *et al.* (2005) and Koh *et al.* (2005) highlight an important feature of incubators and science parks. Unlike standalone enterprises, these entities are deeply embedded in the socio-political system. Publicly-supported incubators and science parks are regarded as tools for economic development and political bargaining. First, there is an active internal bargaining process for resources, broadly defined as recognition, networking with external contacts, services and so on, largely within the strategic core. There is also an external bargaining process with resource providers (governments, other companies, labor market, etc.). These processes are not necessarily driven or mediated by market forces because the combination of public funds and the political interests that control the disbursement of those funds mean that the 'efficient price' signal for a resource allocation decision becomes more noisy. Therefore, it may be that if incubators exist at the behest of political interests then without the support of those interests, incubators as an organizational form may not be very viable, which is often the case for non-profit incubators (Lendner and Dowling, 2003). Putting all this together, one can reasonably ask if an appropriate research question may not be whether incubators lead to higher rates of success among startup firms but rather in what ways do incubators confer legitimacy to the political interests that support them.

Continuing with the theme of assisted entrepreneurial value creation is the paper by Bollingtoft and Ulhoi (2005). Employing a qualitative methodology, the authors show that the "networked incubator", which they uncovered in their research, is a new hybrid form based on territorial synergy, relational symbiosis and economies of scope. Using social capital[6] theory they conducted an ethnographic study of a single incubator and show that entrepreneurial economic decisions are made in a sociocultural and emotional (i.e. non-economic) context. The existence of network ties between those involved individuals and organizations in the incubator suggests that the exchange of information and resources between firms in the incubator is influenced by social norms, social structure and individual power. These, in turn, are determined by access to and relative position within the social network.

We believe that the contribution of Bollingtoft and Ulhoi (2005) is to characterize the incubator as a means to address the liability of "newness" that all startups experience. In this context, newness refers to the lack of market visibility and connectedness with a resource network. The authors demonstrate that network theory and social capital theory can account for much of the social and business activities in a business incubator. On the other hand, their discussion forces us to ask if there is a theoretical

---

[6] Resources embedded in a social structure and made accessible and mobile by purposive actions.

difference between incubators and VC partnerships, corporate internal venturing units and governmental economic development agencies. If the definition of an incubator has to be more precise, then on what basis should this be done?

Sociologically, incubators can be seen as micro-communities of firms and individuals. As such, we anticipate that future studies will increasingly adopt the social network approach exemplified by Bollingtoft and Ulhoi (2005). It is appropriate to think more carefully about this approach, precisely because it appears to be so apt. First, social networks and the accompanying analytical approach is a formal descriptive methodology for mapping out the relationships between entities that are tied together by resource and information flows. How do the results of such analyses lead to normative theory, which should be the natural outcome of such research? Second, is the network an appropriate metaphor for the incubator? An incubator is a self-contained organization with an identity, set of routines and a strategic core. It has an administrative center, a distinct mission and interacts with the external environment as a unified entity. In many ways, the *incubator* (ignoring the differences across profit/ non-profit, university or company based, etc., for now) is really a company and is organized as such. On the other hand, a true network has relatively more porous boundaries, is more informally organized, and is potentially more embedded than an incubator. In short, the level of analysis question has to be asked first.

An agenda for future research

So where do we go from here? The papers we highlighted address typical questions in the research. In that sense, we do not think that that core questions related to the purposes, processes, structures and outcomes of business incubator research would change very much. While there have been a proliferation of research in the last 30 years, these questions remain in the literature. Theory continues to be relatively weak, while the structure of incubators and science parks continue to rapidly evolve. The empirical evidence is more robust today because of the efforts of the National Academies, National Science Foundation, National Bureau of Economic Research, the European Union and various national governments to systematize data collection. The search for 'best practices' continues unabated but with little effect, as performance indicators from around the world continue to show.

Papers on incubators and science parks typically begin with two features: an enumeration of different types of incubators and a list of antecedents and consequence of some measure of success (sometimes, self-reported measures). For example, Clarysse *et al.* (2005) identified three types of incubators relating to the development of spin-outs from research institutions, with the level of assistance ranging from perfunctory provision of physical space to detailed hands-on involvement. In contrast, Koh *et al.* (2005) suggest three *dimensions* that can describe most science parks. This suggests that the organizations we are dealing with are sufficiently idiosyncratic to ensure that developing a unified theory of incubators and science parks may be very difficult.

On the other hand, there are existing organizational theories that we can exploit. A general model of incubators and science parks should allow us to answer the following questions, which are standard for research into other organization forms but would represent advances to the extant research on this topic. The first question is why do science parks and incubators exist, given that there are already markets for the exchange of resources typical of those provided by incubators? One might argue that high-technology incubators address an innovation market failure, if the commercial value of the technology being promulgated is so uncertain (in the sense of Knight, 1921) as to thwart the calculation of a discount rate. Hence, market forces do not result in financial and other support for the commercialization of the technology. In particular, if the likely social returns to the innovation would greatly exceed the private returns to these activities (see Mansfield *et al.*, 1977 for an elaboration) an incubator, which is essentially an indemnification of the entrepreneur's risks from the public purse, may be the only solution. In practical terms, the incubation process may be the only way a startup that exploits an embryonic technology can emerge.

An extension to this question may be to ask if one can describe the ecology of incubators and science parks as a market for tenant firms. With the exception of the work by Westhead and Storey (1994) on U.K. science parks, there is little existing evidence on the search processes adopted by firms concerning their decision to locate on a particular science park or incubator, and the intermediaries involved in the process. Theoretically, we can build models that characterize science parks and incubators as being in competition with each other and with other organizations such as corporations to attract tenant firms to co-locate in them. Research has shown that knowledge spillovers occur whenever agglomeration occurs. Therefore, these 'economic network effects' suggest that the larger the size of an incubator or science park, *ceteris paribus*, the more valuable the geographic location and hence, the rents that can be extracted from tenants. Researchers can even contemplate the possibility of a cooperative, rather than a competitive solution, to this problem, which moves the level of analysis up a level to the network of science parks or incubators in a geographic region. Such approaches would augment the property-based studies that have been the mainstream of such research, but on a more appealing theoretical foundation.

Finally, in proposing that incubators and science parks are solutions to market failure, one can consider the *types* of innovation market failure (Martin and Scott, 2000) that they are designed to correct. Given the existence of quasi-organizational forms such as virtual networks, online marketplaces, application service providers (ASP) or other forms of exchange, a model must be capable of answering the question. "Why incubators and science parks are *uniquely* able to solve these types of market failures". One way to approach this question is to show that without incubators, a more efficient way to organize resources, whether by market exchange or a unitary hierarchy, would not occur because of information asymmetry, asset specificity and/or resource stickiness. More specifically, because there are transactions costs attached to any organizational solution to market failure so an assessment of its efficiency and thus viability has to account for the economic value that it creates.

In addition to the market failure approach, we can also employ a strategic approach to building models of science parks and incubators. Here, we are concerned with issues of resource substitution and complementarity. Specifically, we can consider whether science parks and incubators substitute for institutional voids (Khanna and Palepu, 2000) and how they offer something that is different from what is not available, or complementary, elsewhere. For example, to what extent are incubators and science parks substitutes for or complementary to venture capital firms? We believe that to the extent VCs and incubators are driven by different strategic objectives, the two types of accelerator organizations are complementary in the value chain of entrepreneurial value creation.

The issues surrounding the unique contribution of science parks and incubators and of substitution and complementarity raise a key concern about the nature of their resources and capabilities. Science parks and incubators may be able to create greater value in the firms located on them if they possess specific, rather than general non-specific, resources that are not available elsewhere. But their ability to learn from experience and develop their capabilities is also important in enhancing their ability to create value for their tenant firms. This highlights the need to consider the absorptive capacity of the science parks and incubators, and notably of their managers. Absorptive capacity relates to the ability of firms to recognize the value of new information, assimilate it and apply it to commercial ends (Cohen and Levinthal, 1990). We may also which to consider what Zahra and George (2002) refer to as "potential absorptive capacity", which comprises knowledge acquisition and assimilation capabilities, and realized absorptive capacity, which centers on knowledge transformation and exploitation. Crucially, the former provides organizations with the flexibility to adapt and evolve in changing environments (Zahra and George, 2002).

Increasingly, as the research has spread around the world, papers are being written about science parks and incubators in different environmental and institutional contexts. It is evident that there are similarities and differences between science parks located in the same geographic region and between science parks located in different geographic regions (Clarysse *et al.*, 2005; Koh *et al.*, 2005). This points to the need for a structural contingency perspective that relates the different types of science parks and incubators to different institutional contexts and objectives. For example, not all science parks and incubators focus exclusively on promoting technology intensive firms.

We suggest that if the institutional context is important, we should explicate it in the models that we test. It is also important to recognize that these environments are themselves changing as, for example, government policy objectives change or venture capital firms adapt their approaches to investing in companies located on science parks and incubators. In the light of our previous comment that the capabilities of science parks and incubators may develop over time through a process of learning, a central issue relates to the co-evolution of science parks and incubators and the institutional and environmental context in which they operate.

We need to consider the nature of the co-evolution of the resources and capabilities of both the science parks and incubators, and their tenant firms. A co-evolutionary perspective (Lewin and Volberda, 1999, 2003) suggests that organizations and their environments evolve together and are inter-dependent. Longer-term survival involves organizations reconciling potentially conflicting pressures between stability and change to achieve fit with a dynamic environment. Such an approach may help, for example, in understanding how resource or competence deficient incubators (Clarysse *et al.*, this issue) are able to enhance their competitive positions in the market for tenant firms.

In conjunction with the issue of institutional contexts is the level of analysis problem. Specifically, because incubators and science parks encompass independent organizations, they can be examined at different levels of analysis. These are the systems or national innovation level, the university or regional level, the science park or incubator level, the incubator firm level, and the entrepreneur and team level. The cited papers in this chapter deal with the systems and to a lesser extent, university or regional levels. Indeed this reflects much of the extant work because data is more readily available (e.g. governments regularly collect such data as part of accountability audits). This means that future research should move on to the incubator or science park and lower levels of analyses.

At the highest level of analysis is the issue of the ownership and control. The differing and sometime conflicting objectives of the stakeholders in science parks and incubators raise questions about their governance. Rules concerning how long firms can stay on in an incubator are driven by governance imperatives and thus the governance mechanisms for monitoring the productivity of science parks and incubators becomes an important research question. In this regard, we feel that agency theory is an appropriate lens to frame the relationship between incubator and science park management and their stakeholders (e.g. Jensen *et al.*, 2003 in the context of the university TTO). One can foresee how agency problems might be exacerbated in publicly subsidized incubators and science parks.

That is because information on the value of resources and opportunities may be unreliable. This may result in a situation in which those firms least able to exist without subsidies are more likely to bargain hardest for resources and are consequently more likely to receive them.

Given that incubators and science parks are often the result of public–private partnerships, it is likely that there are multiple principals. This gives rise to a "principal–principal" agency problem (Young *et al.*, 2008) where the primary agency problem is not the failure of professional managers to satisfy the objectives of diffuse shareholders, but rather the opportunistic behavior of the controlling shareholders (Shleifer and Vishny, 1997). We expect that the magnitude of principal–principal conflict will be related to the extent to which each principal is able to maximize its parochial interests and also to the scope and value of the resources they provide. More importantly, because the value of particular resource bundles change as an incubator or science park evolves (and the firms in them), the relative bargaining power of the principals will also vary over time. Therefore, to the extent that principles of good corporate governance[7] are formalized and embedded in the management routines of these organizations, one can expect minimal impact from principal conflict. To the extent that they are not, principal conflict will lead to inefficiency in the resource allocation decisions of incubator and park administrators.

A research agenda is not complete without an in-depth discussion of the relevant dependent variables. In our introduction, we stated that there continues to be a question of the appropriate dependent variables and we believe that until there is progress on this issue, the models that we build can be challenged on grounds of theoretical validity. First, there is a need to consider survival *per se* versus wealth or job creation. The relative importance of these dimensions may be closely associated with the objectives of different science parks and incubators. We should also assess political, social and economic objectives, and the interactions among them, which may influence the attention given to survival *per se*. The end result is that a more precise and meaningful evaluation of a science park

---

[7] Encompassing questions of board arrangements, balance of stakeholder representation, board processes, strategic objectives, incentives and the incentive setting process for managers of science parks and incubators.

or incubator would be based on broader outcome indicators including activities that are more likely to generate social returns or externalities to the region.

As an example, Siegel *et al.* (2003) examined whether companies located on science parks report higher research productivity than comparable firms not located on these facilities. Their results suggest that science park firms are indeed more effective than non-park firms, in terms of generating new products, services and patents. These findings imply that university science parks could be an important mechanism for generating technological spillovers to local firms and regions.

Many studies on tenant firms use longevity or tenure as a dependent variable. This measure deserves further theoretical explication. For example, firms that depart from science parks may not exit as a result of failure but due to acquisition. This group may be either highly attractive firms with good economic prospects or may possess valuable intellectual and human capital even though they may not be financially viable as independent entities. One approach to investigating this issue is to use event history analysis in which a hazard function[8] is derived to explain the impact of various independent variables or covariates on incubator firm longevity or productivity (see Kaplan, 1991; Wright *et al.*, 1995; Lichtenberg and Siegel, 1990; Harris *et al.*, 2003 for example on how this is used).

On the other hand, firms that have had a long tenure in science parks may choose to remain because they cannot operate without the benefits of subsidized resources. Additionally, any explanation of the mobility of science park firms has to also account for the incentives of science park managers to maintain full occupation capacity. In the UK, only 49% of incubators in 2002 had a formal graduation or exit policy.[9] There are two issues embedded in this observation. The most obvious is the governance question of incentives and measures of science park or incubator performance. The second, less obvious, has to do with the yet unanswered empirical question of whether these organizations possess the capabilities to develop their tenant firms to the point of graduation (Vohora *et al.*, 2004).

---

[8] Defined as the probability of event A, say the incubator firm living for another year, occurring given the known probability that it has survived to the current time period *t*.
[9] http://www.ukbi.co.uk/.

The upshot is that without more fine-grained and longitudinal data, it is inappropriate to compare the performance of such firms. For example, recent research on habitual entrepreneurs (Westhead and Wright, 1998) suggests that portfolio entrepreneurs, in particular, may start multiple activities on science parks and incubators as "experiments" and then close or merge them according to how they develop. This emphasizes the need to treat the entrepreneur as a level of analysis apart from that of the incubator firm because there are substantive implications for performance measurement. In sum, we believe that a fruitful research direction lies in the identification and examination of the 'threshold' issues related to venture firms' entry into and exit from science parks and incubators.

Conclusion

Merriam-Webster's Collegiate Dictionary (2003) defines an *"in•cu•ba•tor: one that incubates: as (a) an apparatus by which eggs are hatched artificially (b) an apparatus with a chamber used to provide controlled environmental conditions especially for the cultivation of microorganisms or the care and protection of premature or sick babies"*. Created by public institutions and private firms, incubators and science parks attempt to create munificent environments in which new ventures are nurtured. Our current level of understanding of this process of 'cultivation' and 'care and protection' of premature businesses is still at the phenomenological stage. In this chapter, we have attempted to demonstrate how some research has contributed to a more sophisticated theoretical discussion of this rapidly growing literature. We also provide some suggestions for a research agenda to leverage the work that has already taken place.

We argue that science parks and incubators are important links in the entrepreneurial value chain at the national or environmental level of analysis. A theoretical model to explain the existence of such organizations has to account for the political and social institutions in which they are embedded. As a result, we believe that more theoretical rigor should be associated with the choice of a dependent variable in studies of science parks and incubators. For one thing, this variable will determine the generalizability of the models we construct. More critically, the dependent variable will drive the choice of our theoretical lenses, of which many can be brought to bear in developing such a model. Institutional theory may view incubation as an accelerated (albeit artificial) way to institutionalize new ventures. With respect to resource dependence theory, incubation may constitute a means to create resource buffers to absorb uncertainty. For agency theory, the incubating relationship could be modeled as way for venture capitalists to monitor entrepreneurial effort. Organization learning may characterize it as a form of knowledge accumulation and hypothesis testing.

Another issue we have identified concerns the multiple levels of analyses inherent in research on these property-based institutions. Incubators and science parks are obviously distinct organizations. However, they typically operate within officially or unofficially designated incubating regions — another level of analysis. Equally important is the notion that incubation is a form of individual mentorship between the incubator and science park managers and the entrepreneur or entrepreneurial team. Incubation can be a discrete activity, an ongoing process, or a context; all of which can be formal or informal, deliberate or emergent, rational or non-rational.

In conclusion, we observe that the theoretical questions and approaches are myriad, limited only by a researcher's imagination and analytical tools. Hence, the opportunities for innovative, theory building and empirical analysis are enormous. Such a body of literature is required to understand the purposes and values of these organizational arrangements and its role in entrepreneurial development.

References

Association of University Technology Managers (AUTM) (2000). The AUTM Licensing Survey, Fiscal Year 1999.

Battelle (2013). *Driving regional innovation and growth: The 2012 survey of North American university research parks.* Columbus: Battelle Technology Partnership Practice. http://www.aurp,net/battelle-report [Last accessed 9 February 2014].

Bercovitz, J., Feldman, M., Feller, I., and Burton, R. (2001). Organizational structure as determinants of academic patent and licensing behavior: An exploratory study of Duke, Johns Hopkins, and Pennsylvania State Universities. *Journal of Technology Transfer*, 26: 21–35.

Bøllingtoft, A. and Ulhøi, J. P. (2005). The networked business incubator — leveraging entrepreneurial agency? *Journal of Business Venturing,* 20(2): 265–290.

Bray, M. J. and Lee, J. N. (2000). University revenues from technology transfer: Licensing fees vs. Equity positions. *Journal of Business Venturing,* 15: 385–392.

Clarysse, B., Wright, M., Lockett, A., Van de Velde, E., and Vohora, A. (2005). Spinning out new ventures: A typology of incubation strategies from European research institutions, *Journal of Business Venturing,* 20(2): 183–216.

Cohen, W. M. and Levinthal, D. (1990). Absorptive capacity: A new perspective on learning and innovation. *Administrative Science Quarterly,* 35: 128–152.

Ensley, M. D., Pearson, A. W. and Amason, A. C. (2002). Understanding the dynamics of new venture top management teams: Cohesion, conflict and new venture performance. *Journal of Business Venturing,* 17: 365–386.

Franklin, S., Wright, M., and Lockett, A. (2001). Academic and surrogate entrepreneurs in university spin-out companies. *Journal of Technology Transfer,* 26: 127–141.

Gaglio, C. M. (1997). Opportunity Identification: Review, critique and suggested research directions. In Katz, J. A. (Ed.), *Advances in Entrepreneurship, Firm Emergence and Growth,* JAI Press, Greenwich, CA, pp. 119–138.

Harris, R., Siegel, D., and Wright, M. (2003). Assessing the Impact of Management Buyouts on Economic Efficiency: Plant-Level Evidence from the United Kingdom, mimeo.

Jensen, R., Thursby, J. G., and Thursby, M. C. (2003). The disclosure and licensing of university inventions: The best we can do with the S**t We get to work with. *International Journal of Industrial Organization,* 21(9): 1271–1300.

Kaplan, S. (1991). The staying power of leveraged buyouts. *Journal of Financial Economics,* 29: 287–313.

Khanna, T. and Palepu, K. (2000). Is Group Affiliation Profitable in Emerging Markets? An Analysis of Diversified Indian Business Groups, *Journal of Finance,* 55(2): 867–891.

Knight, F. (1921). *Risk, Uncertainty and Profit.* Augustus Kelley, New York.

Koh, F. C. C., Koh, W. T. H. and Tschang, F. T. (2005). An analytical framework for science parks and technology districts with an application to Singapore. *Journal of Business Venturing,* 20(2): 217–239

Lendner, C. and Dowling, M. (2003). University Business Incubators and the Impact of Their Networks on the Success of Startups: An International Study. Paper presented at the 2003 International Conference on Science Parks and Incubators, Rensselaer Polytechnic Institute, Troy, NY.

Lewin, A. and Volberda, H. (1999). Prolegomena on coevolution: A framework for research on strategy and new organizational forms. *Organization Science*, 10(5): 519–534.

Lewin, A. and Volberda, H. (2003). Beyond adaptation-selection research: Organizing self-renewal in co-evolving environments. *Journal of Management Studies*, 40(8): 2109–2110.

Lichtenberg, F. and Siegel, D. (1990). The Effect of leveraged buyouts on productivity and related aspects of firm behavior. *Journal of Financial Economics*, 27(1): 165–194.

Link, A. N. and Link, K. R. (2003). On the growth of U.S. Science parks. *Journal of Technology Transfer*, 28: 81–85.

Lumpkin, J. R. and Ireland, R. D. (1988). Screening practices of new business incubators: The evaluation of critical success factors. *American Journal of Small Business*, 12(4): 59–81.

Mansfield, E., Rapoport, J., Romeo, A., Wagner, S., and Beardsley, G. (1977). Social and private rates of return from industrial innovations. *Quarterly Journal of Economics*, 91: 221–240.

Markman, G. D., Phan, P. H., Balkin, D. B., and Gianodis, P. T. (2005). Entrepreneurship and university-based technology transfer. *Journal of Business Venturing*, 20(2): 241–263.

Martin, S. and Scott, J. T. (2000). The Nature of Innovation Market Failure and the Design of Public Support for Private Innovation. *Research Policy*, 29(4–5): 437–448.

Mian, S. A. (1997). Assessing and managing the university technology business incubator: An integrative framework, *Journal of Business Venturing*, 12(4): 251–285.

Mowery, D. C., Nelson, R. R., Sampat, B., and Ziedonis, A. A. (2001). The growth of patenting and licensing by U.S. universities: An assessment of the effects of the Bayh–Dole Act of 1980. *Research Policy*, 30: 99–119.

National Business Incubation Association (NBIA) (2015). Available at: https://www.inbia.org/resources/business-incubation-faq [Accessed January 5, 2016].

Nerkar, A. and Shane, S. (2003). When do startups that exploit academic knowledge survive? *International Journal of Industrial Organization*, 21(9): 1391–1410.

Saxenian, A. (1991). The origins and dynamics of production networks in Silicon Valley. *Research Policy*, 20(5): 423–438.

Shleifer, A. and Vishny, R. (1997). A Survey of Corporate Governance. *Journal of Finance*, 52(2): 737–783.

Siegel, D. S. (2003). Data requirements for assessing the impact of strategic research partnerships on economic performance: Analysis and recommendations. *Technology Analysis and Strategic Management*, 15(2): 207–225.

Siegel, D. S., Waldman, D. A., Atwater, L. E. and Link, A. N. (2003a). Toward a model of the effective transfer of scientific knowledge from academicians to practitioners: Qualitative evidence from the commercialization of university technologies. *Journal of Engineering and Technology Management*, 21(1): 115–142.

Siegel, D. S., Waldman, D., Atwater, L., and Link, A. N. (2003b). Commercial knowledge transfers from universities to firms: Improving the effectiveness of university–industry collaboration. *Journal of High Technology Management Research*, 14: 111–133.

Siegel, D. S., Westhead, P., and Wright, M. (2003). Assessing the impact of science parks on the research productivity of firms: Exploratory evidence from the United Kingdom. *International Journal of Industrial Organization*, 21(9): 1357–1369.

Storey, D. J. and Tether, B. S. (1998). Public policy measures to support new technology-based firms in the European Union. *Research Policy*, 26: 1037–1057.

U.K. Business Incubation (UKBI) (2003). Available at: http://www.ukbi.co.uk/

Ucbasaran, D., Lockett, A., Wright, M. and Westhead, P. (2003). Entrepreneurial founder teams: Factors associated with member entry and exit. *Entrepreneurship Theory and Practice*, 28(2): 107–128.

UKSPA (2015). Available at: http://www.ukspa.org.uk/members/our-members (Accessed 15 January 2016). The United Kingdom Science Park Association, Birmingham.

Venkataraman, S. (1997). The distinctive domain of entrepreneurship research: An editor's perspective. In Katz, J. A. (Ed.), *Advances in Entrepreneurship, Firm Emergence and Growth*, Vol. 3. JAI Press, Greenwich, CA, 119–138.

Vohora, A., Wright, M. and Lockett, A. (2004). Critical junctures in the development of university high-tech spinout companies. *Research policy*, 33(1): 147–175.

Westhead, P. (1997). R&D 'Inputs' and 'Outputs' of Technology-based firms located on and off science parks. *R&D Management*, 27: 45–62.

Westhead, P. and Wright, M. (1998). Novice, serial and portfolio founders: Are they different? *Journal of Business Venturing*, 13: 3, 173–205.

Westhead, P. and Storey, D. J. (1994). *An Assessment of Firms Located On and Off Science Parks in the United Kingdom*. HMSO, London.

Wright, M., Thompson, S., Robbie, K., and Wong, P. (1995). Management buy-outs in the short and long term. *Journal of Business Finance and Accounting*, 22: 4, 461–482.

Young, M., Peng, M. W., Ahlstrom, D., Bruton, G. D. and Jiang, Y. (2008). Corporate governance in emerging economies: A review of the principal-principal perspective. *Journal of Management Studies*, 45: 196–220.

Zahra, S. A. and George, G. (2002). Absorptive capacity: A review, reconceptualization, and extension. *Academy of Management Review*, 27: 185–203.

Business Incubation for Technology Entrepreneurship Around the World: Promises and Prospects

Phillip Phan, Sarfraz Mian and Wadid Lamine

This purpose of this book is to highlight the emerging incubation research and practice from around the world. In doing so, we were less concerned about being comprehensive, since the breadth of these activities far exceeds what we can cover in this volume, as we are with illustrating how regions for which this phenomenon is relatively new conduct such work. As such, we have aimed this book at reporting mostly from emerging and developing countries. We discussed the history of incubation research, much of which resides in North America and Western Europe, as a way to establish the literature base for viewing and assessing the newer work. Chapter 1 reviewed three decades of business incubation research and offered a typology for classifying the work, namely, studies on the concept itself, facility design and business models, and those that look at performance assessment and benchmarking best practices. It concluded, as did an earlier review in Chapter 9, that 'the state of the extant business incubation... research lacks... theories, units of analysis, [and]... comparison groups'.

Chapter 9's conclusions, made a decade ago, generally hold true today. This is that our current level of understanding regarding the incubation process is still at the phenomenological stage. While the chapters are still concerned with describing and inventorying the activities and outcomes of incubation from their regions because these are so heterogeneous, some chapters advance the research by anchoring their observations in theory such as institutional theory (Chapter 2) or ecological theory (Chapter 3). Chapter 2's institutional view describes the political and social institutions in which incubators are embedded. Chapter 4's ecological view attempts to explain how these organizational forms simultaneously respond to market forces while fulfilling their mission to protect fledging firms from those forces.

The most important aspect of this research, from a theory-building point of view, is the need for a comprehensive discussion of incubator and incubatee performance. As Chapter 9 states, the dependent variable will determine the generalizability of the models and therefore the choice of our theoretical lenses. For example, if we choose to study incubators from resource dependence theory, then these organizations are the means to create resource buffers to absorb uncertainty. If we model incubators as solving an agent-principal problem, then the incubating relationship is a way for the resource provider to monitor entrepreneurial effort. Agent–principal models are reducible to semi-closed forms (hence tractable) if we make relatively strong but realistic assumptions about information symmetry. Yet, other theoretical perspectives, such as organization learning characterize the incubation journey from the perspective of the incubatee. Such a framework will allow scholars to ignore the specifics of the support services to generalize across types of incubator forms. This was the undertaken task by the authors in Chapter 4, in which they studied networks of incubators to understand the knowledge flows between them and how these flows influenced incubatee performance.

Performance also matters because of questions surrounding the economic sustainability of incubators. The chapters in this volume, notably Chapters 1, 2, 6 and 9, made the point that incubator performance is measured in many studies but the heterogeneity of incubator forms and objectives call into question the validity of the measures. As discussed in the introduction, incubators are policy interventions to address failure in the market for startups. In measuring performance, an important distinction that scholars (and policy makers) need to make is the difference between the performance of the incubatee and that of the incubator. They are distinct. The difference lies in the unit of analysis and the horizon over which performance is measured.

Incubator tenants have relatively short performance horizons, in terms of their status as incubatees. They either graduate from the incubator (i.e. continue to grow and take more space elsewhere, liquidate at a profit relative to the cost of investment capital and so on) or not. Hence, standard measures of entrepreneurial performance (e.g. acquisition of first customer or investor, sales or employee growth and so on) are appropriate ways to assess incubatee performance.

Incubators live beyond the tenure of individual tenants. In the literature, performance has been measured in a number of ways such as the average survival rate of or economic value created by their incubatees over time, employment growth and growth in number of tenant firms, rate at which tenants move from entry to profitable exit, and so on. Earlier research (e.g. Amezcua *et al.*, 2013) has found that the definitions of success (and hence success itself) depend on the match between the needs of the tenants and the competencies of the incubators. The authors in Chapter 3 seem to confirm this notion. They conclude that the variations in accelerator types and objectives imply that different performance measures, some of which are not comparable to each other, need to be considered.

Additionally, it is not reasonable to compare incubators on the same performance criteria across time. Incubators mature, and at different rates, so that the measures on which they are assessed would naturally evolve. As such, we believe that a portfolio governance approach to measuring performance, relative to the objectives and rate of growth of the incubator, is more appropriate. In a portfolio, the relative importance of the factors that matter to performance, forecasting, selection, monitoring and control and management support, are adjusted over time to account for the dynamism of the organizational form. Indeed, Chapter 2 found that the most valuable support services in the European accelerators they studied is the mentorship opportunity afforded by their networks; but we know that the need for mentorship varies by the type and maturity of the emerging firm. In their case, while mentorship meant advice on product development, in other contexts, it could include intellectual property strategy, capital structure and asset management.

From the standpoint of research methods, qualitative techniques prove just as useful and popular as quantitative ones. In fact, again because of the rapid evolving nature of incubator forms, qualitative techniques, as illustrated by Chapter 3, remain the best way to understand the forms, processes and objectives of incubators in different regions. The challenge is to translate the qualitative lessons to generalizable theory and large scale empirical tests of that theory. On this point, the extant research has been less productive or useful. For the same reason that measuring performance across incubators and across time has been challenging, testing theory in this research is even more challenging. To solve the heterogeneity problem, scholars have a number of options to follow. They can hold constant the organizational form of incubation (that is, for example, exclusively examine government funded, information and communications technology (ICT) incubators across regions) or hold constant the strategic objectives of the incubators in a region. The implication is that we may not be able to derive a general, empirically verifiable, theory of incubation. We may have to live with a number of meso-level theories that focused on specific types of incubators or specific regions of the world, the latter sensitized to the stage of economic development of the region.

The research seems to have generated more interest, and influence, among policy makers and practitioners. This has largely resulted from the demand for 'best-practices' that can be quickly adopted, given the pace of rapid growth around the world. For example, Chapter 3's three-archetype typology of accelerators implies actionable principles for specific stakeholder groups such as investors, corporations and government agencies. Chapter 4's findings suggest that incubators should be viewed as part of a network, meaning that their activities should not only be directed inward to tenant firms but also outward toward other incubators and influencers such as government regulators and policy makers; again suggesting actionable strategies and tactics. Chapter 5 made the point that external factors beyond the control of incubator managers are as much to blame for the success or failure of these organizations as internal factors such as managerial competence or organizational structures and procedures. Yet, it also suggests that in periods of macroeconomic uncertainty, incubators can still engage in coalition building to mitigate the effects of resource paucity (Mian *et al.*, 2012). This isomorphic tendency presents an ongoing challenge to scholars because it endogenizes the practice-outcome calculus. One solution is to consider a multilevel analytical approach suggested in Chapter 9 so that even when isomorphism is present in a region, it is less likely (because of the need to respond to local stakeholders) to be present in the organization and individual.

Regardless of the caveats notes in the chapters and in this conclusion, we believe that the future for incubation and its study is bright. The rapidly evolving nature of the phenomenon means rich opportunities for theorizing. The challenges related to empirical testing can be solved by careful identification strategies, the use of multilevel models and careful choices in the performance measurement.

References

Amezcua, A. S., Grimes, M.G., Bradley, S.W., and Wiklund, J. (2013). Organizational sponsorship and founding environments: A contingency view on the survival of business-incubated firms, 1994–2007. *Academy of Management Journal*, 56(6): 1628–1654.

Mian, S., Fayolle, A., and Lamine, W. (2012). Building sustainable regional innovation platforms for incubating science & technology businesses: Evidence from the US and French Science & Technology Parks. *International Journal of Entrepreneurship and Innovation*, 13(4): 235–248.

Author Biographies

Bart Clarysse is a Professor of Entrepreneurship at Ghent University and Imperial College Business School. He specializes in high-tech entrepreneurship with a focus on topics such as identity, entrepreneurial passion, legitimacy and opportunity search. He has published in journals such as the *Journal of Business Venturing, Technovation, Research Policy, Strategic Entrepreneurship Journal* and *Small Business Economics*.

Selma Mhamed Hichri is Assistant Professor of Entrepreneurship and Economics at the Faculty of Economics and Management of Sfax and member of the Research Laboratory of Quantitative Economics of Development. Her principal research areas concern entrepreneurship, innovation and the organizational strategy in the high-tech industries.

Wadid Lamine is an Associate Professor of Entrepreneurship at Toulouse Business School. His research interests include business incubation, high-tech entrepreneurship and entrepreneurial networks. He has received the French National Foundation of Education in Management's best dissertation award. He has published in *International Journal of Entrepreneurship and Innovation, Entrepreneurship and Regional Development* and *Applied Economics Letters*, among others.

Per Lind is a Professor of Industrial Development at Uppsala University and has worked with private sector development for the United Nations. His research covers small business development in Africa, Asia and Latin America. Recently, he has been leading a research team in the Baltic Sea region on university–industry collaboration.

Zouhaïer M'Chirgui is an Associate Professor at Kedge Business School, Marseille, France. His research interests include entrepreneurship, Internet evolution, technology acceptance, strategic alliances, mergers and acquisitions, networks and organizational strategy in the high-tech industries.

Sarfraz A. Mian is a Professor of Entrepreneurship and Management Policy, State University of New York, Oswego, NY. Mian's work on technology business incubation has appeared in books and scholarly journals including *Research Policy, Journal of Business Venturing, Technovation, Journal of High Technology Management Research* and the *International Journal of Entrepreneurship and Innovation.*

Phillip Phan is an Alonzo and Virginia Decker Professor of Strategic Management and Entrepreneurship at The Johns Hopkins University Carey Business School. He researches technology innovation and entrepreneurship, and has published over 100 peer reviewed articles and 10 books. He is Editor of the *Academy of Management Perspectives,* and associate editor of the *Journal of Technology Transfer.*

Guilherme Ary Plonski is a Professor at the University of São Paulo. He serves as Research Director of the Center for Technology Policy and Management and is on the board of the University Institute of Advanced Studies. He was President of the Brazilian Association of Science Parks and Business Incubators (ANPROTEC).

Donald Siegel is a Dean of the School of Business at the University at Albany, SUNY. He has published in the *American Economic Review, The Review of Economics and Statistics, Journal of Law and Economics, Journal of Financial Economics, Academy of Management Review, Academy of Management Journal, Strategic Management Journal, Journal of International Business Studies* and *Journal of Management Studies.*

Goosain Solomon is Lecturer in the Department of Business Management and PhD Researcher at University of Stellenbosch in South Africa.

David Tsiteladze is a Lecturer in the Venture Capital Management Department of the Higher School of Economics in Russia. His key areas of expertise are entrepreneurship education, VC investments and academic entrepreneurship with focus on the development of entrepreneurial capacity in startups. He is publisher of "The Angel Investor" (in Russian).

Jonas Van Hove is a member of the faculty at the Imperial College Business School where he conducts research on entrepreneurial ecosystems, incubation models and academic entrepreneurship. He is managing and designing experiential programs to equip STEM students and academics with an entrepreneurial mindset.

Dina Williams obtained her PhD in Science, Innovation and Technology Management from Manchester Business School. Her key areas of expertise are entrepreneurship development, entrepreneurship education, academic entrepreneurship and university–industry interaction. Alongside academic activities, Dina runs her own training and consulting company EnACT: Enterprise Action Consulting and Training Ltd.

Mike Wright is a Professor of Entrepreneurship at Imperial College Business School, Director of the Centre for Management Buy-out Research, Associate Director of the Enterprise Research Centre and Visiting Professor at the University of Ghent. He is an Editor for the *Strategic Entrepreneurship Journal*, and *Academy of Management Perspectives*.

Ayna Yusubova is PhD researcher at Ghent University, Belgium at the Department of Innovation, Entrepreneurship and Service Management.

Yunhao Zhu is post-doctoral fellow in the School of Management, University of Science and Technology of China, Hefei, Anhui Province. His research interests are in the areas of entrepreneurship and social networks.

Index

Printed in the United States
By Bookmasters